Peter Ellyard is an Australian futurist, strategist, speaker, and author who lives in Melbourne. Originally a biochemist, and a soil and plant scientist, he is a graduate of Sydney University and Cornell University (Ph.D). He formally became a futurist upon his appointment as CEO of the Australian Commission for the Future in 1988. Peter's work seeks to assist nations, organisations, communities, and individuals to construct their own pathways to achieve future success. Before working as a futurist, Peter held CEO positions in several public sector organisations over eighteen years. These included two associated with environment and planning and one with industry and technology. He was also Senior Adviser in the office of three environment ministers in the Australian Government in Canberra. Peter is a fellow of the Australian College of Educators, the Environment Institute of Australia and New Zealand, and the Australian Institute of Management.

He has advised the United Nations system and has acted as a senior adviser/consultant to the UNEP, UNDP, and UNESCO. Peter has worked in several developing and transitional countries in South-East and East Asia and the Pacific. He was a special adviser to the 1992 Earth Summit in the fields of biodiversity and climate change. He contributed to the preparation of the Framework Conventions in both these areas.

He is the father of two grown-up daughters and has one grandson. This is his fourth book on futures.

He has more complete biographies on Wikipedia and at www.saxton.com.au.

To my grandson, Tobias (Toby) King, and his generation.

Peter Ellyard

THE FUTURE KNOWLEDGE COMPENDIUM

A Curriculum for Thriving in the 21st Century

AUSTIN MACAULEY PUBLISHERS™
LONDON * CAMBRIDGE * NEW YORK * SHARJAH

Copyright © Peter Ellyard 2023

The right of Peter Ellyard to be identified as author of this work has been asserted by the author in accordance with sections 77 and 78 of the Copyright, Designs and Patents Act 1988.

All rights reserved. No part of this publication may be reproduced, stored in a retrieval system, or transmitted in any form or by any means, electronic, mechanical, photocopying, recording, or otherwise, without the prior permission of the publishers.

Any person who commits any unauthorised act in relation to this publication may be liable to criminal prosecution and civil claims for damages.

A CIP catalogue record for this title is available from the British Library.

ISBN 9781398419827 (Paperback)
ISBN 9781398419834 (Hardback)
ISBN 9781398419841 (ePub e-book)

www.austinmacauley.com

First Published 2023
Austin Macauley Publishers Ltd®
1 Canada Square
Canary Wharf
London
E14 5AA

Thank you, Robyn Velik Klein, for giving me your loving support in my life and my work. I want to express my deep gratitude to my family, Heather, Sonya, Hannah, Amit, James, and Toby, for their love and support as well. Over decades I have been inspired and enlightened by many people that I have been privileged to know and work with. These include Maurice Strong who demonstrated to me by his own deeds, and through our conversations, that one could aspire to imagine, and seek to build, a future for our planet and for humanity that is worthy of humanity's best self.

Table of Contents

Introduction 15

Twelve Mindsets for 21st Century Futurists 21

Future Knowledge 24

Chapter 1: Exploring Global Trends 26

    1.1. Identity and Change in the 21st Century 26

    1.2. The Birth of Planetism 27

    1.3. Globalisation: Past, Present and Future 29

    1.4. Two Converging Global Trends 42

    1.5. The Nine values of Planetism 44

    1.6. Planetism: The Shaper of Emerging Global Markets and Industrial and Economic Futures 48

    1.7. Fourteen Global Trends 50

Chapter 2: Social and Political Change in Our emerging global village 56

    2.1. Globalisation: Catalyst of the Politics of Hope and Fear 56

    2.2. The Birth of Planetary Politics 59

    2.3. The Politics of Resistance to Global Integration 61

    2.4. Adapting for Success in a Global Village 71

    2.5. The Decline of Ideology and the Rise of Ideals and Values-Driven Politics 77

    2.6. Governance in Our Emerging Global Village 83

Chapter 3: Self-Knowledge for Future Shapers 94

    3.1. Knowing Yourself. Exploring Personal Identity 94

    3.2. Three Selves, Three Sights and Three Dialogues 95

3.3. Hindsight in Action: Exploring Derivations	*96*
3.4. Insight in Action: Exploring Destinies	*97*
3.5. Foresight in Action: Exploring Destinations	*99*
Chapter 4: Shaping the 21st Century	**101**
4.1. Charting Destinations	*101*
4.2. The Six Future Questions and the Six Futures	*101*
4.3. Integrating the Six Futures into a Unified Toolkit	*104*
4.4. The Six Future Shaping Tools	*108*
4.5. Shaping Futures: Rethinking Management and Leadership	*109*
4.6. From Visualisation to Realisation	*112*
4.7. Optimism, Pessimism and Utopian Realism	*113*
4.8. The Visualising and Realising Mind: Cerebral Intelligence	*114*
4.9. Futures Narratives: Scenario Building for Shaping Futures	*121*
Chapter 5: Relationships in 21st Century Society	**125**
5.1. Two Capabilities That Really Matter	*125*
5.2. The Century of Interdependence	*125*
5.3. The Three Relationships	*126*
5.4. The Interdependent Relationship in the 21st Century	*127*
5.5. Trust in Relationships	*129*
5.6. Committing Ourselves to a Relationship	*130*
5.7. Collaboration to Shape the Future	*132*
5.8. Seeking Win/Win	*132*
5.9. Interdependence and Maturity	*134*
5.10. Communicating in a Global Village	*140*
Chapter 6: Imagining and Building a Liveable Planet	**145**
6.1. A Liveable Future	*145*
6.2. Defining Liveability: The Six Pillars of Liveability	*147*

6.3. Building an Ever More Liveable Planetary Society	147
6.4. The Liveability Economy: Our Industrial Future?	148
6.5. Exploring the Six Pillars of Liveability	149
6.6. Mindsets for Building a Liveable Future	153

Chapter 7: Reimagining Sustainability: Sustainable Behaviour, Sustainable Prosperity — 156

7.1. Sustainability: Do We Need to Reinvent It?	156
7.2 Sustainable Prosperity	160
7.3. Economic Prosperity and Economic Poverty	161
7.4. Ecological Prosperity and Ecological Poverty	165
7.5. Exploring Social and Cultural Prosperity and Poverty	168
7.6. Social Prosperity and Social Poverty	169
7.7. Cultural Prosperity and Cultural Poverty	169
7.8. Sustainable Prosperity	170
7.9. Sustainable Individualism	171

Chapter 8: Abating and Adapting to Three Global Challenges: Global Pandemics, Global heating and Demographic Ageing — 173

8.1. Three 21st Century Global Challenges	173
8.2. Creating a Pandemic-Safe Planet	175
8.3. Innovating and Building a Climate-Safe Planet	177
8.4. Demographic Ageing in an Emerging Global Village	187

Chapter 9: Renewing the Agents of Change: Innovation and Technology Futures — 197

9.1. Renewing the Agents of Change	197
9.2. Social and Technological Innovation: Which Drives Which?	197
9.3. Social Innovation: The Five Social Drivers of Innovation	199
9.4. Technological Innovation: Four Generic Technologies	200

9.5. Technological Convergence — 205

9.6. Embedding Technology into 21st Century Innovation — 206

9.7. Social and Technological Disruption and Resilience — 207

Chapter 10: Renewing the Agents of Change: Education and Learning Futures — 209

10.1. Learning for 21st Century Success — 209

10.2. Knowledge and Wealth — 210

10.3. The Two-Year-Old Learner — 210

10.4. The 21st Century Learning Culture — 211

10.5. The Seven Modes of 21st Century Learning — 212

10.6. Uplifting the Capability and Fulfilling the Potential of Our Mind — 217

10.7. The Four Domains of Holistic Learning — 217

10.8. Learning Innovations for the 21st Century: Effective Learning — 223

Chapter 11: Renewing the Agents of Change: Work and Career Futures — 224

11.1. Worry About Work Futures — 224

11.2. Looking More Closely at Work — 225

11.3. How We Think Matters — 226

11.4. Imagining Emerging 21st Century Work and Career Paths — 229

11.5. Building Exemplar 21st Century Work and Workplaces — 230

Chapter 12: Renewing Our Economic Mindsets for Building and Managing a Planetist Global Village — 234

12.1. The Growing Planetist Moral Compass — 234

12.2. Following in the Footsteps of Three 20th Century Visionaries — 236

12.3. Realising the Vision of Kenneth Boulding — 237

12.4. Consolidating the 21st Century Cosmonaut Economy — 242

12.5. Investing in the Planetist Future — 246

Chapter 13: Conclusion 252

Appendix: The Future Knowledge Curriculum 258

By the same author

- Ideas for the New Millennium (1998, 2001)
- Designing 2050: Pathways to Sustainable Prosperity on Spaceship Earth (2004)
- Destination 2050: A Concepts Bank and Toolkit for Future-Makers (2012)

I think of what the world could be
A vision of the one I see
A million dreams is all its gonna take
A million dreams for the world we're gonna make
They can say, they can say it all sounds crazy
They can say, they can say I've lost my mind
I don't care, I don't care, so call me crazy
We can live in a world that we design.

(Benj Pasek and Justin Paul
A million dreams from *The Greatest Showman*)

Introduction

In February 2022 Vladimir Putin shocked the world by launching an attack to conquer and subjugate Russia's neighbour, Ukraine. His actions were shocking to most of humanity because it believed that this kind of uncivilized European behaviour had been left well behind in the 20th century. His actions were reminiscent of a Hitler blitzkrieg. However, Putin does not see himself as a Hitler. He even claimed he wanted to de-nazify a Ukraine led by a Jewish president and a Jewish prime minister. In fact, Putin is emulating earlier war making icons. He apparently sees himself as a 21st century reincarnation of the 18th century Tsar, Peter the Great. Putin faced not only a totally resistant Ukraine but also a unified and resolute global community. He became an instant global pariah. His rival in the war, Volodymyr Zelensky, the Ukrainian president, simultaneously became an instant 21st century global hero.

At this writing the war continues. However, I am confident Putin will fail in his mission and will face humiliation and punishment by the rest of the world. Putin has not seemed to recognize how much the world has changed and that aggressive acts which might have worked in the 20th century will not work for him in the 21st century. This book will examine the world in the 21st century and why Putin will be recognized as a yesteryear man, a 21st century misfit.

In early 2020, our world was endangered and traumatised because somebody ate a wild animal, an endangered pangolin, in Hubei Province in China and became sick as a result. Our whole interconnected and interdependent world suddenly became vulnerable to the action of one person who merely continued to do what he or she had probably been doing for years. This was a new situation for all of us: a new 21st century form of collective endangerment. This was not a 20th century type endangerment caused by a conflict between two different parts of humanity. Here, we were all endangered. We could only blame our collective selves, even though some unconvincingly sought to blame China and the WHO for the crisis.

We were also all victims but there were no victors. It was not possible for anyone to opt out, to declare themselves 'neutral' as they did in a 20th century war, or cut themselves off from the world as North Korea has done for decades.

North Korea was as susceptible and endangered as everyone else. Our global society had to behave like a village that is being flooded. It was a case of all hands to the dykes and the pumps, friends and enemies alike. And like the other great current 21st century challenge, global heating, we have no option but to work and collaborate with others we do not necessarily want to work or collaborate with. The reality is that we have all become more vulnerable and more easily disrupted because our world has changed: our ever-growing interdependence and shared vulnerability in an emerging global village was starkly revealed to us. We have been found not to be up to the task of sufficiently protecting ourselves.

What is extraordinary is that we could have been and should have been better prepared. But we were not prepared. We could have had a vaccine ready for such an event, but we did not. We were disrupted to the point that we are now also experiencing the shared punishment of a global economic recession. This failure was a consequence of our continuing to use yesteryear mindsets, our failure to think and collaborate in the 21st century-relevant way that henceforth will be required if we are to be successful in dealing with similar future threats.

The good news is that we are already adapting and becoming more future-ready. Scientists such as those in the non-profit New York-based Eco Health Alliance and the Wuhan Institute of Virology are cooperating to hunt for both unknown coronaviruses and coronavirus antibodies in bat caves in Yunnan China. Over 15,000 different coronaviruses in bats have so far been identified. These can now be assembled into a genome bank and database of these coronaviruses. This work is likely to provide a basis of a new global pandemic prevention and abatement system. Scientists never have problems in collaborating in such multicultural research programs. The problem that often prevents such collaboration is the mindset of some of their political masters.

When the history of the 21st century is written, three issues: the COVID-19 pandemic, Putin's aggression against Ukraine, and the reality that humanity is facing the shared endangerment of global warming, will be seen as catalytic events shaping the future of humanity in the 21st century.

Consequently, what do we need to do differently, stop doing, or begin to do, and what new thinking, new concepts and tools are needed to both prevent and abate such global challenges and enable all of us to be the most 21st century-ready and successful people we can be? This is a core question this book will seek to answer.

Over the past 30 years, much of my work has been directed towards answering a single question: *what knowledge and skills do people need to possess so that they are as successful as they can be in the future?* As I sought to answer this question, I also recognised that the 'future' I was considering is an emerging 21st century society. I recognized that I would need to develop a better understanding of the 21st century and how it differed from the 20th century, the century in which most of my own thinking was moulded.

This work commenced in earnest in 1989 when I began working as the Executive Director of the Australian Commission for the Future that had been established by the Australian Government to bring a longer-term perspective to public policy making. I had been challenged by the comments of a prominent Australian conservative politician who saw little value in my work. He believed that we would never be able to predict the future, that the work of futurists was basically a waste of time and that our visualisations of the future and of our strategic actions to realise these visualisations could never be more than guesswork. I dearly wanted to prove him wrong.

Most futurists then and now are interested in predicting the future by examining how new innovations and emerging technologies might change our future world. Many if not most futurists also seek to be prophets and believe the work of a futurist is mostly about predicting the consequences of adapting to, and avoiding disruption by, social and technological change.

I had a different aspiration. I wanted to discover a means that would enable all who wished to, to become futurists themselves, to develop a set of concepts and tools that could be used by all of us: to enable each of us to become effective shapers of our own futures. I also saw my task as conceiving the means to not only shape our own futures but also the future of the world which we all share, including making a future world that is better and more liveable for all than it is now. I believed that the work of the futurist should include how we can better fulfil our dreams and aspirations as well as becoming resilient to social and technological change. When I articulated this goal, I was met with considerable cynicism including from some of my political masters at the time.

All of us want to be able to build future success for ourselves and for those we love and have responsibility for. And because there is no clearly recognized existing suite of capabilities needed to accomplish such a task, important though this clearly is many, if not most, of us have a limited capability to do this. This 'us' here applies equally to individuals, groups, communities and organisations, and to governments as well. Many people I meet in all walks of life are continuously disappointed by the lack of vision and the absence of inspiration present in most government, corporate and community leadership.

As I began the task of developing such a suite of key future-shaping capabilities, I began to recognise that there are many people in different careers and with very different personal histories who might benefit if such a suite of capabilities were to become available. These might include young people thinking about what might become their future life and career path by making a choice about their tertiary education. They might include *second chance* people who are seeking to rebuild their lives, people such as ex-prisoners and refugees, or people charting a new 21st century-relevant life path out of broken relationships or disadvantage. And they might include young would-be investors who will be some of the fortunate recipients of the more than $100 trillion that will be transferred between generations in the next decade, and who want to invest in ventures that are 21st century-relevant, ethical, and environmentally wise.

I already recognised that many of us devote huge amounts of time to shaping the future: managers, leaders, planners, designers, innovators, and educators among them. All these professions have developed future-shaping concepts, methodologies, and toolkits within their own professional domains. But most of these professional people do not fully recognise that these professions share a common goal: they all aspire to shape the future, and to uplift our ability to achieve future success and build a better tomorrow.

All of us make decisions every day about what we will do and what we will seek to achieve in the future: tomorrow, next week, next year or even decades ahead. And most of us would also recognise that we could probably do this better than we are currently doing. To me, it is most amazing to find that education organisations everywhere, which after all are all dedicated to giving us the knowledge and skills to maximise our capability to be more future successful, have not sought to develop and place into their curricula concepts and tools their students could use to shape the future. This book offers a basic curriculum that might be considered to fill this void.

In this book, I am describing for the first time a collection of concepts and tools designed to enable readers to answer questions in six key areas:

- Understanding global trends. *What are the long-term trends shaping society in the 21st century? What kind of world is emerging from these 21st century trends? What opportunities and threats will consequentially emerge from these trends?*
- Changing human behaviour and politics. *How are human behaviour and politics changing in response to increasing global integration and the birth of a 21st century global society?*
- Knowing ourselves. *How can I find my place and role in the emerging world? What is my identity? How do I describe myself? How might I best prepare myself so that I can become the most effective shaper of my future life and career path I can be in our emerging 21st century world?*
- Shaping the future. *What mindsets, concepts and tools do I need to have at my disposal to be an effective shaper of the future in the emerging realities of 21st century global society?*
- Building and nurturing relationships. *As I often also seek to shape the future with others, what can I do to ensure our relationships in these circumstances are as productive and harmonious as they can be?*
- Building a liveable future. *What are the key ingredients of a global liveable society that is worthy of the best of humanity? How might we ensure that the society emerging from our collective future-shaping work maximises this liveability?*

These six questions will be explored in the first six chapters of this book. This book is designed to serve two purposes: as a stand-alone book, *The Future Knowledge Compendium*, and as a knowledge and learning resource for *Shaping the Future* products and services, such as the podcasts, webinars and future-shaping software that will become available from a new online facility, the *Future Knowledge Academy*.

I have sought to give specific and memorable names to these core concepts and tools, for there are 69 of them, so they can be more easily referred to and discussed. I have also given each a number between FUTK01 and FUTK69 for easy reference for when these concepts and tools are incorporated into other products and services. Finally, I have sought to use alliteration, acronyms, and other mnemonic devices as aide-memoires. I hope that by doing this I can assist people to use these concepts and tools better and to enable each of them to be more easily retrieved when they wish to shape their future lives, work, and world.

Peter Ellyard
December 2022

Twelve Mindsets for 21ˢᵗ Century Futurists

This book has been created for a particular purpose: to provide all people with a set of concepts and tools which will enable all who wish to do so, to be capable of successfully shaping the future and to thrive there. These twelve Future Knowledge Mindsets below are a preview of some of the key concepts and tools of future knowledge. If we wish to become effective futurists and thrive in the emerging 21ˢᵗ century society, these are mindsets each of us should embed in ourselves. They will be listed and given a brief explanation now. The book that follows will provide full explanations of these mindsets and many more besides. Here they are:

1. Maximise your imagination. Imagination is to the future as memory is to the past. We cannot build a future that we do not first imagine. Einstein tells us that imagination is more important than knowledge.

2. Be both prophet and visionary. The question the Prophet in each of us asks is *what will* be the future? The question the Visionary in each of us asks is what *should/could be* the future? The futurist in each of us should ask and answer both these complementary questions.

3. Be both a manager and leader of self and other. Management perfection is the resilient future taker. Leadership perfection is the purposeful future maker. The first task of good management and leadership is to become an effective manager and leader of self.

4. Embody planetist values. Planetism is a new 21ˢᵗ century paradigm. It involves giving first allegiance to Planet, just as tribalism involves giving first allegiance to the tribe (one's tribal, cultural, or religious identity), and nationalism involves giving first allegiance to nation. The paradigm of planetism embodies nine core values. If we want to be the most 21ˢᵗ century relevant and successful person we can be, we should put planet first.

5. Build positive futures rather than eliminate negative futures. As we shape futures, we should aspire to build positive futures and not just ameliorate negative futures. Ending war does not create peace. Ending poverty does not create prosperity. Ending illness does not create wellness. Ending cruelty does not create kindness.

6. Embed sustainable behaviours in yourself. Sustainable behaviour causes zero net collateral harm to life and zero net collateral damage to place. In the 21st century humanity will innovate the means to achieve this.

7. Understand and grow interdependence. The interdependent relationship is the most critical relationship in emerging 21st century society. This requires that we practice the golden rule, make mutual obligations to shared destinations, and seek win/win outcomes. This is the *Interdependence Trio*.

8. Value questions and treasure reflection. Most futurist activities commence with a question. And to answer these questions well we should give ourselves reflective time. Ask yourselves what were you doing when you had your best ideas about your work? It is unlikely that you were working.

9. Be a utopian realist. Sociologist Anthony Giddens coined the concept of *Utopian Realism*: imagining utopian ends and crafting realistic means to achieve these ends. High achieving futurists will be *Utopian Realists*.

10. Expand your circle of identity. Ethicist Peter Singer encourages us to fully explore what and whom we care about and what and who we do not care about, and why. He created the concept of the *Circle of Concern (FUTK34)* and suggested we should over time expand our *Circle of Concern* to care for all of life capable of suffering. This book's *Circle of Identity* (FUTK32) is concerned about the human part of life, and recommends that over time we expand our *Circle of Identity (FUTK35)* to all who are different so that it eventually includes all of humanity.

11. Recognise the role of and embody the six future shaping tools. There are six tools for shaping the future: management, leadership, planning, design, innovation, and learning. Successful futurists will be able to use these six future shaping tools.

12. Build a liveable future. A liveable place, precinct, community, nation, and planet is prosperous, harmonious, inclusive, sustainable, healthy, and secure. These are the *Six Pillars of Liveability*. All of us want to live in communities that are as liveable as we can make them. The uplifting of liveability will become a key shaper and purpose of the 21st century global economy.

Future Knowledge

This book contains a coherent set of transmissible *concepts* and *tools*. *Concepts* are social innovations to structure and change the way we think and to improve our understanding of the world around us. They also enable us to share our thinking and discuss our perceptions and visualisations with others. *Tools,* on the other hand, are social or technological innovations that can enable each of us to strategically intervene in trending events and initiate the changes we want to make and to shape the future.

There are 69 concepts and tools offered in *The Future Knowledge Compendium*, but I haven't nominated which of them is either a concept or tool. This is because a concept to one person might be a tool to another and vice versa. We all think and act differently, in ways probably unique for each of us.

Richard Buckminster Fuller, known as Bucky Fuller to his millions of admirers and followers, said: *'Wealth consists of two components, the Physical (material resources and ecosystems) that must be conserved, and the Metaphysical (knowledge and ideas) that can only grow.'* Bucky Fuller is one of two intellectual giants of the 20th century who has been a constant source of inspiration for this writer.

Future Knowledge is knowledge assembled and used to achieve a future-related purpose. Our future wealth and prosperity will be overwhelmingly determined by what we know now or will know in the future and by how we use this knowledge to shape the future. It can consist of many different forms of knowledge. It includes self-knowledge: understanding oneself more completely so that one can become a more effective shaper of one's own future. It can be knowledge about a particular knowledge domain. It might be, for example, what we can call Tropical Knowledge: all the relevant knowledge we have relating to tropical environments, so we are able to build and manage infrastructure and develop communities in tropical environments while conserving tropical natural heritage and biodiversity. Or it might be relationship building knowledge or cultural knowledge of one kind or another.

Future Knowledge can be knowledge built into tools such as a design, a pattern, an algorithm, or a technology that can assist us to accomplish a particular future-shaping outcome. Or it could be management knowledge, leadership knowledge, planning knowledge, design knowledge, innovation knowledge or learning knowledge.

Our knowledge, what we know, determines how we look at our world and our future. What we know also shapes our values, what we believe or care about, or do not believe or care about. We care more about global heating when we become more knowledgeable of, and therefore more aware about, the potential impact of global heating.

Values are expressions of what we *value* highly or regard as being precious. As something becomes more highly *valued* or precious to us, it will considered to be more *valuable*. And what is becoming increasingly *valued by* and *valuable to* more of us, more of us will want to acquire. That in turn will determine what others will seek to supply to the market. So what we know shapes what we *value*, and this in turn shapes markets and emerging economies, and our industrial, social, and ethical futures. And we can accomplish this through the use of *Six Future Shaping Tools* that will be described in Chapter 4.

We will either shape the future or the future will shape us. The following are four core domains of philosophy that collectively describe how we turn our knowledge about a situation into future shaping action based on this knowledge:

- *Metaphysics*: which asks and answers the questions, *What do we know? What are the facts?*
- *Epistemology*: which asks and answers the questions, *How do we know? Are our sources of knowledge reliable?*
- *Reason:* which asks and answers the questions, *What can we conclude? What sense can we make from what and how we know?*
- *Ethics*: which asks and answers the questions, *What should we do? What is the right thing to do?*

This philosophy-driven thinking pathway that links what we know, our knowledge, to sequential action will be discussed further in Chapter 4 and in several other places in this *Compendium.*

This is all the up-front material I will provide for now. Hopefully, it is sufficient to convince readers to read on. Now I want to move on to the first big piece of Future Knowledge, a detailed discussion of 21st century global trends.

Chapter 1: Exploring Global Trends

What are the long-term trends shaping society in the 21st century? What kind of world is emerging from these 21st century trends and what opportunities and threats will emerge from these trends?

1.1. Identity and Change in the 21st Century

The first component we will consider we can call *Global Change Knowledge*, and the first concept we will explore is *Identity*.

Throughout history, humans have identified themselves as being similar to some, and different from many. How we identify ourselves and our place in the world is critical to how we consider, initiate, or respond to change. We all identify ourselves in our ever-changing world, both through the cultures of groups we belong to or choose to join, and this identity informs and guides many of our individual and collective perceptions and actions.

Our identities are based on our heritage and our past experiences, and also by our aspirations and our hopes for the future. We bond more with those we regard as similar to us and less with those we regard as different from us. This has been the human experience for the whole of human history. And our cultural and religious identities and our attitude to difference have too often catalysed human conflict over centuries. If less so than in the past, we are still doing so.

Our identities do not remain static. We often change them, and whether we seek to change or are willing to change them can make a big difference to whether we are likely to succeed or fail in the ever-changing unfolding future world.

In his book *The Expanding Circle*, the ethicist Peter Singer described what he called the *Circle of Concern*. Inside this Circle, we include all the things we care about and outside the Circle are all the things we don't care about. Singer invited us to expand our *Circles of Concern* so we could include ever more of life within this circle. Singer was considering the welfare of all of life that is capable of suffering. People with large *Circles of Concern* are more likely to be vegetarians or vegans.

However, even though all of life matters, in this book I am focusing on the human species rather than all of life. So I have modified Singer's phrase, *Circle of Concern* (FUTK34), to *Circle of Identity* (FUTK35). We identify with those we include inside our *Circle of Identity*. They are our 'us' while everyone outside our *Circle of Identity* is our 'them'. If we have a small *Circle of Identity* there will be a few 'us' and many 'them' and we will be more likely not to trust or even be hostile to many, if not most, of 'them'. And vice versa for those with a large *Circle of Identity*

Some people with a large *Circle of Identity* still might not trust or respect some of 'them' because their actions do not engender trust or respect. But they will be unlikely to judge *all* of 'them' as untrustworthy or threatening simply because they do not like or disrespect *some* of 'them'. In the past we did not trust many who were different simply because they were different. We were often hostile to 'them' unless they were able to convince us not to be. Now the opposite increasingly prevails; ever more of us only distrust those who are different if their behaviour gives us reasons to do so.

I believe that people willing to expand their *Circles of Identity* are more likely to be successful in the emerging multicultural 21st century world than those who are not.

Commencing in the last three decades of the 20th century and continuing during the first two decades of the 21st century, social change is rapidly undermining this millennia-long traditional pattern of caution about, distrust of, and hostility to, difference. This undermining process began at Christmas 1968.

1.2. The Birth of Planetism

It was Christmas 1968, and the astronauts aboard Apollo 8 came from behind the moon to witness a remarkable new vista. The Mission photographer Bill Anders grabbed his camera and took a photograph we now know as *Earthrise*. Fifty years later, on Christmas 2018, Anders wrote:

The Earth we saw rising over the battered grey lunar surface was small and delicate, a magnificent spot of colour in the vast blackness of space. Once-distant places appeared inseparably close. Borders that once rendered division vanished. All of humanity appeared joined together on this glorious-but-fragile sphere.

We set out to explore the moon and instead discovered the Earth.

Fifty years later, "Earthrise"—the lingering imprint of our mission—stands sentinel. It still reminds us that distance and borders and division are merely a matter of perspective. We are all linked in a joined human enterprise; we are bound to a planet we all must share. We are all, together, stewards of this fragile treasure.

That moment jolted humanity's consciousness and opened the door to a subsequent and still-continuing global consciousness transformation. The narrative of this transformation and its implications for understanding the 21st century will be told in this chapter. This transformation is changing how we see ourselves from a past self-perception based on our national, ethnic, cultural, and religious identity to humanity seeing itself as a single humanity sharing a planetary home and with shared future. The former identities emphasise the differences that have generated and still generate competition and conflict with each other. The emerging identity emphasises humanity's oneness, an identity that can generate cooperation and collaboration with each other.

Some cynical or sceptical readers might not accept this proposition. If you're one of them, try to read on for a while. *Sceptics* are left-brain dominant people who need to be convinced by reason and evidence. *Cynics* tend to be right-brain dominant people who are disillusioned idealists; they can be re-illusioned by processes that can give them reasons to hope.

The transformations triggered by the tipping point of *Earthrise* are generating social and cultural seismic shifts, and everywhere we can find evidence of these shifts. There are many who are already expanding their *Circles of Identity* who are welcoming this progression; there are also some who are retaining their current *Circles of Identity* and resisting these changes. This section describes this transformation, examines its status at the beginning of the third decade of the 21st century, and explores the implications of its continuance into the future.

For 1,500 years, all of humanity has been aware that there is a fascinating world beyond our tribal and national borders. But for the most part, except for some historic conquerors humanity stayed at home. For most of history, though as we shall soon see not all of it, humanity has sought to compete with, wage war against, and exploit those who are different. We even thought this was a morally acceptable way to behave. For centuries our most heroic people were war heroes. Even when we were contemplating the shared harm that conflicts between different parts of human kind have caused and could further cause, we didn't regard this as anything but normal behaviour.

We identified ourselves through our difference from others. Our identity stopped at our borders, and we believed those on the other side of our border could be a potential enemy. And we did not consider questioning this thinking even though some of our religions told us we should question it. That is except for John Donne! He wrote in 1624:

No man is an island entire of itself; every man is a piece of the continent, a Part of the main; if a clod be washed away by the sea, Europe is the less, as well as if a promontory were, as well as any manner of thy friends or of thine own were; any man's death diminishes me, because I am involved in mankind. And therefore, never send to know for whom the bell tolls; it tolls for thee.

Probably very few nodded their heads in agreement when he wrote these words. Those who did would have been regarded by others as hopelessly unrealistic dreamers. Yet today we can nod our heads in agreement to these prophetic words without being regarded as unrealistic dreamers because today there are billions who agree with Donne's worldview. With the emergence of more planet wide challenges such as global heating and the COVID-19 pandemic the number of people who think this way is increasing.

The world is rapidly being transformed through a combination of two drivers of change: *Globalisation* and *Interconnectivity*. First, we will discuss globalisation.

1.3. Globalisation: Past, Present and Future

Globalisation is the most significant force shaping our 21st century world. Unfortunately, it has a chequered history.

Over the past 600 years, it has mostly involved the exploitation of the weak by the strong, the conquered by the conqueror. It generally delivered wins to the conquerors and losses to the conquered. This form of globalisation was often so brutal that until recently many people could only associate globalisation with conquest, colonialism, and exploitation, and with socially bad outcomes rather than socially good ones.

Exploitative Globalisation, or European-initiated globalisation, began in the 15th century after the voyage to the Americas by Columbus in 1492. Columbus' voyage to the Americas opened the doors to an exploitative globalisation based on the repression, religious conversion, and colonisation of those who were different. These conquerors carried with them a special kind of blindness to the often-towering achievements of many of these civilisations. The Spanish and then other European nations utilised this exploitative globalisation from 1492 onwards, during what is euphemistically referred to as the *Age of Discovery,* as they sought to conquer these newly discovered civilisations in the Americas and other parts of the planet.

The darkest aspect of the exploitative globalisation era involved the enslavement of those who were different. This was usually a consequence of colonisation. Non-European slaves provided labour in many parts of the world, in European-run plantations and mines. The transport of African slaves to the Americas is just one well-known example. The fact that national leaders such as George Washington and Thomas Jefferson owned slaves showed how totally acceptable slavery was in the 18th and 19th Centuries.

Virtually every colonising power promoted slavery. The British colonists, for example, transported Indians to plantations they owned in Fiji, Guyana, and Sri Lanka. And the British in colonial Australia kidnapped Pacific Islanders and transported them to Queensland to work in the sugar cane industry. But probably the most reprehensible enslavement misdeeds of the era of slavery involved the enslavement of the people of the Congo River Basin by the King of the Belgians, Leopold 11. The Congolese were brutally enslaved in their own land in a colony that Leopold personally annexed and owned.

This kind of globalisation softened many of its more exploitative practices towards the end of the 19th century, but it continued in less repressive ways until it was ended in the mid-20th century after World War 2, when global public opinion could clearly see how reprehensible these activities were.

During this time global trade continued to increase. Some of this trade was not exploitative but much of it was, and given the opportunity to do social bad, the ethics of the time did not discourage this bad behaviour or seek to punish those who acted badly. It was a winner-take-all world.

In the two decades post World War 2, many nations achieved independence, including much of East, South-East and South Asia, Latin America, and most of Africa. Political freedom was still rare until after World War 2. At the end of this war there were only 12 fully-fledged democracies. Today there are more than 130 of them, even if many of these are very imperfect democracies.

However, there is a history and narrative of globalisation that goes back 1000 years before 1492. This was a globalisation based on mutual respect and on collaboration for mutual benefit. This was what some historians call *Archaic Globalisation*. It will be described briefly here. Those readers who wish to know more about *archaic globalisation* can explore the work of John D. Hobson and Mousumi Ghosh.

Archaic Globalisation began in the second century BC. It was not exploitative. Instead, it sought to offer mutual enrichment to its participants while not destroying cultures and environments. It involved peaceful trade that respected and did not threaten difference. This *Archaic Globalisation* linked East Asia and South Asia with Europe. Muslim and Jewish traders used both sea and overland trade via the *Silk Road* to link the East and the West in mutually beneficial trade.

Many new innovations originating in East Asia were introduced into Europe through Southern Spain. Europe massively benefitted from this trade. These Muslim and Jewish global traders mostly respected each other, and respected difference, and many of them cohabited with Christians in Southern Spain for centuries until the Spanish Inquisition, initiated by Ferdinand and Isabella, began to persecute them in 1473, just before Columbus' voyage to the Americas. The intolerance and brutality of the Spanish Inquisition established an ugly moral code that travelled to the Americas with Columbus and with those who followed him, including to other parts of the planet. The year 1473 was a tipping point that influenced the following five centuries.

Archaic Globalisation sought to produce mutual benefit and win/win. *Earthrise* was also a tipping point, a catalyst for a value-shift now transforming globalisation for a second time. This transformation is recreating a 21st century form of archaic pre-Columbus Globalisation, a new emerging era of non-exploitative form of globalisation based on mutual benefit and win/win.

The birth of the Early Modern period (16th and 17th Centuries) that included the Renaissance, the Protestant Reformation, and the Age of Reason, and the late Modern period (18th and 19th Centuries) that included The Enlightenment, the American and French Revolutions, the rise and demise of Napoleon, and the first great age of scientific discovery, contributed nothing to civilising exploitative globalisation. There simply was no appropriate global mechanism present to do this until the birth of international agencies such as the League of Nations and the United Nations in the 20th century. Any behaviour beyond one's own national boundaries was regarded as an amoral zone where piracy could reign and one's military power was the sole determinant of success. There are still some hawkish military and political leaders who continue to think this way today.

However, even if international trade was not open and mutually beneficial, what could and did spread easily and openly across international boundaries were ideas. And there was one big idea that emerged out of the first and second modern periods that did generate global change. It was the birth of *Modernism,* a paradigm that dominated the 18th to mid-20th centuries. A *paradigm* is a group of values that converge and interact to create a single holistic concept or perspective that can be embraced by sufficient people to generate cultural and social change. There were nine core values that composed the Modernist paradigm. These were:

- One's own tribe/culture/nation/religion had first priority
- You should compete with those who are different and seek win (for you) and lose (for them) outcomes
- Individual rights have priority over community rights
- Governance should be via an autocracy
- Humanity is separate from nature, which is to be exploited for our benefit
- Acceptance of unsustainable behaviours
- Gender relationships based on patriarchy
- Conflict should be resolved through confrontation/combat
- Safekeeping by defence

So when international conferences were held, they served national self-interests with winners taking as much as they could get away with from others. A good example of this was what happened at the Versailles Conference at the end of the First World War. The self-interest and vengefulness of the winners was so great, their win-lose decisions so short-sighted and brutal, that they sowed the seeds of the Second World War.

Like every idea at the time, Modernism was deeply rooted in tribal and national cultures. Modernist ideas freely crossed national boundaries and generated global change, but its influence was at the national and tribal level and within some nations but not others. The spread of Modernist thinking continued and was embedded into national cultures by many autocratic modernist leaders, people like Tsars Peter the Great and Catherine the Great in Russia. Such people, despite their being oppressive autocrats, were major initiators of change. Modernist ideas also informed those who sought to overthrow and replace one kind of autocracy with another, such as replacing an aristocratic autocracy with a 'Dictatorship of the Proletariat'. Democracy was rarely the outcome. It would still be decades before any clear internationalist moral compass began to emerge. Modernism did not have any sense of global consciousness.

In the 19th to mid-20th centuries, the modernist concept of *progress* became a mainstream idea. Modernists believed we should replace the old with the new simply because it was new. Old was deemed to be inferior. People believed in 'progress' and established progressive movements and progress associations to promote modernisation, promoting newness everywhere while declaring the old to be 'old fashioned' or 'out of date'.

However, enlightened change was often not the result of these endeavours. Change occurred, yes, but it was not always for the better. Although many different nations and cultures all sought a modern future and modernism as a concept was ubiquitous, conflicts emerged about the best means to achieve a Modern future. These differences generated the great ideological divisions of the 20th century: capitalism versus communism, fascism versus socialism and autocracy versus democracy. Ideology, a concept born out of modernism, began to replace identity (of tribe or religion) as a catalyst for human conflict, as a reason to go to war. These conflicting ideologies all supported what they believed to be modernist ends, but strongly disagreed over the means to achieve them, in vicious struggles that polarised much of the 20th century. Identity and ideology both have for much of the time since continued to provide the major raison d'être for generating human conflict.

By the mid-20th century, modernist 'progress' had developed its own momentum and was continued by the governments of newly independent former colonies as they regained control of their own destinies. In the name of *progress,* we sullied and trashed the global environment and marginalised and even destroyed many indigenous cultures and cultural and religious minorities. At the height of the modernist era smoking chimneys and polluted air and water symbolised 'progress'. This plundering of our planet in the name of *progress* continued into the second half of the 20th century. It continues in some parts of the planet today.

This brings us to Christmas 1968 and *Earthrise*. *Earthrise* generated a shift in consciousness that continues to this day. The human race was forced to recognise for the first time that we can, if we wish to, identify ourselves through lenses informed by our shared humanity.

These new perceptions of a single humanity with a shared home and a common future triggered more global change. This would not have happened unless quickly rising global education levels had reached a point where there were enough people who could see, and be willing to reflect on and understand, the consequences of these changing circumstances. More highly educated people are usually more willing to review their values in the face of new evidence, and observed fact and experience, and to change their views and embrace a new identity that is more commensurate with the changing times. All over the world people began to abandon some of the traditional cultural views that promoted the division of humanity by culture and religion in order to embrace a new identity that looked at the world as a shared home for humanity.

However, in many poor nations with only basic education levels, *Earthrise* transformed nothing. And in these nations cultural and religious identities still provide dividing lines for people to dispute about.

This is still the case but today the ever-increasing rate of global change and the global challenges that result from these changes are forcing more of us, whether we like it or not, to be in the same conference room more often. Today we are being forced to act collaboratively in the interests of all of humanity. When we face shared danger from global heating, a COVID-19 pandemic, economic collapse, or a global trouble spot, we have no choice other than to meet and collaborate with others including with those we do not like.

In 1962 Marshall McLuhan prophesied, just six years before Apollo 8 but after the commencement of the Apollo Program, that humanity was going to become a *global village.* It is important to note that McLuhan called it a *global village* rather than a *global city*. Cities traditionally tolerated exploitation, but this was rare in villages. If one individual exploited another in a village they would become a village pariah, and nobody in a small village wants to be a pariah. Enough of humanity at the time believed McLuhan's idea for it to become a credible prophecy and many were even excited by McLuhan's thinking. This thinking directly challenged the modernist belief that one entity could prosper economically by exploiting another in a win/lose outcome.

Now back to our narrative of global change. A new way at looking at our planet through new conceptual lenses was emerging. This was generated by a combination of globalisation and a massive uplift in mass education. Globalisation and education were combining to generate the huge rise of a global middle class.

This massively growing educated cohort of humanity, a new global middle class, is growing by the population of New York City every three months, and it will number 5 billion in 2030. This cohort has understood the implications of *Earthrise*, that we are one people with a shared planet and a common future. Two issues, global heating and the COVID-19 pandemic, have accelerated this recognition. These two issues are driving an emerging primary allegiance to, and identification with, our planetary future, and this is particularly so in school children and young people.

In late 2019, a sixteen-year-old Swedish girl, Greta Thunberg, challenged the world to change its behaviour because we all now face the shared threat of global heating. She argued that the planet was in danger and nationalist thinking is now irrelevant. A large proportion of humanity agreed with her and shared her rage. When the history of the 21st century is written it is likely that that the two challenges of global heating and the 2020 COVID-19 pandemic, and the economic dislocation and recession generated by it, will be seen as significant catalysts of transformative social change leading to the development of a better governed and managed integrated planetary society in the 21st century.

Around 1970, just after *Earthrise*, humanity increasingly began to be ashamed by the things it did in the name of Modernity. The feeling that accompanied the use of the phrase 'you can't stop progress' shifted from enthusiasm, to resignation, and then to cynicism, a feeling summed up by Joni Mitchell in her 1970 song *'Big Yellow Taxi'*, when she sang that we 'paved paradise and put up a parking lot'.

And about 1970, post-modernism was born. *Earthrise* and the Apollo Program triggered a shift in our consciousness about how we might treat our planetary home. U Thant, the UN Secretary General, emphasised this just three years after Apollo 8. In 1971 and after the Apollo 13 mission nearly ended in the slow deaths of the crew because of the failure of the spaceship's life-support systems, U Thant said in an address to the University of Texas:

The drama of Apollo 13 gave us an exhibition on a small scale of what might easily become the problem of Spaceship Earth. The problem in those agonising days of Apollo 13's return from the moon was basically the uncertain balance between the capacity of the spaceship to support life and the demands made on it by its inhabitants. Until recently, the Earth could without difficulty, meet the needs of all its passengers and could absorb the various waste products that it produced. But now we face a rapidly increasing imbalance between the life-sustaining demands of the Earth, and the demands, industrial, agricultural, technological and demographic, which its inhabitants put upon it. This is an unprecedented challenge to all Earth-people here and now. If we fail to meet that challenge it could become an unthinkable disaster for all our children.

Apollo 13 had behind it a vast and brilliant research and planning organisation and a dedicated and decisive Mission Control whose authority was unquestioned. It also had a home base to return to. On Spaceship Earth we do not have any of these advantages. Indeed, it is strange that while we marvel at, and pride ourselves on, the miracles of invention, planning, technique, courage and teamwork which sustain our space explorers we still accept, for our own Spaceship Earth, the most antiquated systems, the most wretched mismanagement and a level of profiteering, sabotage, self-seeking and indiscipline which would not be tolerated for a second in the Manned Space Flight Centre or at the Soviet Cosmodrome.

U Thant persuaded the UN General Assembly to approve the first global environment conference, the UN Conference on the Human Environment, which commenced on the fifth of June 1972 in Stockholm. The Stockholm Conference began to generate a global effort directed at meeting these newly recognised environmental challenges. It established the UN Environment Program (UNEP). The fifth of June is now celebrated annually as World Environment Day.

Twenty years later, the Earth Summit took place in June 1992, and the World Summit on Environment and Development Brazil Plus 20 occurred in June 2012. Such meetings are now held every 20 years. The Canadian Maurice Strong was possibly the biggest shaper of this transformation during these two decades. Strong was the Secretary General of the Stockholm Conference in 1972, the first Chief Executive of the UN Environment Program, and the Secretary General of the 1992 Earth Summit in Rio de Janeiro.

The idea that a future humanity might give its primary loyalty to planet was first raised by the visionary economist and writer, Barbara Ward, whose seminal book *The Home of Man* was written as a base document for the UN Conference on Human Settlements held in Vancouver in 1976. She wrote:

We have at least reached the point of talking together about the great common tasks of Humanity, preserving the living Environment, feeding the hungry, giving shelter to all our fellow creatures, treating with great care and fraternal sharing the fundamental resources—of water, of minerals, of energy, upon which our common life depends. This dialogue could be the signal of a new but growing loyalty, not to our old divisive nationalisms, but to shared tasks and common membership in the City of Man.

Too vast a dream? Too naïve a hope? Perhaps—yet we can now talk to the ends of the earth as easily as villagers once conversed with each other. Our planetary interdependence is as great as that of earlier states. So are all the preconditions of material existence. If man has learned to be loyal to his family and his town, do we have to argue that no further extension of loyalty is possible to the planet itself, which carries our earthly life and all the means of sustaining it? (p. 294)

In this beautifully written 1976 plea, Barbara Ward was asking us to expand our *Circle of Identity* to embrace our whole planet and all of humanity. In 1976 this was mere hope. But Ward was a remarkable visionary. Today we can recognise that both Singer's *Circle of Concern* (FUTK34) and the *Circle of Identity* (FUTK35) are part of our response to her plea. Singer's *Circles of Concern* (FUTK34) are expanding. More people are becoming vegan and vegetarian. More are concerned about animal welfare and liberation and more people are concerned about the negative environmental consequences of continued meat production and consumption. And our *Circles of Identity* are also expanding as well, as an increasing number of people see humanity as one. I believe that over time both Circles will expand for more people during the remainder of the 21st century.

In the 1990s the time was right for a new paradigm to emerge. *Modernism* was a totally inappropriate paradigm to guide our journey into the future from that point on. *Postmodernism* was born.

Among other things, post-modernists believed we should keep old things of high value and integrate them with the best of the new. So, we retrofitted what we began to call 'heritage buildings' with new facilities rather than demolishing them as we had done during the modernist era. We created new art and music that showed respect for, and even appropriated, the best of the old and the culturally different, and integrated it with the new.

People in developed western nations began to explore the traditional healing and wellness arts and the martial arts of Asian cultures, such as acupuncture, yoga, Ayurveda, taekwondo, Tai Chi Chuan, and Shiatsu. We discovered that these wellness and martial arts can complement the latest medical treatments. We changed many of the words we used to signify that we now valued things we had regarded as having little or no value: *swamp*s became *wetlands*, and *slums* became *heritage precincts*. We began to treasure the cuisines of other cultures as well as our own.

What then will follow postmodernism? Before answering this question, consider what has happened over three centuries:

- The 19th century was the century of dependence. Most people lived in colonies that sometimes were even called dependencies.
- The 20th century was the century of independence. By its end the majority of people lived in independent nations.
- The 21st century is the century of interdependence, where independent entities voluntarily give up some of their independence to seek the benefits and synergies that come from union.

These are also the three stages of maturation of our own species

- Dependence—childhood.
- Independence—adolescence.
- Interdependence—adulthood.

Interdependent relationships are mature relationships, and for success in an increasingly interdependent 21st century we all need to know how to initiate, nurture, and amicably terminate specific interdependent relationships. This progression can be seen as the process of the maturation of humanity so that we become more capable of living successfully and indefinitely in an ever more interdependent future. In an emerging global village, we can no longer afford to have adults, especially political leaders, behaving like self-obsessed children. We will discuss this critical issue of global maturity further later in this book.

Interdependence is the key to describe our emerging 21st century global society: our growing political and economic interdependence, and our ever-increasing awareness that we share an ecologically vulnerable, climate and pandemic endangered planetary home. We cannot any longer tolerate destructive war in a global village. Any nation or autocrat that does not cooperate with others to protect us from shared pandemic or climatic threats will endanger us all.

We must recognise that the actions of a greedy or profligate bank, hedge fund or company, or a selfish nation, can pull all of us down because we are now so financially interdependent and are interdependent in many other ways as well. Many banks and other large financial organisations began to behave badly in the 1980s. They we oblivious to, or consciously ignored, the shifts in values that accompanied humanity's growing global interdependence. Many sought to continue their modernist values informed behaviours. This was particularly true for Wall Street financial institutions. Many financial institutions decided that they could use their critical role in financing and facilitating global development and trade to enrich themselves and their shareholders, even by stealing from their customers.

This reality was marvellously demonstrated in the film *Wall Street* when its lead character Gordon Gecko declared that *Greed is Good*. Many people changed their perception of banks from that of trustworthy mutual benefit seeking institutions, to untrustworthy exploitative institutions. This greed continued until it inflicted two successive financial crises, in East Asia in 1997-1998, and in the western world in 2007-2008. The public standing of banks was severely damaged, and at the beginning of the third decade of the 21st century it has not recovered. And if the emerging blockchain technology and digital currencies fulfil their promise as I believe they will, many private banks will become redundant. The role of private banks will change and their influence will be much reduced. Many of us will no longer need banks as we currently need them now. This revolution is just beginning. This is one emerging innovation arena that will significantly change our world. Another emerging innovation arena I would like to telegraph to the reader now will be the emergence of factory-made food made possible by the emerging precision fermentation revolution which will have massive implications for agriculture, for the creation of a future world of food plenty, and for the realisation of a climate safe future. This second innovation arena will be discussed in Chapter 8 and again in Chapter 12.

At this time we began to recognise that nations and organisations that practice or support nation first or organisation first, rather than planet or global community first, will become planetary pariahs.

Modernist globalisation, which was merely a less brutal version of earlier exploitative globalisation, was still driven by competition, conflict and win/lose. This began to recede and give way to an emerging post-modernist globalisation driven by a more collaborative humanity that was seeking to base its relationships on mutual obligations, mutual benefit, and win/win. And it began to change capitalism itself, as we shall explore later in this book.

Many did not want to recognise this new reality and many still don't to this day. They continue to perceive themselves through their national, cultural, and religious identities and still seek to confront and compete with and seek win/lose outcomes from those who are different. In the next chapter, and others as well, we will discuss a hindsight process I call the *Derivation Duo*, which includes identifying one's *heritage and baggage*. *Heritage* represents the collective elements from our past that are priceless and that we should keep and nurture, while *baggage* is the now worthless elements from our past that, if we are wise, we will eliminate from our lives. Many of these people are holding onto what they perceive to be tribal, religious, and cultural *heritage* when in fact through social change this *heritage* has now become *baggage*.

However, others expanded their *Circles of Identity* and with this change commenced to transform their behaviour and ethics. A new planetary consciousness was born and a new planetary moral compass began to emerge. Many of us recognised for the first time that planet must come first: the paradigm of what I call *Planetism* was born. *Planetists* know that they must give their first allegiance to planet: to prioritise planet over nation (*Nationalism*) or tribe, ethnicity, culture, or religion.

In the third decade of the 21st century, there is now an emerging planetist majority, one that seeks to shape the future through collaboration and cooperation and, if necessary, negotiation, and though the seeking of mutual benefit and win/win. Greta Thunberg is one such planetist and so are her supporters. Many of the young, mostly students challenging Modernist Chinese rule in Hong Kong in 2019, are Planetists as well. I believe that a global planetist majority will be present by 2030.

If humanity is to succeed in this emerging Planetist world, its agenda must now include answering a question posed by Garrett Hardin in his 1968 essay *The Tragedy of the Commons*, to wit: 'what forms of mutual coercion can we mutually agree upon?' The answer will be the basis of many of our global negotiations from now on. This will be the case whenever we need to collectively confront shared endangerment from global heating, pandemics, global economic meltdown, or from destructive wars within our emerging global village. And it will also be the case when we wish to build, or secede from, a personal, business or political relationship.

Sometimes crafting win/win outcomes will be exceedingly difficult. But from now on we can no longer be winners and losers as was the case in the Modernist era. Now the only choice before us is to create outcomes that permit us all to win together or eventually we will all lose together. As humanity becomes more interdependent, unless we find the means to achieve mutual benefit there will be no agreement. Unfortunately, there are still many political leaders who have not yet recognised this reality.

The new integrated, interdependent *Global Village* first predicted by Marshall McLuhan in 1962 is an emerging reality. Moreover, our collective interdependence and interconnectivity has already grown sufficiently for us to be able to collectively punish planetary rogues and pariahs by:

- Applying trade sanctions against them.
- Boycotting products and services they market
- Withholding investment capital from them.
- Freezing their bank accounts in other countries.

These punishments are the *Planetary Pariah Punishments* (FUTK11). As our interdependence increases in the coming decades these punishments will increase in both number and power. The ever-increasing interconnectivity and interdependence of the global trade and investment system will provide enough power to bring most planetary rogues and pariahs into line.

Wars were created to settle disputes—certainly humanity's stupidest solution to a problem. Now there are many other means to settle disputes, and the basis of most of them is that in the 21st century we have now become so interdependent that war is no longer a feasible option as a conflict-resolving tool. This was a major motivating factor for the creation of the Europe Union: so that France and

Germany, who had had three wars in the previous century, would never be able to afford to go to war again. Now, even if there is a war between nations, it is rarely a fight to the finish but is used to position oneself for the negotiation that global public opinion will pressure the participants to undertake.

If the parties involved continue with war, they will be forced to face the *International Criminal Court (ICC)*, which can punish people who commit crimes against humanity such as genocide. I will show that in the 21st century there will be a widening gap between the concepts of defence and security. In our emerging 21st century global village defence is in long-term decline, but security is something we must become collectively much better at accomplishing if we are to remain fully secure as our global village emerges and develops.

The global community is now considering establishing a new addition to this international legal infrastructure, an *International Anti-Corruption Court*. This will be a very useful addition to the emerging infrastructure for facilitating greater and more secure global interdependence and for punishing Planetary Pariahs. Other similar new pieces of legal and governance infrastructure will be added in the coming decades. The governance and the political, social, physical, and technological infrastructure to engender a free and fair, collaborative, interdependent and functional global village will be in place by the year 2050.

1.4. Two Converging Global Trends

The birth of the paradigm of Planetism in the late 20th century and its further development in the early 21st century is a consequence of the convergence of two long-term global trends:

- *From modernism to postmodernism to planetism*
- *From first allegiance to tribe, to nation, to planet*

The first of these trends is the shift from the paradigms *of Modernism (circa 1800-1970), to Postmodernism (circa 1970-2020) to Planetism (post 2020).* These three paradigms are the only paradigms we can call truly 'global' paradigms, ones that have had or are having a significant influence on a large proportion of the Earth's peoples, and that extend beyond just a few nations or cultures. Paradigm shifts occur when people witness a world which challenges their concept of what ought to be. For example, Vladimir Putin holds onto a now archaic idea about a Russian Empire continuing into the 21st century. The disaster that is the Urkrainian war is the consequence. More flexible people will review their mindsets. Some, like Putin and Trump, will refuse to move on, and actually change, their mindsets: these are the people who will be left behind by a changing world.

Modernism, the paradigm that drove global Modernisation in the 20th century was progressive in its outlook: it believed in 'progress' or change, even if only for its own sake. Modernisation produced countless positive benefits to society, and for decades the shadow of Modernism was neglected. Modernism did successfully challenge humanity to conceive that the future could be different from more of the same, and it commenced liberating humanity from the shackles of the aristocratic autocratic political order and other forms of traditional thinking. But as we have already discussed it also came at a cost. Modernity was a European construct that caused many negative changes in much of the rest of the World. And as we have already discussed it legitimised the destruction of environments, societies, and cultures all over the planet.

By the early 21st century, progressive people, the people who had benefited from globalisation thus far and who saw it as a good albeit a still imperfect mechanism for raising global prosperity and opportunity, had moved on embrace the paradigm of *Postmodernism*. *Postmodernism* is functionally a form of *multicultural humanism*. It respects both nature and cultural difference, whereas modernism disrespected these. Postmodernism values democracy, intercultural and interreligious respect, believes in gender equality and promotes development, production, and consumption that is sustainable.

Many people think democracy is a modernist concept. At the end of the Second World War, after more than two centuries of modernity, there were still only a dozen democracies in the world. This is despite many seminal events such as the American and French Revolution, the Revolution of 1848, and the Russian Revolution. Modernist dictators of all kinds were strongly socially autocratic and repressive and yet were technologically progressive, embracing for example the latest communication and military technologies.

Today, modernist values are still embedded in, and inform the identities of, many conservative and fundamentalist people. Of course, there are still a few who would still not qualify even as Modernists, and who might more appropriately be described as pre-modern, those such as ISIS and other extremist religious groups. However, here we are talking about those who still see themselves as participants in mainstream society, not those who have chosen to isolate themselves from this mainstream society. Many of these mainstream people are still wedded to past values. Some of the people in this category include some older and many poorly educated people. These people mostly will resist global integration with those who are different because they continue to believe these people pose an existential threat to them.

We will discuss in the next chapter the politics of global integration and the conflict between those who support global integration and those who are resisting it. These politics are likely to produce further conflict for a while. However, I believe that most of these issues will be resolved within two decades at the most.

Most of educated humanity, both progressive and conservative in political terms, want a future that is fairer for all than the present. They want to ensure that current globalisation lessens injustice by ensuring the rising tide of globalisation lifts all boats and not just some boats.

1.5. The Nine values of Planetism

Postmodernism is the paradigm of transition in global values occurring between the years circa 1970-2020. It has facilitated the decline of Modernism because Modernism is now an inappropriate paradigm for a 21st century global society. Postmodernism is a paradigm of transition. It rejects Modernity but it is not of itself a worthy successor to Modernity. It is a paradigm for disassembling Modernism, but it does not embrace a new global perspective that can genuinely replace Modernism. Postmodernism is now itself giving way to a new emerging paradigm that worthy of replacing Modernism, to which I have given the name Planetism.

Postmodernism is the paradigm of transition from a global culture based on Modernist values to global culture based on Planetist values. Planetism is the emerging paradigm of the cosmonaut, the member of the crew of 'Spaceship Earth', and the values of this emerging paradigm are already held by most highly educated people, young and old, rich and poor.

The table below summarises this shift in global culture:

Nine values Shifts from Modernism to Planetism (FUTK05)

From the cowboy culture /Modernism (1960)	To the spaceship culture/Planetism (2025)
First priority to tribe (culture, nation, religion.)	First priority to planet.
Compete with and seek win/lose outcomes against those who are different.	Collaborate with and seek win/win outcomes with those who are different
Individualist. Individual rights have priority over community rights.	Communitarian. Community rights have priority over individual rights.
Governance through autocracy	Governance through democracy
Humanity is separate from nature. We can exploit and destroy nature to advance human wellbeing.	Humanity is part of nature. We must protect and nurture nature to advance human wellbeing
Accepts/condones unsustainable behaviours.	Promotes/innovates sustainable behaviours
Gender relationships based on patriarchy	Gender relationships based on equality
Resolve conflict through confrontation/combat	Resolve conflict through collaboration/negotiation
Safekeeping through defence	Safekeeping through security

Until recently it was seen to be normal behaviour for everybody to put national or tribal interest first. But now we are recognising that our ever-increasing levels of interdependence require us to recognise that such self-interested behaviour will be regarded as selfish, hostile, and even as bullying because such actions could collaterally harm others. For example, any nation that that continues to claim it has an individual right to build a coal-fired power station or do something else to pollute our shared planetary atmosphere with carbon can increasingly expect an ever more hostile response from the rest of the world. We have banned smoking in public for the same basic reason. These are just two examples of why global culture in the 21st century must become ever more communitarian. From now these kinds of problems can only be successfully overcome through collaboration and by putting planet first. In the future, if people cause significant and irreversible harm to our planetary home, they will be punished by others who share our planetary home with them, including through the *Planetary Pariah Punishments.*

More of us now celebrate our tribal and national identity in ways that recognise we are also part of a shared humanity. And many of us also recognise that we should look at nationalism and tribalism differently from now on, and we should often subordinate tribal and nationalist identities to our common human identity because we share a planetary home.

These issues include responding to the challenges posed by global heating, pandemics, global financial crises and management issues generated by our ever-growing economic interdependence, the plight of refugees, global terrorism and organised crime, and bringing peace to the planet's trouble spots, while preventing those who seek to initiate wars and punishing those who do. We can no longer opt out by saying any of these issues are not our business. As John Donne, perhaps the world's first Planetist, prophetically said in 1624, 'we are involved in mankind'. Humanity was forced to recognise this reality during the COVID-19 pandemic.

While most of the Planetist values listed above are self-evident, one that is less well-understood is *Communitarianism. Individualism* believes that individual rights are paramount and that if there is conflict between individuals and groups the rights of individuals should prevail. To many, but far from all, Modernists community rights should be subservient to individual rights. The most extreme version of this perspective is present in English speaking cultures such as the UK and the USA. In other places this perspective of the status of individual rights has not been elevated to such sacrosanct levels. And for some there is no such thing as the community interest or community rights at all. As recently as 2013, Margaret Thatcher said: *And, you know, there is no such thing as society. There are individual men and women and there are families.* Communitarianism is the opposite of individualism. For communitarians, community rights should take precedent over individual rights if they conflict.

And community rights can extend to nature as well, recognising that rivers, other species, and whole ecosystems should have the right to thrive on our shared planet as well. This has always been the view of all first-nations peoples. To deal with such dilemmas humanity, post Earthrise, has conceived new concepts such as those of sustainability and heritage that are now major components of global ethics and public policy. These will be discussed in detail later in this book.

Over the centuries different cultures have arrived at different places as they have sought to achieve an appropriate balance between individualism and communitarianism. What balance between individual freedom and community responsibility should we seek to achieve to create a society that works well for all? The English culture and those derived from it, in answering this question have emphasised the importance of individualism most, while other cultures such as the German, French and Chinese have emphasised that we should tip this balance towards communitarianism to varying degrees. Those who want to explore individualism and communitarianism more fully should look at the exceptional work of Charles Hampden-Turner and Fons Trompenaars.

Over the coming two decades, if we want to develop a global village that works for all we will all need to become more communitarian and less individualistic. Communitarianism recognises our fundamental interdependence. The issues of communitarianism and interdependence are major facets of emerging 21st century global society. This will be discussed more fully in other chapters of this book.

In mid-2019, at the G20 meeting in Tokyo, Russian President Vladimir Putin said: *The liberal idea has become obsolete. It has come into conflict with the overwhelming majority of the population.*

Putin's beliefs are the opposite to those of Margaret Thatcher. At home he is a communitarian autocrat. But he an individualistic autocrat in international affairs. He believes that while he has scant respect for individual human rights inside Russia, Russia has the right as an individual nation to do whatever it likes in our emerging interdependent global community. He has no problem in bullying others and waging war to promote Russian national interests as he has done in Chechnya, Georgia, Crimea, and Ukraine. Russia's internal and external governance values are inconsistent. Russian internal culture has always been an autocratic and communitarian one. The cultural evolutionary journey that Russia will make in a post-Putin era will be from autocratic communitarianism at home and autocratic individualism abroad, to democratic communitarianism in both arenas.

The UK and the US, on the other hand, will move from democratic individualism to a greater measure of democratic communitarianism. To create a Planetist harmonious sustainable global village humanity will most likely evolve a mainstream global culture based on democratic communitarianism.

Democratic communitarianism already thrives in many nations such as Germany, France, and Japan.

1.6. Planetism: The Shaper of Emerging Global Markets and Industrial and Economic Futures

After this discussion of values shifts in the late 20th century and the early 21st century we can now consider how global values shifts and transformations might influence and shape our futures and our lives in our emerging global village. I believe we can predict the economic and industrial consequences of the emergence of the global paradigm of planetism. We can predict what people might want to buy and sell in the next few decades. And if we can do this, we can also predict what new products and services and technologies will be in demand in the emerging markets of the coming decades, and what new industries and vocations might emerge to supply these markets.

The *nine values of planetism* will spread to more people over time as an increasing number of people are uplifted into greater prosperity through globalisation and the spread of mass education. As the proportion of planetists increases in coming decades the combined purchasing and investing power of this cohort of the world's population will increase.

Can we understand what this ever-increasing number of more prosperous first-allegiance-to-planet people will want to buy in increasing quantities in emerging global markets? The answer can be found through exploring the meaning of and joining the dots between five related words: *values, value, valued, valuable, and evaluate*. The connection is that:

- Our *values* determine what we *value* or what we regard as of little or no *value*.
- What we *value* more we will *evaluate* more highly and then seek to acquire more of.
- As more of us seek to acquire what we increasingly *value* it will become increasingly *valued* and *valuable*
- What we *evaluate* as more (or less) *valued* and *valuable* we will seek more of (or less of) in markets.
- Others will then create organisations and vocations to imagine, innovate, and market infrastructure, products and services that can provide us with what we regard as becoming more *valuable*.

To take the next step, we need to consider innovation: innovation is what we do to create new products and services that will be demanded in emerging markets. As we mentioned in the foreword and will explore further in Chapters 4 and 9, innovation is one of the six tools we use to shape the future.

I would like to offer the reader one item from the future knowledge curriculum now. This is how we can understand and predict how our knowledge that something is becoming more valued and valuable can be turned into products or services to supply global markers and what innovations could be developed to supply a market that is seeking more of what is becoming increasingly valued. This is the concept of the *Innovation Duet: Ways and Wares*.

- *Ways* are *social innovations*: innovations to what we do, to how we change our behaviour so that we can better realise our aspirations or purposes. These might include new ideas, and events of all kinds such as a discussion, a meeting, a political movement, a workshop, or a publicity campaign.
- *Wares* are *physical innovations*: innovations to what we *use, the tools we use,* to achieve our aspirations and purposes. Such tools could be a development, a technology, a methodology, an algorithm, a pattern, a design or a plan.

An example:

- A *water conservation way*: shortening your time in the shower
- A *water conservation ware*: a low volume showerhead.

Together, these enhance water conservation. How many other water conservation ways and wares can you imagine?

Though this mechanism, we can understand how the paradigm of Planetism with its nine core values will shape our emerging 21st century society and which goods and service will appear in coming decades. Markets that will be increasingly moulded by the nine values of planetism will, for example, demand more and better *sustainability ways and wares,* more and better *security ways and wares,* more and better *gender equality ways and wares,* and more and better *democracy ways and wares*. The rich detail about how this is manifested in our emerging industrial, economic, and vocational futures will be provided in many different places in this book.

1.7. Fourteen Global Trends:

The narrative of the birth and rise of planetism is based on an examination of global change and trends occurring in the world between 1960 and current times and is based on projecting them forward to the year 2050 and beyond. Some of these trends slowed down during the COVID-19 pandemic but are continuing in the post COVID-19 pandemic era. Here is a list of fourteen global megatrends (FUTK02) that are currently transforming the world. Judge for yourself whether or not you believe that these trends are real. Here they are:

1.7.1. Growing interdependence and interconnectedness: A single integrated global society, a global village, is being created through globalisation. Our world is becoming ever more:

- *Interdependent*. The interdependent relationship based on the Golden Rule of mutual obligations to shared aspirations, and win/win benefit is becoming an ever more dominant global model in personal, business, workplace, and international relations, and
- *Interconnected*: There has been a massive uplifting of humanity's capacity to communicate and exchange ideas through digital and communications technologies, and social and global media.

Humanity is innovating the means to enable it to build and manage its relationships in our emerging global village so that these relationships become as effective and rewarding in a global village as they were in a village of 500 people a millennium ago.

1.7.2. Rising educational levels: A massive expansion of education is under way, both in terms of its geographic spread (more and more people are being educated,) and in terms of its depth, (more and more people are being educated for longer). Primary education is universal. Secondary education is almost so. And Tertiary education is expanding massively. As they become more educated people increasingly look beyond their own cultural roots and they begin to see themselves as part of a single humanity that simultaneously respects and celebrates both cultural diversity and human unity. Education is currently the second largest industry in the world and is likely to become the biggest industry in the coming decades.

1.7.3. Increasing global wealth: Wealth is increasingly being generated from new innovations, new products and services that are created from new knowledge and new ideas, from *metaphysical resources*. This is a consequence of rising education levels and can be expected to continue as global education levels continue to rise. Therefore, wealth can be potentially unlimited. In the past when we thought wealth was primarily created from the 'exploitation' of *physical resources* we assumed that wealth would always be limited, and poverty would always be present. In the 21st century, the creation of universal economic prosperity has become a realisable goal for humanity.

1.7.4. A growing educated middle class: There has been a substantial growth of the educated middle class because of a spreading of prosperity generated by globalisation. This educated middle class is growing by the population of New York City every three months. There will be 5 billion educated middle class people in the world in 2030. There are 5000 millionaires being created in China every week. The result is that the values of the educated middle class are becoming the values that inform both global public opinion and global investment patterns. This has major implications for global paradigm shifts and the creation of a sustainably prosperous global society.

1.7.5. A single integrated global marketplace: A single integrated global marketplace for ideas, products and services is emerging, one that is increasingly informed by a global public opinion embodying planetist values. The collective purchasing power and investment power of the global educated middle class that is informed by these planetist values is increasingly shaping global markets and the global economy.

1.7.6. Growing communitarianism: Communitarianism (giving priority to community rights over individual rights when these are in conflict) is growing and there is a relative decline in its opposite, individualism. There is an increasing recognition that global issues such as global heating, pandemics, global trade, and delivering a peaceful future, can only be effectively achieved if all humanity collaborates as a single global community. A modified form of individualism is emerging —*sustainable individualism*—that condones only individual behaviours that do not cause net collateral harm to life or net collateral damage to place.

1.7.7. Rising democracy: There is rising global support for democratic governance. Popular movements are challenging both democratic and autocratic administrations everywhere: those who feel they are being left behind by or not benefitting from globalisation are using this same democratic power to try to improve their situations. The number of democracies in the world has increased from just twelve in 1945 to about 130 in the second decade of the 21st century. Many of these democracies are still imperfect democracies, with autocratic leadership being elected by imperfect electoral means.

As global education levels continue to rise and the electorate becomes better informed these imperfect democracies will become better democracies. Highly educated people do not like being ruled by autocrats. Although there are some who are concerned by an apparent rise of autocratic governance in the early 21st century, I believe democracy will continue to consolidate itself. Democracy is now on the threshold of becoming the global norm.

1.7.8. New planet-wide punishments: There is an increased use of a new suite of measures that use ever growing global interdependence, global public opinion and shaming and international collaboration to penalise rogue leaders, nations, companies, and organisations. These interdependence-based punishments include trade sanctions, customer boycotts, strikes on capital investment, and the freezing of bank accounts. The threat of being tried in the International Criminal Court (ICC) is beginning to provide an added incentive to encourage autocrats to leave office without resistance and hand power to democratic movements.

1.7.9. Increasing multilateralism: There are a mounting number of multilateral agreements that collectively increase global interdependence. These include bilateral and multilateral trade agreements and agreements to effectively manage, trade in, and protect the functioning of our shared planetary home and better manage our emerging global village. This is eroding the power of national governments to act without giving sufficient cognisance to the rights of other nations and the global community. The power of the individual nation state is in relative long-term decline.

There is also an increasing development of international and regional forms of governance. Entities such as the EU and ASEAN, The Transpacific Partnership (TPP), the G8 and the G20, the World Bank, the WTO and the International Criminal Court, and Global NGOs such as Oxfam, World Vision, Amnesty International, Transparency International, and the WWF, are increasingly influential in world affairs. The complexity of international issues and the level of interdependence between nations means that it is no longer possible for individual nations, even superpowers, to be successful if they do not have the support of other nations. All these multilateral organisations and agreements are continually lifting their entry requirements. So while people were once concerned that globalisation would encourage a race to the lowest ethical bottom, the opposite is the reality.

1.7.10. An emerging integrated global financial and investment market: An integrated and interdependent global investment and financial system is evolving. It increasingly operates under one set of rules, and will force international responsibility on all financial institutions whether they like it or not. Speculation on the value of currencies will slowly decline as the number and power of national currencies decline, and speculative transactions are discouraged by taxation and regulation. Our increasingly integrated interdependent global financial system is still vulnerable to being destabilised by self-interested financial corporations, but these will increasingly risk being designated planetary pariahs.

Rogue banks and financial traders are being judged as harshly and subjected to as much negative collective global public opinion as is directed at autocratic governments bent on repressing their own people. It is likely that a global central regulator and a universal second currency will be realities within ten years. A new international anti-corruption court has been proposed. New means based on blockchain technology and digital currencies have been created that can enable secure financial transfers to occur that do not need the involvement of banks. These changes will collectively work to further minimise financial corruption and theft.

1.7.11. An ageing planetary population: More people are joining the global middle class and more women are seeking long-term careers. Therefore, they are having fewer and better-educated children. The consequence of these changes is that populations are ageing in many parts of the world. This in turn is leading to a massive increase in automation and robotics and the use of artificial intelligence and other technologies to ensure that increasing productivity per working person offsets the decline in workforce numbers. The rate of growth of the planet's population is slowing and will stabilise around 10-11 billion about 2070. It will then begin to decline. Ageing as an issue has major implications for the future of transnational migration and for the realisation of 21st century economic prosperity.

1.7.12. Religion under pressure: There is growing support for religion that respects difference, and there will be escalating opposition to and increasing pariah status for religion that does not. Fundamentalist religion in all its forms is increasingly being challenged by its more tolerant alternatives and by international public opinion. There is still much division and even conflict both between religions and within each religion. There also has been an increase in secularism, a significant increase in the number of people who state they embrace no religion and who see all religion as promoting division and conflict based on difference.

1.7.13. Rising sustainability: Products and services that realise sustainable production, trade, consumption, development and lifestyles are proliferating in global markets. These new innovations will be designed to create new coteries of products and services that cause zero net collateral harm to life and zero net collateral damage to planetary places. The creation of an ever more sustainable future will be a major component of the 21st century global economy.

1.7.14 A global village customised for difference: In the 21st century, globalisation is integrating our world into a single global village with a shared global market. Our differences, and our cultural and individual differences in particular, are becoming ever more precious. Therefore, there has been an increased customisation of products and services to respect and honour these human differences. *Economies of Scale* that promoted *a one size fits all* production have been replaced by *Economies of Scope* where manufacturers and services are now becoming ever more capable of providing products and services customised for both cultural and individual difference.

These include the development of what can be called world industries, such as world music, and world or multicultural food halls that simultaneously celebrate both tribal and cultural difference and human unity. In coming decades, this trend of the cultural and individual customisation of products and services will enlarge and deepen and become a major facet of the planet's industrial and educational futures.

Chapter 2: Social and Political Change in Our emerging global village

Changing human behaviour and politics: *How are human behaviour and politics changing in response to increasing global integration and the birth of a 21st century global society?*

2.1. Globalisation: Catalyst of the Politics of Hope and Fear

As global integration continues unabated, and as the 21st century commences its third decade, the world has divided into two camps. Some support further global integration and some oppose it. I believe that those who support further global integration have been willing and able to expand their *circles of identity* and have begun to recognise that they should now give their primary allegiance to planet. And as they make the critical shift from putting nation or tribe first to putting planet first, they are simultaneously embedding in themselves the *nine values of planetism.* Those who are resisting or opposing global integration for the most part continue to hold on to their primary allegiance and nation or tribe, to their tribal/national identities, and to Modernist values. A new form of global politics is emerging that reflects this division in global public opinion.

Thirty years ago, most of our news was national news. Now our news is increasingly generated from beyond our national borders. Our emerging global village is already so interconnected and interdependent that a decision made somewhere can produce both positive and negative consequences anywhere. This was perfectly illustrated by the global COVID-19 pandemic. Our politics is being increasingly shaped by different perceptions of the causes and consequences of these changes.

For most of human history, humanity believed that an exploitable world existed beyond one's national boundaries where military power and piracy could flourish and that winners could take all. We believed that we could 'throw away' into the apparently vast planetary commons that are the planet's atmospheric and oceanic domains anything we did not want: nobody 'owned' these domains, so we treated them as planetary cesspools without any threat of retaliation. In the 21st century and for the same reason, we now are treating outer space as a cesspool (or a junk yard) where we feel we can dump anything we don't want. Humanity sometimes can be a slow learner.

We mostly have regarded politics to be something we did within our national boundaries and did not practice beyond them except to protect our own national interest. Even today there are some conservative political leaders who see global politics only as a mechanism to settle disputes between conflicting national self-interests. The concept that humanity might share a collective responsibility for the governance and future of our shared planetary home is an idea that is still not yet embraced by many who continue to see the world only through their nationalist or tribal lenses.

In the last chapter, we examined how planetist values are now spreading from the global margins into the global mainstream and how this will influence global markets and humanity's industrial and economic future. In this chapter we will examine how humanity is responding to these changes and how this is creating a 21st century politics that is truly global. These new politics are *planetary politics*, the politics of our shared planetary home.

It is important that we all recognise the sheer economic and political power of the forces driving our increasing global integration, interdependence, and interconnectivity, that in turn is shaping our emerging global village. Much of this is occurring despite the action of governments and not because of them. This is because both commercial corporations and humanitarian NGOs have stepped up to the plate and are now shaping our global cultures even more than governments. Most of the biggest commercial corporations in the world are also the wealthiest corporate entities that have ever existed. They are collectively creating what I call call *planetary interconnectivity ways and wares*. It is not surprising they are so successful and wealthy. At the beginning of the third decade of the 21st century these corporations are providing the infrastructure to interconnect humanity into a single global village. These include companies such as Google (Alphabet), Facebook (Meta), Microsoft, Samsung, Huawei, and Apple. They are prospering because they are innovating and marketing these *planetary interconnectivity ways and wares* to a global market that is insatiable for these ways and wares. *Social media ways and wares* and *global trading ways and wares* are just two other groups of innovations uplifting our collective capacity to communicate and trade as effectively in an emerging global village in the 21st century as we once did in a small village 100 years ago.

Our genes have not changed and our basic needs for connection, love, intimacy, friendship, privacy, and trade, have not changed. What has changed is that people want to communicate, conduct relationships and trade with others as effectively in our emerging global village as they did in a small village a millennium ago. The conversations people have on social media today are very similar to the conversations they would have had around the kitchen table or in pillow talk a century ago. This is precisely why social media was invented. The aspiration to fulfil humanity's genetically based needs in the emerging global village has created a market-driven innovation and economic juggernaut that cannot be stopped.

Further global integration and the emergence of a multicultural global village are both desirable and inevitable futures. Global integration will continue because the universal benefits gained from its continuance massively outweigh the costs, even though we also know these costs are growing and could in future become significant threats, particularly if we do not sufficiently collaborate to meet these emerging global challenges. This is what occurred with the COVID-19 pandemic. There are many places in this book where we will focus on how we need to do things differently so that we do not harm both ourselves and our shared planetary home as we seek to build shared future prosperity.

There are some who do not want to live in this emerging global village. They prefer yesteryear. They continue to hold on to their tribal/national identities and to their modernist values and they are not interested in expanding their *circles of identity*. Many others, however, are welcoming the ever-increasing opportunities offered to them by global integration. Many of those resisting global integration are threatened by the fear they will not be able to re-anchor themselves successfully and find a secure place for themselves in this emerging global village. They fear that they will be forced to mix with many people who are different from them and whom they fear and cannot trust. They still prefer to remain with their own.

As will be shown shortly, there are changes afoot in our emerging global village that will cater for their needs, for there are means being developed that can enable them to have their own tribal/national precincts in a global village if they wish to. However, these people will still need to be willing to accept the governance rules of this emerging global village if they want to be accepted by others as worthy occupants of it.

This book aspires to provide each of us with the concepts and tools so that in the future we can thrive in this emerging global village and become ever more successful in a rapidly changing 21st century. We can all embed in ourselves concepts and tools to enable each of us to be the most 21st century successful person we can be. And 'person' here can be a collective as well as an individual. It can be an organisation, a community, or a nation.

When we look at how much of our politics is now dominated by global issues, we can conclude that most of the big issues we are facing are truly global in nature and cannot be solved by individual nation states, no matter how powerful these nation states are. We cannot reverse global heating without unprecedented collaboration. And we can't overcome global pandemics like COVID-19 without collaboration. We cannot deal with a global economic recession without collaboration. And we can't bring peace to trouble spots without collaborating to prevent or stop a war. We are now beginning to recognise that from now on national politics will need to obey new emerging global political rules and agreements, just as over the last century, regional and state/provincial politics gave way to national politics for basically the same reason. From now on, planet must come first.

In Chapter 5, we will discuss the key issues of interdependence and trust in global relationships. Here, and in later chapters, we will discuss matters such as our changing patterns of trade and investment, and how these will be uplifted in the next two decades to create ever more free and fair models of globalisation. Those who imagine, build and market *interdependence ways and wares* and *trustworthiness ways and wares* will do economically well by doing global good. Just as extraordinary wealth has accrued to those corporations that have innovated *planetary interconnectivity way and wares*, there will be virtually no limits on the potential size of the market for the building of connectivity, interdependence, harmony, and trust in relationships across the planet. Economic benefit will accrue to those who innovate and market *the ways and the wares* enabling humanity to accomplish these outcomes.

2.2. The Birth of Planetary Politics

In 2019, a sixteen-year-old girl from Sweden, Greta Thunberg, lectured a room full of national leaders at the UN Climate Conference. Many of them were there to protect their own national interests and surrender as little as possible to planetary interests. She spoke of her disgust at the collective delinquency of the people in that room for failing to make our planet climate safe. Greta Thunberg is a fully committed planetist and she speaks for much of her generation and for at least a billion older people who are already giving their first allegiance to planet. She condemned her audience for lacking the vision, the aspiration, and the political will to put planet first. Planetary politics had truly arrived.

The planetary politics that is emerging is much more than the politics of the resolution of differences between competing nation states and tribes. It is the politics driven by the ever-growing numbers of planetists, those who put planet first when this is required, rather than consider political issues only through national or tribal eyes.

Planetary politics is the unique politics of the 21st century. The human race has never known it before. Those who look at politics through national and tribal eyes struggle to understand planetary politics. When Greta Thunberg criticised the leaders of nation states, many national leaders might have been emotionally disturbed by the truths she was uttering but their cerebral adherence to nation and tribe first made them unable to truly hear her message.

At the beginning of the third decade of the 21st century, our world is becoming ever more interdependent and interconnected. Yet too many of our political leaders and many of their followers as well are still looking out at the world through unchanged modernist lenses. They cannot move beyond their own individual national and tribal interests to consider humanity's collective planetary interest: America must come first, Brazil first, Great Britain first. However, their other actions often undermine their own causes, for they continue to sign agreements that interlock all of us into long term trade arrangements and other similar arrangements that collectively deliver ever more interdependence and interconnectivity. Trade wars are increasingly conducted not to win and return to a yesteryear when the nation state was top dog, but to extract a better deal for the future.

Given the nearly 600 years of history of exploitative history of globalisation that was outlined in Chapter 1, it is not surprising that a great amount of distrust of globalisation still exists. Over the last thirty years there have been, and continue to be, many victims of globalisation. However, I believe that between 1970 and 2040 globalisation will undergo a complete transformation from an exploitative *modernist* informed *cowboy globalisation* into a trustworthy future form, a *planetist*-informed *cosmonaut globalisation*. That is where humanity aspires to go, and ultimately will go. This will be further discussed in several places in this book

Planetary politics has been around for some time even if this has not been recognised by many. It is politics that focuses primarily on the future of our shared planetary home, a politics about humanity's collective future not about the future of individual nations and interest groups. In the previous two centuries millions of people were slaughtered or were endangered in battles between competing national and tribal interests. In these wars it was possible to be neutral. No more! First the Cold War changed this reality. The Cold War was a conflict between a few nations. The whole planet was endangered by the threat of nuclear Armageddon because of this confrontation. Then our consciousness was still mostly nation and tribal based. Humanity now faces many shared moments of planetary-wide endangerment such as global heating, pandemics such as COVID-19, and planetary wide economic recessions. At these moments all of us are being forced to recognise, whether we like it or not, that we must collaborate even with people we don't necessarily like, just as we did in a village threatened by a flood or an earthquake in the past. With such challenges all of us are potential victims irrespective of our national or tribal identities or our political, military, or economic power.

In the third decade of the 21st century, shared endangerment is happening ever more often. From now on, we have no other choice than to raise our political consciousness to a planetary level.

2.3. The Politics of Resistance to Global Integration

Since *Earthrise* in 1968, there have been two major examples of genuine planetary politics, and a third example is beginning to emerge. I believe these should be recognised as moments that have given birth to, and have led to the further development of, genuine planetary politics. These two movements have both sought to resist global integration. However, they are driven by polar-opposite agendas.

The first of these in the 1990s was shaped by progressive ideals. This was basically a progressive movement that was focussed on the perceived unfairness of globalisation. This globalisation was regarded as being too dominated by large *Modernist* informed corporate power and by the then prevailing form of conservative economic neoliberalism. These anti-globalisation activists regarded globalisation as too ruthless: our trade was free, but it was not fair. The political activists who sought to change globalisation were early adopting *planetists* who believed that the wrong people had their hands on the levers controlling the evolution of the global trading and investment system. They saw this group as a greedy and unethical *Modernist global elite* in large commercial corporations and large financial institutions who were hijacking globalisation to deliver winning outcomes for themselves and losing outcomes, and even victimhood, to others.

This anti-globalisation movement wanted to change this dominant modernist globalisation so that it delivered win/win rather than win/lose outcomes. They believed that if this situation persisted globalisation would continue the same exploitative trajectory that it had followed for the last 500 plus years. Many of them would have known the history of the early form of mutually beneficial archaic globalisation and perhaps they were inspired to recreate it in an appropriately updated form in the late 20th and the 21st centuries.

This anti-globalisation movement was driven by ideals, it was an agenda shaped by what are basically planetist values. Its advocates were socially progressive change makers and future makers, rather than socially conservative change takers and future takers.

In the first years of the 21st century, a Postmodern concept of *fair trade* was added to the already existing Modernist concept of *free trade* and this combined concept has now become mainstream thinking. We began to recognise that we should seek to eliminate win/lose from global trade and investment and begin to embrace universal win/win. This movement accomplished much of its mission, and it began to wither in the first decade of the 21st century. Now many of these same people continue to work in global and national NGOs to further reshape, humanise, and civilise, globalisation.

In the second decade of the 21st century, a second movement of resistance to globalisation began to emerge. This second anti-globalisation movement is perceived to come from the ideological opposite pole to the first anti-globalisation movement, from those who have had a history of being politically powerful but who now have a growing fear that they are losing their political power and becoming increasingly vulnerable to global integration. In contrast to those who initiated and drove the first anti-globalisation movement, these people are socially conservative change takers and future takers.

While the first anti-globalisation movement was an anger-driven reform movement, this second anti-globalisation movement is a fear-driven resistance movement. Its supporters voted for politicians who, for the most part, wanted to continue the unfairness of the current systems that delivered win/lose outcomes, but with them being able to get back on the winning side. In a rational world these fear-filled people would be supporting those who were seeking to make the globalisation fairer for all. But they are wedded to the Modernist-informed politics of fear and resentment that continue to generate competition and conflict, and particularly conflict with those who are different. The first movement in contrast was driven by a planetist informed socially progressive politics that sought collaboration with other.

The supporters of this fear-driven second anti-globalisation movement really don't want a universally fairer world at all but a world with a different division of the spoils. They care little about whether fairness is universal or not. They just want it to be fairer for themselves even if it remains unfair for others. And the political leaders they support simply want to return to a yesteryear that was even less fair but where they were usually winners. But this was also a world where those who were the losers were those they did not care about, and who, for the most part, were ethnically or racially different. This resistance to globalisation or to what they referred to as 'Globalism', comes from people from the traditional ideological right, but also from a smaller, but still significant, rump from the traditional ideological left as well.

In a less ideological 21st century, these former ideological enemies could now share the same aspirational political space and collaborate to fight for a common cause. Some have described these anti-globalisation activists as *the identitarian movement.* I will call these people *Modernist populists* and their shared political cause *Modernist populism.* They carry embedded modernist values and see those with planetist values as their political enemies. Modernist populists believe:

- The mid-20th century concept of 'progress' should continue in the 21st century. We should expect that collateral harm to peoples and environments might be an inevitable consequence of industrial and economic development.
- The nation state should continue to be the dominant global organisational entity into the future. We should oppose continuing

- global integration and the creation of single integrated global society because these processes will weaken the nation state.
- We should look at and interpret global trends through the lenses of competition between different nationalist/cultural/religious/ethnic identities and seek win/lose, rather than through the lenses of collaboration on a shared planetary home and seek win/win, as do planetists.
- Global challenges that pose shared endangerment, such as global heating and pandemics, and that require universal unprecedented collaboration including with traditional enemies for their abatement, might be hoaxes. Scientific and technological progress that fits into traditional international competitive models such as a cure for cancer or a new digital breakthrough will be supported, but scientific evidence that requires us to change our behaviour and work collaboratively with others who are potential enemies, or who are different, will be denied.
- We should see all security in terms of defence against threats from those who are different, and in terms of continuing competition and hostility between tribes and nations. A collectively secured and collaborative future world without intertribal hostility and competition is, to them, inconceivable.

That exemplar Modernist populist Donald Trump promotes all the above. The metaphor used by him for cleaning up Washington was 'draining the swamp'. This is 1950's language. Planetists no longer use the word 'swamp'. They use the term 'wetland' for an entity we do not drain but should instead conserve and protect. Trump said he wanted to *Make America Great Again*; that is, he wanted to return to a yesteryear when America was top dog in the world. Jair Bolsonaro in Brazil believed levelling the Amazon rainforest to produce beef in an ever more vegetarian 21st century is 'progress'. Vladimir Putin continues to build a Russian economy that is a product of mid-20th century thinking. Putin does not need to be a *Modernist populist* for he does not need to seek votes in a democratic process. Putin is *a Modernist autocrat*, pure and simple. Russia has a mostly yesteryear economy. It is highly dependent on its exports of fossil fuels, on fertilisers derived from fossil fuels, and on military hardware that largely lacks sufficient 21st century subtilty, for it causes too much mass collateral damage to be usefully utilised for securing a 21st century global village.

Modernist populists continue to carry mid-20th century mainstream values into the third decade of the 21st century. Many modernist populist leaders such as Trump admire autocratic rather than democratic political processes and tend to admire other autocrats more than other democratic leaders. M*odernist populists* eventually will be removed from office by the growing numbers of assertive planetist voters, and because the numbers of modernist supporters will further decline. These supporters already know that their days are limited. That is why there are many of them trying to gerrymander electoral boundaries in the USA. They are seeking to make it more difficult for their potential political opponents to vote.

Modernist populists oppose planetists, whom they call 'globalists', and whom they see as an *elite*. In fact, many of those they see as this political elite include many of the people who initiated the first anti-globalisation movement and who were seeking a fairer form of globalisation. These second wave anti-globalisation activists and Modernist populists usually blame others for their predicaments.

This movement continues to give priority to nation or to ethnic culture before planet. Most of those in this movement still identify themselves by the cultural and national identities of their parents and grandparents. They are *identity unadaptable*. They have not sought to expand or shift their *circles of identity* in any way. They are still locked into, and even hold grimly onto, these nationalist or ethnic identities. They see globalisation as disrespecting and undermining these core identities. They seek to live among others who are like them, not different from them.

Some of them even want to ethnically cleanse their communities of people who are different from them. They have consciously chosen to keep these nationalist or ethnic identities because they believe this will enable them to anchor themselves more securely in an increasingly dynamic and challenging 21st century. They often feel they are disrespected but when it comes to disrespect of difference these people themselves are often living paragons of disrespectful behaviour. They hold on to their modernist values of disrespecting difference.

Many practice the politics of *downward envy,* where they blame people who are even more disadvantaged than they are, people such as poorer people, those who are culturally, racially, and religiously different, and refugees. This contrasts with the traditional *upward envy* of current holders of political and economic power that was a core mindset of the 20th century *ideological left*.

I am uncomfortable with the name *identitarian* because it implies that only these people, and not others, are concerned about their identity. In fact, all politics is shaped by identity. We all treasure our identities, for we need them to make sense of our world and anchor ourselves securely in a world of rapid change. Without an understanding of who and where we are, we cannot evaluate and interpret the social, cultural, and political change going on around us. Planetists have identities as well. Planetists identify themselves as giving first allegiance to our planetary home and their primary concern is focussed on its future and to ensuring that this future will be fairer for all, and will provide an ever more liveable home for humanity.

Many believe that this *Modernist populist* movement is becoming more powerful and influential. However, I believe this is not really the case. What has changed is that many of them feel that they and the modernist values they hold are under siege and as a result they have become more politically active in promoting their interests. They are reactive, not proactive people. Unlike those in the earlier anti-globalisation movement, they are future takers and change takers rather than future makers and change makers.

I believe that as globalisation itself becomes fairer and people become more educated and more 21st century-prepared, and therefore able to gain access to better 21st century opportunities, the number of people feeling threatened by globalisation will decrease.

However, some of those threatened by globalisation have become more politically active because their numbers have increased in relative terms, although not in absolute terms. Many well-educated and more 21st century prepared people who once lived with them have emigrated to seek opportunities elsewhere. A major consequence of the European ex-Soviet Union nations joining the European Union has been a massive emigration of many of their young and better-educated people to Western Europe. They have left behind them the less well-educated and less 21st century employable behind.

Since the fall of the Berlin Wall, there has been a catastrophic fall in the populations of many of these countries. These population decreases include a decline in Latvia by 27%, Lithuania by 23% and Bulgaria by 21%. Over 3.5 million Romanians have migrated to Western Europe since Romania joined the European Union in 2007. Many of them are well-educated and highly skilled pro-European young people who carry planetist values and who have the linguistic capabilities to work elsewhere. They have expanded their *circles of identity* and now see themselves as Europeans as well as Romanians or Lithuanians, and they give their first allegiance to Europe and then to Planet. They are confident they can thrive in other parts of Europe and no longer need to live in their own ethnic cultural domains. They feel that they can flourish better by emigrating to places that give them more opportunity.

As the young leave their home nation, these same home nations demographically age and begin to lose their vitality. The more socially conservative people remaining at home have an increasing fear of a weakening national identity because of this depopulation. Many of them can't see themselves as Europeans. They continue to give first allegiance to Nation. This sense of vulnerability also generates increasing opposition to the immigration by people who are different into their communities. They would prefer their own émigrés to return home rather than include refugees from outside Europe. They might feel threatened by their depopulation, but they do not want to repopulate their countries with culturally/ethnically different people. The migration of Central and Eastern Europeans into Western Europe has been much greater than the migration into Western Europe of more racially and ethnically different immigrants. This not sufficiently recognised by many observers, who for the most part recognise as genuine immigrants only those immigrants into Western Europe who are racially or religiously different. After all, the movement of people throughout Europe is lawful and even encouraged, and immigration from other parts of the planet is not.

The net result of this depopulation of nations in Eastern Europe has been an increased relative empowerment of people left behind who are carrying embedded anti-EU and intolerance-to-difference mindsets. The pro-European emigrants who have left them have simply moved to seek opportunities that are not being given to them by their own home governments.

In Chapter 3, I will discuss a concept called the *Derivation Duet (FUTK22)*. This refers to two elements of our experience and learning from our past that we take with us as we plan and seek to shape the future. *Heritage* is the collective experience, knowledge, and understanding we bring with us from our past and that we highly value, even priceless. We believe we should retain this heritage because it can enable us to become more future successful. *Baggage* is the experience, knowledge, and understanding we have brought from our past, that we should now eliminate from our lives because it can disable our capacity to become future successful.

Over time, much of what we once thought to be *heritage* can become, through social change and the passage of time, *baggage*. Modernist populists have simply not sufficiently recognised how much times have changed. I believe that many values-based beliefs and some cultural and national identity beliefs previously regarded as heritage in the mid-20th century have become baggage in the 21st century. Many Modernist populists have not recognised this reality. All the nine values of Modernism will become baggage in the next decade as well. Anti-globalisation Modernist populists are holding onto identities and values of the past that are becoming ever more inappropriate for the present and the future.

If we are not identity adaptable, including by being willing to expand our *circles of identity*, and if we continue to adhere to Modernist values, we will become ever more vulnerable to social change and ultimately be severely disrupted and disadvantaged by it. Fortunately, however, more of us are also becoming more *identity adaptable*. *Identity adaptable* people are willing and able to review and expand their *circles of identity*. They have expanded their *circles of identity* to the point that they now see themselves as part of a multicultural humanity that gives first allegiance to humanity's shared planetary home.

Identity unadaptable Modernist populists in the USA put America first and hard-line Modernist populist Brexiters put Britain first, or more precisely England first. There are equivalents in France, Hungary, Austria, Australia, Italy, Bulgaria, and Brazil. They mostly loathe multiculturalism and do not welcome refugees who belong to other cultures and races living with them in their communities. Many have identified themselves as members of Modernist populist political parties and movements that in traditional ideological terms belong to both the far right and the far left.

I see them as holding tenaciously to Modernist values. These Modernist populists would like to reverse the current patterns of globalisation that are steadily integrating the world's peoples into a multicultural global village. They would like to return to a yesteryear of cultural apartheid that to them were halcyon days. These Modernist populists have not learned from the story of King Canute and the waves that humans are not omnipotent.

Many of these people cannot see any possibility of themselves being able to thrive in this emerging global village. As a result, they have become fearful, resentful, and angry. Many are victims of the failure of their governments to adequately prepare them for an ever more borderless world and vanishing trade barriers. But they have also failed themselves by being unwilling or unable to expand their own *circles of identity* and embrace the concept of an emerging tomorrow based on the oneness of humanity. They grimly hold on to a yesteryear based on hostility to racial, cultural, and religious difference.

Modernist populists are mostly people who are not well prepared to thrive in an emerging interdependent 21st century society. Their jobs are often in those industries that are increasingly 21st century threatened and irrelevant and that will further shrink in the future. They do not trust governments that are piloting the big changes described in this book and that they fear threaten them. They use their identity to rationalise their opposition to the further integration of nation states into larger multicultural entities such as the European Union and through the entering into evermore multilateral trade agreements.

A good example of this movement is the so-called *Yellow Vests* movement in France in 2018-2019: a combination of far-left and far-right groups that last century were vehemently opposed to each other and who are, early in the 21st century, fighting a common cause. This movement opposes what they see as threats to them, namely the further integration of Europe and the arrival of refugees who are different from them and who they fear will steal their often now more vulnerable jobs. They often belong to nations that have stagnant and even declining populations, such as those in Eastern Europe. They mostly do not articulate what they support but strongly articulate what they oppose. Some are virtually nihilistic.

The traditional far-right populist and conservative parties and some far-left populist parties of Hungary, Poland, Bulgaria, France, Germany, Spain, and Italy are all part of this movement as are many US Republicans who want to put America First. They also include many white supremacists and Christian, Islamic, Jewish, Buddhist and Hindu extremists who fear that religious power is declining in an increasingly secular 21st century. They will resist surrendering their political power to any new multicultural or multi-faith macro entity.

Many people with progressive mindsets regard them as bigots, racists, neo fascists or neo communists, but people are actually recalcitrant modernists in an emerging planetist 21st century. In the coming two decades, the proportion of those resisting these long-term trends will steadily decrease and as general education levels rise so will tolerance to difference.

The politicians who have attained power through offering Modernist populist 20th century solutions in the 21st century will eventually fail as well. Their politics is the politics of grievance, and they have no solutions except to promise to undo some of the social change that has already occurred. They are yesteryear people with yesteryear solutions. The world has moved on. The better educated children of these Modernist populists will leave this now self-harming mindset behind them and will expand their *circles of identity* and then tread the same pathway to success already taken by others into the multicultural global village of tomorrow.

Sadly, *Modernist populists* who remain such are change takers and future takers. In Chapter 4 we will discuss future taking and change taking, and its opposite, future making and change making.

The rise of planetism will continue. It contains a set of values that is appropriate for guiding our behaviour as we seek to build and tread a pathway to success in our emerging 21st century global village.

Modernist populism will begin to wither and die in the next 10 years. In this same decade billions will learn a lot more about how to better prepare themselves for, and grow the capabilities to thrive in, our emerging interdependent interconnected global village.

Governments are now collaborating to remove many of the impediments undermining this transformation. They are doing things like negating the actions of cultural, racial, and religious extremists on the Internet, and the actions of those who want to exploit our increasing interconnectedness to benefit themselves at the cost of disadvantaging others. This removal of impediments to increasing global integration is vitally important and will continue unabated.

This book is full of concepts and tools designed to assist us to flourish in this ever more interdependent emerging future. My aspiration is to provide a new curriculum that enables all of us to thrive in our emerging 21st century global village. If we don't set out to change ourselves, and prepare ourselves appropriately for living in our emerging 21st century global village, we will be in danger of being side-lined, or of being significantly disrupted and disadvantaged, by social and technological change. One major part of changing ourselves is to review our identities and adapt them for the emerging 21st century realities.

When we face collective danger, such as the case during the COVID-19 pandemic or when we contemplate living on a planet that is being warmed by collective human activity, we will be reminded by the sometimes intolerant and denying behaviours of Modernist populists that their mid-20th century mindsets are part of the problem and that they offer no solutions. We will recognise that modernist thinking and nation-first modernist behaviours will worsen the situation. We will conclude that we must put planet first and collaborate with all of humanity to create a climate-safe and pandemic-safe planet, and an ever more prosperous global society on an ever more liveable planet. If we are reflective, we will also conclude that a moral compass guided by planetist values can enable humanity to collaborate effectively to meet the 21st century challenges that it will face.

Our emerging global village also needs to develop new forms of planetary governance that can enable humanity to become more effective in dealing with planet-wide challenges and shaping the future of our global village. With our growing level of interdependence, we only need one rogue war-mongering government or recalcitrant population for all of us to be endangered. We cannot manage 21st century situations with 20th century management processes. In the post-COVID-19 emerging planetist era, we need to collaborate ever more to create new world governance arrangements and even a *New World Order* for trade and investment that will enable our diverse humanity to move forward and collectively create shared success.

Global integration has already proceeded too far to be unmade and reversed by anybody, even the most powerful Modernist populists. It cannot be stopped by them or anyone else. Even the most severe economic turndown we can experience will only slow down global integration. It will not stop it.

2.4. Adapting for Success in a Global Village

We have just discussed the significant cohort of humanity who are see global change as a threat or who fear they will be disadvantaged by it. However, there are also millions and even billions who are either consciously or unconsciously adapting their mindsets so that they can reposition themselves to enable them to become ever more 21st century successful.

When we change our identities and mindsets and therefore how we perceive our place in the world, we often seek to change some of our key relationships as well. A party in a relationship might see its current interdependent relationship as becoming ever more stifling of its aspirations, just as can be the case in an interdependent marriage relationship. So that party will divorce itself from a current relationship and subsequently enter a new interdependent relationship that offers it more promise for the future.

This kind of shift in both allegiance and identity is now becoming a major, but not yet fully appreciated, new trend in planetary politics. It is the politics not of negative resistance to change, but instead of changing ourselves and reimagining our aspirations so we can chart more promising pathways to future success in our rapidly changing 21st century global society. This trend will become as least as significant in the next two decades as the two just-described anti-globalisation movements over the past three decades.

When one gives first allegiance to a multicultural entity like Europe, or to the whole planet, this does not mean one is less (say) Swedish, Greek or American, just differently Swedish, Greek, or American. Each of us who embeds the values of planetism will retain a second identity as a member of our national or tribal culture. And for some, such as most Europeans, their national or ethnic culture will become their third allegiance behind their first two allegiances to Planet and to Europe.

So far, we have discussed identity change at an individual level. But it is also occurring at a collective level and even across whole cultures as well. Such a constant unmaking and remaking of international relationships between nations and cultures will become a significant component of 21st century social and political change. I call this process *identity renovation*. And most of us know that the ending and remaking of an interdependent relationship can be traumatic, just as it is in a failing marriage.

Relationships that worked in the modernist 20th century might not flourish in a planetist 21st century unless all parties in the relationship commit themselves to renegotiating and renewing the relationship so that it is a more 21st century appropriate one. And if there is little willingness in at least one party in the relationship to change and negotiate a new relationship, separation will be the only option left on the table.

With *identity renovation*, there might be more than just two parties separating. The Soviet Union split into 15 different nations in the early 1990s. After its collapse in 1989, most people recognised that the operating system at the centre the Soviet social, political, and economic culture, a system based on centralised planning, state capitalism and the subordination of those who were not Russian, to be deeply flawed. The light that inspired ex-Soviet nations which were geographically part of Eastern Europe was the emerging European Union, which provided them with an attractive democratic alternative form of governance.

Mikhail Gorbachev, who began the dismantling of the Soviet Union, was a visionary who saw a future association of ex-Soviet nations in a voluntary long-term interdependent and an ultimately democratic union that would become an Eastern equivalent of the European Union. His successor, Boris Yeltsin, tried to change things too fast. He created an economic and socially chaotic Soviet Union that triggered its own collapse. The social and economic mess that followed facilitated the hijacking of state assets by corporate criminals and caused a massive rise in poverty which reignited a yearning amongst Russians for the certainty of the past. This rendered impossible the realisation of Gorbachev's vision. Vladimir Putin, Yeltsin's successor, would, if he could, recreate a new version of the Soviet Union as an autocratic union dominated by the Russian Federation.

Putin is not an ideological being. He is simply behaving as a Modernist populist autocrat who rules with a mid-20th century Modernist mindset in a 21st century environment. This is why in early 2020 Putin sought to change the democratic constitution to enable him to maintain his autocratic rule indefinitely.

It is noteworthy that the ex-Soviet nations in eastern Europe have always identified themselves as European, in that they have traditionally looked westwards in terms of their primary international relationships and inspiration rather than eastward towards Russia. They had little choice previously other than being drawn into a close association with Russia because they were all occupied by the Soviet military at the end of the Second World War. But after the collapse of the Soviet Union in 1989, each of these nations sought to jettison its Soviet identity and divorce itself from Russia and reclaim its own identity to become Poland, Hungary, and Estonia. Each of them then set out to join the European Union.

The next involuntary interdependent union to break up was Yugoslavia between 1990 and 1992. It split into seven separate ethnic independent nations. The name of Yugoslavia has receded into history. And the so-called 'Balkanisation' once seen as a prescription for instability and continuing conflict in the 20th century is now producing significant political stability in a very different 21st century. All the former Yugoslav states have joined, or plan to join, the European Union. In 1993 Czechoslovakia split peacefully and amicably into the Czech Republic and Slovakia. Both immediately joined the European Union.

Independence movements in Scotland and Catalonia are seeking the same end: to become a uni-cultural tribal state by seceding from an existing multicultural state so that they can then join a bigger multicultural community where they would be treated as equals rather than subordinated by another dominant culture. The Scots have gone back to the future, redefining themselves as Scots because they do want to be British anymore: they knew that being *British* really meant mostly doing what the *English* wanted them to do. Not surprisingly, the Scots do not want to have their future determined by the English.

Significantly, in the EU Referendum in 2016 the people of Scotland and Northern Ireland both chose to remain in Europe because they believed it was in their interests to do so. Not surprisingly, these two nations did not appreciate having their wishes ignored by the English. Brexit was never a British movement, but an English movement of about half the English population. The people who have lost most from a British secession from Europe have been the less well-off and the less well-educated hostile-to-difference socially conservative English nationalists, many of them in the north of England. Sadly, many of these people have been the strongest supporters of Brexit. These people are also strongly identity unadaptable. They have been unwilling or unable to expand their *Circles of Identity* to embrace a European identity let alone a planetist identity. Their frozen identities have led them to following a pathway that is probably not in their own or their children's interests.

Scotland's succession from Great Britain will be part of the same *identity renovation* process. But a divorce from Great Britain will be messy and could cause significant damage to the relationship between the three nations of England, Scotland and Wales that will need to find the means to successfully coexist on a shared island.

Spain foolishly resisted Catalonia's attempted secession and tried to bully Catalonia into submission. In October 2019 the leaders of the Catalonian secession movement were given jail sentences of more than 10 years by Spanish courts. These actions have killed off any semblance of trust between the two parties. They have ensured that, when the separation does eventually come, the divorce will be messy. That such divorces can be amicable has been shown by the Czechs and the Slovaks, whose collaborative mindsets set the bar high.

At the beginning of the third decade of the 21st century, Ukraine is also in danger of separating into two entities. Depending on the eventual peace settlement that ends the Russia-Ukraine war, what might happen is that the Russian-speaking East Ukraine, the Donetsk region, will form a new union with Russia, while the Ukrainian-speaking region joins the European Community as a new member. The Russian-speaking people of Ukraine are split, with some (mostly Modernists) wishing to join with Russia, and some (mostly emerging Planetists), seeking to remain with Ukraine and become Europeans.

The names of the Soviet Union, Yugoslavia and Czechoslovakia have disappeared from our atlases. How many more like them will follow? I believe that in the next two decades there will be many, including in Africa and in Asia. Hopefully more will have a peaceful dissolution like Czechoslovakia rather than a conflicting one like Spain. In a world that is becoming ever more interdependent the long-term result of *identity renovation* and secession followed by a new interdependent relationship with a more 21st century compatible entity, will be more likely to create peaceful, stable, and prosperous outcomes.

All the cultures that have seceded from their former multicultural nations wanted to renovate their identity: Lithuanians did not want to be Soviet first and Lithuanian second. They wanted to be European first and Lithuanian second. Catalans want to be Europeans first and Catalans second, rather than Spanish first and Catalans second. The Scots want to be Europeans first and Scots second, not British first and Scots second. The problem for the English has been that too many English people have never seen themselves as European first and English second, but the other way around.

Increased prosperity will accrue to parties treading this divorce and remarriage pathway. However, future relative impoverishment might be the consequence for parties who choose to leave one union but not enter another, as Great Britain has done. This is because their bargaining power in future trade and other global negotiations will be much diminished.

This *identity renovation* will proceed further in Europe and elsewhere. It is not difficult to imagine more cases like Scotland and Catalonia in the years ahead. It is possible that Italy might split into many of its pre-unification components, with each then separately joining the European Union. The good news is that a state that follows this *identity renovation process* is likely be too small to seriously threaten or bully another. The peace dividend of this identity renovation process could be considerable, and the outcome would be greater politically stability with greater harmony.

Ideology is no longer the motivator of social change that it was in the 20th century. Both ends of the political ideological spectrum, the far right and the far left, will be perceived to be too undemocratic and disrespectful of difference, and sometimes too violent as well to be respected by an evolving and more mature global civil society. The more democratic forms at the centre of the weakening ideological political spectrum both recognise that free market capitalism and not state initiated command capitalism will be a continuing engine for uplifting prosperity, and humanity's task in the 21st century is to ensure that both globalisation and collaborative capitalism delivers to all a more equitable and prosperous future.

This trend of *identity renovation* will spread further and eventually become a whole-of-planet process over coming decades. It will reach into Africa, Eastern Europe and Central Asia, the Middle East, and East, South and South-East Asia in coming decades as global integration continues to grow. Many nations have old colonial heritages with borders bearing no relationship to culture, even entrapping different tribes into living uneasily together.

The war in South Sudan after its separation from Sudan is an early example of an intercultural breakup outside Europe that could become a long-term trend in many parts of Africa and perhaps elsewhere as well. The South Sudanese identified themselves collectively as African Christians when they sought to secede from the remainder of mostly Arabic Islamic Sudan. However, after a successful separation they then recognised they were also members of 60 different ethnic tribes. And many of these had long-term historical and unresolved grievances with each other. The two largest of these, the Dinkas and the Nuers, then decided to go to war again immediately after their secession. Their tribal identities and attitudes had been frozen in time and had not evolved through their expanding their *circles of identity*.

Clearly, *Earthrise* had no impact in South Sudan. Mass education had not reached the level that enabled the South Sudanese to recognise a bigger vision that could involve building new relationships with others beyond their national boundaries. Interestingly, after the secession of South Sudan, new democratic green shoots commenced appearing in previously autocratic Sudanese politics.

What will follow in the coming decades? Is it too hard to imagine a fully interdependent African Union or even a North African nation seeking to join the European Union? Both are possible scenarios and over time will become probable scenarios. The long-term trend is likely to be more individual national members of the UN, all of them joining with other nations and cultures in long-term interdependent multicultural unions. But an increased investment in education and particularly in educating women must come first. We will come back to this issue later when we consider educational futures.

I have outlined two opposite responses to global integration in this chapter: one of these (*identity renovation*) is supporting and adapting to it and one (*Modernist populism*) is resisting. Both of these political processes are still operating in the 2020s and both will strongly influence planetary politics over the next two decades. The table below set out some of the key points of these two different responses:

Identity adaptable/identity renovation	Identity unadaptable/Modernist populism
Pro global integration	Anti-global integration
Expanding circle of identity	Frozen circle of identity
Change maker, future maker	Change taker, future taker
Postmodernist, Planetist	Modernist
Collaborate and harmonise with those who are different	Confront and be hostile to those who are different
Build interdependence, seek win/win outcomes	Retain independence, seek win/lose outcomes

The *identity unadaptable/Modernist populist* movement will have its moments in the sun in the next decade. But the mindsets of those belonging to this movement are the mindsets of yesteryear. Over time their presence in global politics and their political influence will decline. The moral compass that will inform 21st century relationships, trade and exchange will be based on Planetist values. Modernist populism will eventually wither as education levels continue to rise. Circles of identity will continue to expand for an increasing number of people, and globalisation itself will generate fairer outcomes. Identity renovation will persist. It will continue catalysing the unmaking and remaking of nation states and generate and shape more political and social change.

2.5. The Decline of Ideology and the Rise of Ideals and Values-Driven Politics

In a speech to the World Economic Forum in Davos in 2000, on the cusp of the new century and millennium, British Prime Minister Tony Blair told his audience that *the 20th century was the century of ideology* and that *the 21st century would be the century of ideals*. Blair created a form of politics he called the '*third way.*' The *third way* involved using capitalism and economic public policy to shape the future instead of using ideologically fashioned means.

Ideology focuses on means, not ends. All ideologies offered alternative routes to a Modern future. Ever since Karl Marx launched the politics of ideology, a core aspiration of the political ideological left has been to enable those who are disadvantaged by the current political regime to confront the existing holders of power and seek to build a more equitable and modern future for themselves. This included seizing the reins of power by force if it were necessary to achieve this aspiration. In the 20th century, change was largely created by competition and confrontation. Win/lose and winner take all was usually the norm. The 21st century tools of collaboration and win/win were not part of anybody's vision. These were simply too idealistic. This aspiration of the ideological left to confront and become winners against the ideological right applied to both autocratic and democratic forms of socialism.

The political ideological right also sought a Modern future but sought to achieve this through the traditional politics of leadership by the aristocratic privileged and those with plutocratic, kleptocratic, and military power. Putin's Russia is today an autocratic state governed by plutocratic, kleptocratic, and military power. All Modernist autocrats and Modernist populists wanted a Modern future but rarely an inclusive one, for they showed little interest in consciously seeking to uplift overall equity. They regarded exclusiveness as the norm, as they also believed that wealth would always be limited and they wanted the lion's share for themselves, and win/lose outcomes.

Indeed, all these 20th century approaches embedded in themselves hostility to those who were culturally different, different in class, and often to women as well. It was only after *Earthrise* and the birth of postmodernity, that greater inclusion and uplifted rights for women and of the culturally different, including giving recognition of indigenous peoples as first-nations people, undertook its journey from the political margins to the political mainstream. At the beginning of the third decade of the 21st century modernism is finally declining and planetism is beginning to blossom.

In contrast to ideology, ideals focus on ends, not means. Ideals answer the question: *what kind of world would we like to create for ourselves and for others?* Tony Blair told his audience in his Davos speech that these ideals should be 'pragmatic'; that is, realistic. Blair and the British Labour Party had learned from the political success of Australian centre left governments under Bob Hawke and Paul Keating.

Sociologist Anthony Giddens, who worked with Blair to define and promote the socially progressive and centre left political movement that they called *The Third Way,* tells us we should aim higher than this. He said we should be *Utopian Realists*, envisioning *Utopian ends* and devising *Realistic means* to realise these ends. I believe that the values of Planetism and Planetist informed *cosmonaut capitalism* could be regarded as a core ingredient of a *utopian realistic Third Way politics*. We will discuss *utopian realism* more completely later in this chapter and again in Chapter 12.

Planetist values are now permeating the political mainstream and being embraced by educated and socially progressive people everywhere. The values of Modernism remain the values of many, but far from all, socially conservative people, some of whom also hold planetist values. But as more people are uplifted by globalisation and are educated for longer, there will be more people who will assume 21st century relevant socially progressive values: Planetist values.

With the arrival of post-modernity and the emergence of Planetism, our planetary politics have been dramatically transformed. At the beginning of the third decade of the 21st century, we can see many strange political events occurring that defy explanation in traditional ideological terms.

In the UK, there was a political polarisation between modernists and planetists. The two mainstream political Parties, Conservative and Labour, were split down the middle over the issue of Brexit to the point that their future as political parties could have been endangered. There are *remainers* and *leavers* in both parties. If we examine this situation a little more closely, we can discern that the more highly educated tend to be socially progressive *remainers*. This includes most of the better-educated young, particularly the urban young. The less well educated of both the ideological left and right identify as socially conservative *leavers*, many of whom are less well-educated older people.

Most remainers are Planetists. Most leavers are Modernists. Many supporters of Brexit are those who have a more limited education and who are traditional Labour supporters who were living in 'rust belt' regions with that have declining 20th century industrial bases. Not surprisingly, people who put nation first over Europe (or planet) supported Brexit. Brexiters are a combination of mostly well-educated, traditional, privileged, exclusivist and aristocratic holders of political power, and a less well-educated traditional working-class rank and file who are identity unadaptable. Remainers are mostly well-educated, identity adaptable people who live in large cities, towns and regions and who are usually working in 21st century relevant industries.

In 2019, we witnessed the spectacle of a leaver majority parliamentary Conservative Party being led by a reluctant remainer (Teresa May) and a remainer majority parliamentary Labour Party being led by a reluctant leaver (Jeremy Corbyn).

In 2019, Italy was governed by a coalition that included a far-right party, The League, and a far-left party, The Five Star Movement. Many thought this arrangement could not last and it didn't. From traditional 20th century ideological perspectives, that it existed at all is astonishing. However, both these ideologically driven parties are Modernist populist parties united by their 20th century Modernist mindsets and their promotion of a nation-first agenda. They were united by their shared opposition against what Modernist populists call 'globalism' and they supported their own brand of 'nationalism', namely Italy first. This is why they could collaborate in a less ideological 21st century.

Neither of these parties had any vision or strategy for constructing a viable standalone 21st century Italy. These people might not like some of the characteristics of the Europe they live in, but they are unlikely to do much more than blame others for their situation. They will not leave Europe, for unlike the Brexiters they know they will lose too much. They merely wanted to strengthen their negotiating power. The government of Italy led by Giorgia Meloni elected in 2022 is composed of different elements of Modernist populism. It is composed solely on centre right and far right political parties. It is too Modernist, and it won't last either. Political stability in Italy will only emerge if Meloni, or somebody else, forms a new centre government containing more Planetist components, that is similar to the Macron Government is France.

It is likely that the net political outcome of this Modernist populist challenge will be an even more integrated Europe with a European parliament that is more powerful than it is at present and with Planetist pro-global integration majorities contesting with Modernist anti-global integration minorities from many countries.

In the Australian elections in 2019, in an election where the political left focussed on fairness and dealing successfully with climate change, many well-off electorates voted for more progressive parties in support of these ends and many poorer electorates containing people fearful of losing their mostly 20th century jobs (such as in the endangered coal industry) voted for conservative parties. In the election of 2022 this trend continued with well-educated mostly female Planetist candidates, calling themselves *teal independents,* defeating Modernist candidates in prosperous, traditionally conservative but highly educated electorates. This resulted in the defeat of a conservative government that was punished by the electorate for holding onto too many of its Modernist values. It was replaced by a progressive Labor government with a Planetist agenda

In the 2016 US elections many of the poorer, less well-educated, and less-advantaged regions swung to the conservative Republicans and the well-off areas swung to the progressive Democrats. This election elevated Donald Trump into the presidency. However, Trump did not win the popular vote. He won through a decision by the politically undemocratic and archaic electoral college. This undemocratic process artificially extended the reign of Modernist populism in the USA. In the 21st century, it will not be the levels of prosperity or poverty or the patterns of advantage and disadvantage that will cause major shifts in voting patterns, though this is how those who look through ideological lens will continue to see this shift. From now on it will be the levels of education existing between different regions and the speed with which education is uplifting people that will shape election patterns. This book has already described how education levels are being uplifting everywhere. This fact and its consequences is a major theme of this book. In November 2022 in the US midterm elections and five months after the Australian trends just mentioned, conservative Republicans were severely punished for holding on to too many Modernist values. This election rejected the trends that characterised voting patterns in most previous midterm elections, which traditionally react negatively to the policies of the current president. But this time Donald Trump and his Modernist populist followers were punished by the more educated and more Planetist components of the US electorate. The values that informed those punishing Trump and his political movement were those relating to private gun ownership, climate change denial, antiabortion and anti the protection of women's right, autocratic winner-take-all political mindsets that undermine democracy. In an increasingly better educated 21st century, ideology will cease to be a factor that will shape electoral voting patterns in an increasing number of places. Instead, it will be planetist ideals that will inform voting patterns.

In Europe, many disadvantaged people are increasingly voting for conservative Modernist populist parties even though these parties do not offer them any 21st century realistic solutions for their economic and social disadvantage. Most of these conservative parties are much less committed to building a stronger European community and clearly believe that the solution to their problems involves returning to a yesteryear where nation came first and could stand alone, and cultures were homogeneous. They offer implausible yesteryear solutions for building tomorrow-year success, and they also seek to prosper by feeding on people's fear and grievances and their hostility to people who are different, including refugees who are different.

People who are prospering in emerging 21st century society are voting for political parties that are socially progressive and have core values that are planetist. Many elections in the next decade will be influenced by values clashes between the declining numbers of Modernists and the increasing numbers of Planetists.

These examples illustrate the relative decline of ideology and the relative rise of ideals and values in determining how people vote. Blair's year 2000 prediction that the 20th century politics of ideology will give way to a 21st century politics of ideals is becoming a reality. Extreme views of all kinds will decline. The politics of the ideological centre will remain, and this will be increasingly influenced by Planetist values. This can already be seen with Macron, who is not an ideological driven politician, but is one whose ideas are informed by Planetist ideals and values.

Planetists want a tomorrow-year that is prosperous, inclusive, harmonious, sustainable, healthy, and secure for all. In short, they want a more *liveable* tomorrow-year for their children and for future generations. If they could clear their minds of resentment, it is likely that many Modernist populists would want this as well. Planetists are motivated by hope and aspiration rather than fear and resentment. They want to live in tomorrow-year on a planet that is more liveable for all and is also climate and pandemic safe. We will discuss liveability in detail in Chapter 6.

The remaining Modernist minority will further decline as globalisation lifts more people into prosperity. Many of the children of Modernist populists will not follow their parent's pathways because they will seek, and they will have, opportunities to be better educated. I believe these battles will slowly be resolved by the further spreading and deepening of education. A mass investment in education is the best way to create a more prosperous, more inclusive, more harmonious, and climate-safe, global village.

Political movements in the 21st century will now be more defined by values, ever more by ideals, and ever less by ideology. The route to creating an ever more thriving planet is more of the same in terms of globalisation but it will require a different mode of globalisation. I call this different mode *cosmonaut globalisation*, Planetist-informed globalisation, the emerging globalisation of tomorrow-year, as distinct from *cowboy globalisation*, modernist informed globalisation, the receding globalisation of yesteryear. We will discuss cosmonaut and cowboy globalisation further in Chapter 12.

2.6. Governance in Our Emerging Global Village

One of the nine values of planetism is democracy. A rising, ever more highly educated middle class will only support forms of governance that are more democratic. The higher the proportion of well-educated people, the more stable democracies will become, and the better democracies they will also become. Educated people who are working in the knowledge-based, metaphysically resourced industries that provide the main routes to 21st century economic prosperity will not want to live and work in autocracies.

As discussed, our emerging global village is becoming ever more interdependent. I believe interdependence is based on three elements I call the *Interdependence Trio*. These are:

- The *Golden Rule*, treat others as you would like them to treat you
- The *making of mutual obligations* to realise shared aspirations
- Seeking *win/win*, not win/lose in all outcomes (FUTK08)

This *Interdependence Trio* has the potential to evolve into a new planetary moral compass, a trio of good behaviours for the 21st century. Those who consciously breach these rules will be cast as *planetary pariahs.*

Our 21st century global society will continue to become ever more interdependent. Of course, interdependence is a voluntary relationship that can be dissolved by any party in the relationship. If one party in an interdependent relationship tries to bully another to achieve win/lose the most likely outcome will be lose/lose.

Could a would-be autocratic leader continue to repress the people he leads while relating to the rest of the world with behaviours based on the Interdependence Trio? Perhaps yes, but only for a short time. This outcome will become increasingly less possible in the future. And over time, all the *nine values of planetism* will inform an emerging planet wide moral compass of good planetary behaviour.

There are still many nations that have autocratic forms of governance. However, their days are numbered. As stated previously, the number of governments that are officially democratic has risen from 12 at the end of World War 2 to about 130 today.

Certainly, many of these are very imperfect democracies and there are many autocratic leaders who seek to manipulate the electoral process and utilise selective forms of repression to ensure that they continue to rule. However, the long-term trend will be towards better democracies as well as more democracies. There will be no reversal of these trends leading to the establishment of more autocracies. Even the most autocratic nations such as Saudi Arabia or China are slowly loosening the strings of autocracy and permitting behaviours that would not have been thought to be possible a decade ago. That is how planetary public opinion informed by an emerging planetary moral compass is influencing the behaviours of even the most recalcitrant autocratic leaders. I believe that despite the efforts of would-be Modernist populist autocrats to slow or reverse this trend, it will continue unabated. They will become planetary pariahs.

The global economy of the 21st century will generate most of its wealth from knowledge, from metaphysical rather than physical resources. Knowledge-based economies are realised from the minds of educated people. These generators of metaphysical wealth want to live in places that are democratically governed, where both ideas and people are nourished not repressed. If these conditions are not present, they will leave. It is interesting to note that repressive autocracy can still work to a degree in nations with economic bases based on natural (physical) resources. However, the more knowledge-based an economy is, the greater is the likelihood that it will have democratic governance.

Global integration will largely be driven by the voluntary actions of individuals, organisations, communities and nations to build interdependent relationships and conduct interdependent trade. All of these will be based on the *Interdependence Trio*. If an interdependent relationship begins to deliver win/lose outcomes the relationship will not last. The conflict between Catalonia and Spain is a good illustration of this. Coercive integration will also fail. A good example of this is what is occurring in Han-dominated China, where China is trying to repress and forcibly 're-educate' Muslim Uyghurs so that they can be more easily integrated. China's ends might be desirable, but their means are certainly not.

These measures generate win/lose, not win/win outcomes. They are not likely to produce stable outcomes, because on one side there will be resentment. And such actions will also receive increasing disapproval from global public opinion in coming decades. Those nations still seeking to bully others rather than collaborate with them will slowly be relatively disempowered. The USA under Trump sought to bully Mexico to get his way and Russia under Putin has sought to bully Ukraine to get his way. Making long-term enemies just across your national border is not at all wise. This leads to discontented and antagonistic neighbourhoods rather than contented and synergistic neighbourhoods. With antagonism, we cannot thrive together.

In the 21st century, most nations, global businesses, and global NGOs understand that belonging to interdependent international global and regional entities or joining global or regional trade agreements will offer them more security and prosperity than by going it alone. Any nation that is a planetary pariah will have no option but to behave as a good planetary citizen to be rehabilitated into a worthy and respected inhabitant of our emerging global village. These nations will have to embed into their behaviours the three components of the *Interdependence Trio* if they want to be invited to live in our global village. These nations include current planetary pariahs such as the DPRK (Democratic People's Republic of Korea) or potential ones like the military autocracy currently governing Myanmar. As the 21st century proceeds and our emerging global village society further consolidates our planet will also become an ever-more-lonely place for those who remain locked out of this village.

If a nation initiates a trade war in an ever more interdependent global society, it will more likely weaken itself rather than seriously damage others. A more intelligent approach to realise future prosperity would be to encourage collaboration with others to build a thriving global village that works for all its occupants. That is what the European Union, for example, seeks to do. The European Union knows that despite its relatively large size and global power, it will need to be a benign giant because its internal governance is based on intercultural respect, interdependence and win/win, not intercultural disrespect, independence and win/lose. Consistency in behaviour will increasingly matter as the 21st century progresses. As the European Community can't bully its own member states, it knows it would be hypocritical to bully external states. Europe will ensure that its external behaviour mirrors its internal behaviour. It will sit down and negotiate with external entities of all kinds just as it does with its own members.

The politics of the 21st century has been dominated by the extraordinary rise of China. The evidence is that China, despite being a socialist Modernist autocracy today, is carefully preparing itself to be a collaborative inhabitant of an ever more Planetist global village: for the nation that best collaborates and builds the most long-term interdependent relationships with others will thrive best in a global village. The use of brute power will not guarantee anybody's success in a global village.

China learned from the spectacular collapse of the Soviet Union under Yeltsin, who tried to make change occur too rapidly. It is orchestrating change deliberately, slowly, and continuously. China has a clear view about managing the rate of developmental change: it must be neither too fast nor too slow. It is consciously slowly abandoning command capitalism and replacing it with free market capitalism.

China has also learned from its humiliation by others, particularly in the 19th century when it was economically colonized by Europeans. Events such as the Boxer Rebellion and the Opium Wars are now deeply etched in its cultural memory. China is resolutely determined that in future it will not be exploited or humiliated again this way. And despite the concerns of many democratic nations that it seeks to oppress other nations, I believe China will not seriously threaten others this way. China sees itself as a good global citizen even if many others do not see it this way.

Thus, China is contributing significantly to the shaping of an interdependent global society through its immense *Belt and Road Initiative (BRI)*. This initiative seeks to create a 21st century version of the archaic collaborative globalisation of the *Silk Road.* The BRI is an interdependent, mutually beneficial trading program linking China with more than 80 nations. More than US$12 trillion will be invested on ports, roads, railways, power stations, and telecommunications. This infrastructure provides the very *planetary interconnectivity ways and wares* needed for the realisation of an integrated interdependent global village. The program is scheduled to end in 2050.

These collaborative actions are inconsistent with China's current bullying and repression within its borders. With its *Belt and Road Initiative* China is implementing what is essentially a China-led loyalty scheme that locks all these nations into long-term interdependent relationships with it based on the three elements of the *Interdependence Trio*. China might bully others today, but it clearly understands that there will be a time when it will no longer be able to get away with doing this. It clearly understands what it needs to do to become to be 21st century successful even if some of its current behaviour appears to be contrary to this.

In contrast to Europe, which seeks to ensure that its external relations behaviour mirrors its internal relations, China will seek to do the opposite. China will have no choice other than to make its internal behaviour a mirror of its external behaviours. If it wants to have long-term interdependent relationships with other nations through its *Belt and Road Initiative,* it will need to show the world that it is fully trustworthy; that its internal and external behaviours are consistent. It will eventually show this by building interdependent trusting relationships with all the non-Han people within its borders, including the Uyghurs and Tibetans. China is today still largely autocratic and modernist. However, as said, it is slowly and consciously changing itself to prepare for life in a global village.

China will be the home of more than a billion educated middle class people by 2030. These educated middle class people will be building China's metaphysical industrial future. Most highly educated people will not support autocracy. China will therefore need to slowly democratize itself. In 2019 and 2020 the political crisis in Hong Kong showed to both the Chinese and world the future of China itself. The demand for democracy was led by young, educated Planetist university students seeking a democratic future in a movement that, as I have already said, unfortunately conflicts with China's own preferred timelines.

This Hong Kong democracy movement wants a democratic Hong Kong now. However, I believe China is pursuing a harmonisation-and-inclusion-by-force strategy to slow this movement down so that the rate of change is better synchronised with its own preferred timeline for shaping the future of the whole of China. It will take another 15 years to enable the rest of China to reach the point where Hong Kong is now. It is notable that the Chinese government has avoided a too-hostile repression of dissident students in Hong Kong. This is in contrast with how it brutally responded to a similar student uprising in Tiananmen Square in 1989.

Thirty years after Tiananmen Square, in 2019, China openly defended its ruthless behaviour in repressing students in Tiananmen Square, calling it 'correct' public policy. They might have added that though they thought it was 'correct' then, they know that murdering its own citizens in the streets is not 'correct' today. Times have changed. China will now have to limit the force it uses to contain this inconveniently early democracy movement because it does not want to destroy Hong Kong's capacity to remain the essential global financial and trading centre it has become. If it represses Hong Kong too much, it will totally undermine some of its other global initiatives to prepare itself for a more interdependent future.

By about 2035 at the very latest all of China will demand what the youth of Hong Kong wanted in 2019. I believe that China recognises the inevitability of the arrival of an interdependent, and even democratic, global village. And they are making themselves ready to thrive in this emerging world. With its *Belt and Road Initiative*, China is building a major new component of the 21st century global trading system. It is constructing a 21st century *Silk Road* to suit itself, with China at one end of the road and most of the planet at the other end. The indications are that China is implementing a clearly thought-out plan for shaping its future in a 21st century global village.

The government of China is facilitating the creation of a 21st century advanced knowledge, metaphysically resourced China. It is doing this in three ways. Firstly, it is opening a new university almost every week and will continue to do this until at least 2030. China now has 37 million university students. One in every five university students in the world is Chinese. Secondly, it is now seeking to entice back to China many of the outstanding Chinese scholars, researchers, and academics who are living outside China. Thirdly, China has actively encouraged its young to study at universities in democratic nations outside China. In 2018, 1.5 million Chinese were studying in overseas higher education institutions in democratic nations. It is seeking to have continuous and productive dialogues with these students while they are away from China. These graduates will be welcomed back to China when their studies are complete. Their return will catalyse the development of an ever more knowledge-based economic future and with it a future democratic nation. These returning students will return carrying embedded planetist values and will become major drivers of the transformation of a modernist autocratic China into a planetist democratic China.

This democratic transformation process will be largely completed by 2050. The year 2050 is also the year when the *Belt and Road Initiative* is expected to end. In 2050 China will ensure it can have mutually beneficial interdependent relationships with at least 100 other nations. While Modernist populists elsewhere are trying to resist humanity's transformation into global villagers, China is consciously constructing this global village. The Chinese will by 2035 have contributed significantly to shaping the global future by helping to completely bury 600 years of brutal European initiated *cowboy globalisation* and replace it with a 21st century version of the mutually beneficial trading system of the ancient *Silk Road* which I call *cosmonaut globalisation*. China is getting to the future first.

The birth of democracy in China will follow the pathway used by the Republic of Korea (South Korea), which amended its constitution in 1987 and instantaneously turned an autocracy into a democracy in a single stroke of the legislative pen. Here a stable democracy was quickly established after more than three decades of growing prosperity based on a massive investment in higher education under an autocratic regime that led to the creation of a large educated Korean middle class.

China is very future perceptive. It knows that if its rise is to continue in an emerging planetist future it will soon have to open itself to more democratic forms of governance and be based on inclusion that is voluntary, not enforced. China is currently well back in this field, but it will close this democracy gap rapidly in the next decades. China is on the verge of becoming one of the most 21st century ready nations in the world. It is being an exemplar purposeful-future-maker as it seeks to consciously shape both its own future and, through its Belt and Road Initiative and other actions, the future of our emerging 21st century global village.

The Chinese government is very aware that managing the shift from autocracy to democracy will be challenging. However, even it was surprised by a challenge that that emerged in late 2022. In late 2022 urban populations all over China began to protest, initially about its still autocratic COVID driven lockdowns, but also to demand a more rapid transition to democracy. This same challenge was also emerging simultaneously in Iran and for the same reasons. It is a 21st century fact of life that educated people do not like autocrats and autocracies. This is the reason why this democracy movement is now a global movement, one that, except perhaps for a few totalitarian backwaters, will be completed by the year 2050.

However, for now there are still some unable or unwilling to adopt such proactive future shaping roles: they are only willing to be reactive future takers.

Some will change themselves only when there is no other alternative, and they often seek to aggressively shape the future of others, against the others' will. One such group is the Taliban. The Taliban shocked the world in August 2021 by defeating the corrupt and marginally competent Western-backed government of Afghanistan. This government simply collapsed and facilitated the almost bloodless return of the Taliban to power after it had spent 20 years in exile as a planetary pariah.

This Western-backed government, however, had made several important progressive changes. These included liberating women and facilitating their education and establishing an inclusive fledgling democracy. This government gave the people of Afghanistan a hopeful vision of what a 21st century relevant Afghanistan might become, a vision which is now embedded in millions of Afghans. The Taliban have had to recognize this reality, and while in exile have reflected enough to realise that in 2021 neither the global community nor the people of Afghanistan would accept a return of the brutal tribal Taliban of the past. The Taliban that took power was not what we can call Taliban 1.0, the old Taliban, a Pashtun-dominated tribal Taliban hostile to all of those who were different, and one dedicated to the suppression of women. It is, so far not very convincingly, trying to tell the world it is now Taliban 2.0, a nationalist Afghan movement that seeks to include those Afghans who are different and that will lift the status and rights of women. In 2022 and beyond the Taliban will need to demonstrate to the rest of the planet that it is no longer seeking to turn back the clock in Afghanistan to a dark yesteryear. If the Taliban does not do that it will join North Korea as an exile in the 21st century cold. It will need to do at least enough to persuade the world it is a worthy member of humanity's emerging 21st century global village and will do nothing to endanger it. If the Taliban do enough to become this trustworthy, China might offer them membership in its *Belt and Road Initiative,* and others could follow and support Afghanistan's further nation building.

I believe that the government of Afghanistan will ultimately evolve into a somewhat more autocratic version of a democratic Pakistan. Over time it might go even further than this. And unlikely as this might seem to many, I also believe Afghanistan might transform itself sufficiently for it to change sides and collaborate with the rest of the world to reduce and ultimately remove the threat posed by the remaining components of Islamic extremism, until the time comes that these fanatical tribal groups are themselves willing to make a similar self-transformative journey. A transformation into a Planetist Afghanistan is inconceivable right now. However, long term, the Taliban will have no choice other than to undergo this transformation, just as others such as the South Sudanese and the warring factions in Yemen, will need to do if they wish to thrive with others in a global village.

There are other governments still led by autocratic Modernist and mildly democratic Modernist populist leaders, nations such as Saudi Arabia, Iran and Russia, that continue to interfere in politics beyond their national boundaries, even seeking to generate intercultural and interreligious conflict in order to fulfil their own nationalist agendas. So Shia Iran supports Shia Islam in Sunni-dominated Bahrain and Yemen. It supports a Shia Government in an Iraq that has a powerful Sunni minority. Sunni Saudi Arabia supports Sunni Islam against the Shia population in Yemen. Russia supports autocratic socialist leaderships in North Korea and Venezuela and collaborates with an autocratic Shia government in Syria. And Russia also uses cyber technology and targeted assassination to bully potential critics in order to buy time so that the ever more Planetist world will not gang up on it and undermine its own continuing nation-first autocratic governance. The capacity of all four of these nations (Saudi Arabia, Russia, Iran, and Venezuela) to continue to do this will be threatened by the approaching end of the fossil fuel era combined with a lack of diversity in their own industrial bases.

A fossil fuel or weapons export dominated economy such as the Russian economy, unless it changes track to create a more 21st century relevant industrial development strategy, will struggle and then fail in an emerging interdependent 21st century global economy. Not so China. The contrast between a return-to-yesteryear seeking Russia and its former Communist soul mate, a tomorrow year seeking China, is becoming ever more striking.

It is also interesting to contemplate that a major peace dividend might be a significant outcome of the end of the fossil fuel era and the arrival of a solar powered planetary society in the 21st century.

The economic drivers of globalisation, namely trade and investment and the spreading and uplifting of mass education, will continue. As everyone can benefit from its continuation there will be few who will want to stop it. In this emerging global society ever more trade and investment will facilitate the further rise of the educated middle class, the growing development of metaphysically resourced economies, and the further development of a democratically governed global village.

We are at an historic moment. For the first time in history the ever-growing interdependent and respect-demanding relationships *between* nations are beginning to shape the development of interdependent relationships and democratic governance *within* nations. A global village can only function well if it is collaborative and interdependent and has markets that are accessible to all, and processes that can produce shared benefit for all. From now on all the internal relationships within nations will need to mirror this 21st century reality and become collaborative and interdependent as well. Competition and independence will of necessity go into decline, though they will, of course, survive in our society, especially in our games and our sports.

The creation of a global village based on more growing metaphysical resourced economic development, increased education, and ever better interdependent relationships, will in future drive the democratisation of governance within nations. The Planetist values of the educated middle class will determine the global standing of nations and corporations and determine whether they should be rewarded or punished for their behaviour. Planetist influenced disinvestment programs and other *Planetary Pariah Punishments,* and international courts directed against both crimes-against-humanity and corruption, will become the tools of punishment for bad planetary behaviour.

Our future world, including political environments within nations, will be ever more interdependent and will be shaped by a moral compass increasingly based on planetist values. The growth of the educated middle class, as it is uplifted by globalisation and mass education, will eventually undermine any form of autocracy anywhere. In two decades, any autocratic government that represses those who are different will become a *Planetary Pariah*. And that would be China's or Russia's fate if these do not democratise their politics or continue to bully their neighbours. This will not happen in China because it knows what it needs to do and what the timeline is for it to a totally 21st century relevant nation. And if there is a democratic China then it will be much harder for any remaining autocratic governments to resist democratisation.

Dislocating events such as the COVID-19 pandemic health crisis and the resulting economic recessions might slow globalisation briefly. But that is all these events will do. We can't stop globalisation. But we can all adapt to it and even shape its future, just as China is seeking to do. This includes shaping it to ensure that globalisation makes our planetary home and society the kind of place we all want to live in and thrive in, in short make our world as *liveable* as we can make it.

The trends unleashed by *Earthrise* are collectively building an interdependent planetist world with a global market that can be utilised by all who aspire to do so. Ever more of us can build our own future success, and without harming others while we are doing so. These trends are both promising and unstoppable, for they can lead to shared uplifted prosperity and liveability for all. But to become 21st century successful in this way we must become as 21st century prepared as we can be. This is a core purpose of the remainder of this book.

We are now going to commence a different exploration. After two long chapters of examining global trends and concepts for understanding the 21st century, we are going to turn our attention to ourselves, to examine the knowledge and tools we need to thrive in the 21st century. The next three chapters will consider how we can make ourselves as 21st century prepared as possible. There might be some readers who are primarily interested in understanding global trends and social and political change. These readers might like to consider initially skipping the next two chapters and proceed directly to Chapter 5.

Chapter 3: Self-Knowledge for Future Shapers

How can I find my place and role in the emerging world? What is my identity? How do I describe myself? How might I best prepare myself so that I can become the most effective shaper of my future life and career path I can be in our emerging 21st century world?

3.1. Knowing Yourself. Exploring Personal Identity

In the first two chapters, we discussed our cultural, national, or planetary identities. In this chapter, we will be discussing another identity, our personal identity, how we see ourselves in terms of our personal qualities, preferences, aspirations, capabilities, and the work we do. This is what can inform your answer when someone asks you *what do you do?* Or *who are you?*

There is an Ancient Greek maxim that comes from the Oracle in the Temple of Apollo in Delphi: *Know thyself!* Socrates took this thought further and told us that *an unexamined life is a life that is not worth living.* Here, we will discuss the form of *future knowledge* which is *self-knowledge*.

We cannot understand and fully secure our best place in the emerging world unless we have more insight about our *destiny*. Henry Ford said *the whole secret of a successful life is to find out what is one's destiny to do and then do it.* So, all of us can ask this question of themselves: *What is my destiny*, or what *is my calling?* This insight-directed question could be interpreted as asking yourself to consider your unique and special qualities and capabilities: your *gift*s if you like. Many people, particularly young people, often ask this question of themselves, but they are frequently unable to answer it with any degree of satisfaction. But if we can do this, we will become better shapers of and adaptors to change, and enhance our capacity to build successful 21st century life and career paths and fulfilling relationships.

There are three primary tasks we need be able to accomplish. The first task, as indicated, is to know how to understand ourselves as best as we can, whether 'we' are an individual, a group, an organisation, a community, or a nation. It is very important that, before we try to shape our futures, we have the deepest possible understanding of ourselves: our strengths and weaknesses, our abilities and disabilities, our fears and hopes.

The second task, which will be discussed in Chapter 4, is to know how to understand, assemble and utilise some key concepts and tools to shape the future.

The third task, which will be discussed in Chapter 5, is to examine what skills we need to acquire so that we can develop successful, fulfilling, fruitful and 21st century relevant relationships with all the people with whom we share our personal and working lives and with whom we want shape to the future. None of us want to unconsciously undermine our key relationships by making poor choices that lead to alienating those with whom we want to have successful long-term relationships.

Now we will explore and seek to deepen your future shaping capability by introducing you to what the first tools of self-knowledge are: *The Three Sights (FUTK19) and The Three Dialogues (FUTK20)*.

Incidentally, in the next decade, it is likely that what we might call a *self-knowledge industry* will emerge. The five billion educated middle-class people who will live on our planet in 2030 will certainly want more self-knowledge. There are many parts of this self-knowledge industry already present: all counselling and coaching services, for example. There will be an increasing number and array of self-knowledge products and services available in the future that we can collectively call *self-knowledge ways and wares*. Imagine for yourself a self-knowledge industry that will emerge in the next two decades. It might, for example, include what we could call *destiny exploration ways and wares*.

3.2. Three Selves, Three Sights and Three Dialogues

We can envision *Three Selves (FUTK21)*: the past self we can learn from; the present self we can consider and explore; and the future self we can imagine and seek to realise.

To maximise our knowledge of these three selves, we need to utilise our three sights (FUTK19): *hindsight*, to help recall and learn from our past self; *insight* to reveal to us and understand our present self; and *foresight* to imagine and construct our future self.

We sometimes wish we had done something differently and we often seek to learn from past failures and successes. We all look backward (in Hindsight Mode), sometimes with nostalgia, sometimes with happiness, sometimes with pain. And we look forward (in Foresight Mode) as well, sometimes with hope and optimism and at other times with fear and a sense of vulnerability.

But if one wishes to become the best shaper of futures one can be, one needs also to look inwards (in Insight Mode) so one can better understand the present self and one's current standing and situation. As we learn more about ourselves, we can make wiser decisions about what the future self could be and then chart a pathway towards realising this future self.

Fortunately, we have the ability to use *the three selves* (FUTK21) and *the three sights* (FUTK19) repeatedly to more deeply understand and learn from all of these *three selves,* separated as they are by time, experience, and developmental change.

When we wish to take our Three Sights into action mode, into active researching tools, and then use them to shape our future and the future of the world around us, we need to use language that tells others we are now in action mode and actively using *The Three Sights* to understand *The Three Selves.* I refer to these Three Sights or Selves in action mode as *The Three Dialogues. (FUTK20).*

These Three Dialogues are: the *Derivation Dialogue* (working in Hindsight Mode when remembering and learning from the past self), the *Destiny Dialogue* (working in Insight Mode when considering and exploring the present self) and the *Destination Dialogue* (working in Foresight Mode when imagining and constructing the future self).

3.3. Hindsight in Action: Exploring Derivations

Those who do not learn history are doomed to repeat it (George Santayana). How might we learn best from history and our past experiences? There are two things we should identify in our past selves. I call these the *Derivation Duet,* which consists of both *heritage* and *baggage.*

- *Heritage* consists of past experiences, plus what we learn from our understanding of our personal history. Heritage is those elements, including some bad experiences, from our past that make us the people we are today or that we believe have or could make a *positive* contribution to our future lives: what we have been grateful to receive and learn and carry forward with us into the present and the future. We can pull out of our memory banks what we have inherited and learned from our parents and significant teachers and mentors, and have treasured and embedded in our deep knowledge. What have we observed that has become priceless knowledge and understanding? What we have learned from our past can become priceless assets as we journey into the future!

- *Baggage* consists of the experiences, the traumas, the mistakes, the wrong mindsets, even perhaps some good experiences as well, that have made or continue to make, a *negative* contribution to our lives, disabling and disadvantaging us. What in our past experiences has limited or is still limiting our capacity to reach our full potential? We need to first recognise our *baggage* and then take steps to remove its influence from shaping our future lives. In order to continue learning from our past experiences, we should do as George Santayana advised us and not eliminate them from our memories. What we do need to do is to evaluate our past and realise when what we have until now regarded as *heritage* has, because of social change and the passage of time, become *baggage*. And, of course, the reverse can apply. For example, community based adolescent initiation, which we threw out as *baggage* during the Modernist era, we are now seeking to reincorporate into our cultures as *heritage* in the Postmodern era.

We can conduct a *Derivation Dialogue* with others that focuses on learning about our shared *heritage and baggage* from our collective past. We can then embed the *heritage* into our collective consciousness to take forward and eliminate the *baggage* to un-encumber ourselves so that we become the most effective shapers of futures we can be.

3.4. Insight in Action: Exploring Destinies

In this section, we are going to explore more about the present self. Mostly, this will involve encouraging you to do so by utilising both thinking and feeling, just as we can also explore the past and future self by using both our cerebral and our emotional intelligences.

However, our learning about ourselves can also be improved if sometimes we consciously set out *not* to think. Meditation is an excellent way of doing this. It encourages us to be present in a continuing present while we are sitting on a cushion or in a chair: to consciously 'be' where our body is, not somewhere else in our imagination. It is similar when one is practicing yoga or a martial art.

Thinking is an incredibly powerful tool, but it is even more so if we can use its full power when we wish to and not at all when we don't wish to. Our mind can both empower us and disable us, and it can both heal us and harm us. The more mastery we can have over our minds the healthier we will be and the more effective shapers of future we can become. We will soon discuss how freeing our minds from thinking about our current tasks and problems can enable our minds to release from our unconscious into our conscious mind some very powerful and even life-changing insights and ideas. However, having said all that, here we are going to focus on thinking about the three selves and informing ourselves about each of these.

We are now going to use our thinking to consider the present self. Here we place ourselves into *Insight Mode*. We will succeed best if we use our insight first to know ourselves better before we use foresight to shape our future. If we can grow our knowledge and understanding of self, we will be more likely to realise a fulfilled, fruitful, and productive future self.

Firstly, what are your aptitudes (what you are good at doing)? Secondly, what are your passions (what you love to do)? Because this combination gives you your likely destiny, I have called this the Destiny Duet *(FUTK12)*. Try imagining sitting in a circle with the people who know you best. You talk about your *aptitudes and your passions* and others can give you their views of your current loves and hates, and abilities and disabilities. After you have done this, describe your destiny in just two words: a *Domain Descriptor* (an adjective) plus an *Activity Descriptor* (a noun) (FUTK13). Examples would be social entrepreneur, relationships counsellor, environmental assessor, investment broker or urban planner.

You may find that you have identified a destiny that is not recognisable in terms of a current work or career description. But coming to such a conclusion is a good prognosis for your future success. Just because your chosen destiny is not currently a recognisable career does not mean that it won't be in the future.

This uplifted level of self-knowledge will spark your imagination and can activate your vision of your future self. So, when somebody asks you about what your career plans for the future are, you can say I am seeking to become XY where X is your Domain Descriptor and Y is your Activity Descriptor. If you do this, you might be surprised by the conversation that follows.

When we consider destinations and emerging opportunities we will see that knowledge of your destiny can open a pathway to real options for your future life and career paths. In the remainder of this book, we will list many potential career and industrial futures that do not currently exist. It is not wise to limit your career considerations only to currently recognisable occupations. Most of the occupations that will exist in a generation's time have yet to be invented. And as we shall see soon, we can gain a clear understanding about emerging labour markets and industrial futures from some of the curriculum described in this book. The 21st century will present to you, if you are well prepared, an increased number and a greater variety of work possibilities than at any other time in history. And in these circumstances, any *Destiny Dialogue* can kick-start the construction of a realistic individual future career pathway or an organisational or community social or economic future.

We can all benefit by reviewing our destiny from time to time as we tread our future life and career paths. We are always changing and our destiny will change as we experience more and we learn more about ourselves and the world around us.

Once we have completed our exploration of self in a destiny dialogue, we can take this awareness forward when we switch from insight mode to foresight mode to explore future possible destinations.

3.5. Foresight in Action: Exploring Destinations

When we take on *foresight mode*, we activate the futurist in each of us. This futurist is part *Prophet* and part *Visionary*. What's the difference?

- The *prophet* asks *what will be the future?* We answer this question by developing predictions of what *will be,* the future. This is also the foresight way of the *Manager* in each of us.
- The *visionary* asks *what could be the future?* We answer this question by developing *visions of what could be,* the future. This is also the foresight way of the *leader* in each of us.

These two parts of ourselves were described thus by George Bernard Shaw:
You see things and you say, why?
I dream things that never were, and I say, Why not?
(G. B. Shaw – *Back to Methuselah*)

Thus far in Chapter 3 we have learned how to know ourselves better. Now we can move on to exploring our next task. This task is to consider the concepts and tools we need to have at our disposal if we want to shape the future so that we can thrive in the 21st century

Chapter 4: Shaping the 21st Century

What mindsets, concepts and tools do I need to have at my disposal to become the most effective shaper of the future I can be in the emerging realities of 21st century society?

4.1. Charting Destinations

The next component of Future Knowledge to be considered is *Shaping the Future Knowledge*. We have just discussed two parts of *The Three Dialogues (FUTK20)*, namely the *Derivation Dialogues* based on *Hindsight* and the *Derivation Duet* (FUTK22) and *Destiny Dialogues* based on *Insight and the Destiny Duet (FUTK12)*. Now you'll be introduced to the third part of *the Three Dialogues,* namely the *Destination Dialogue* based on *Foresight* and the *Destination Duet.*

You have already been introduced to the concept that the Futurist in each of us is *Part Prophet and Part Visionary*. We will now take this concept further by introducing you to two major components of *Future Knowledge: The Six Future Questions* and *The Six Futures (FUTK41) and The Six Future Shaping Tools (FUTK40).*

4.2. The Six Future Questions and the Six Futures

When we seek to shape the future, we usually start with a question. The question we ask will depend on our dominant mindsets, including whether we are operating in *future taking/change taking mode* or *future making/change making mode*. Each of the questions we ask about the future will lead to a different future scenario. There are six core future questions that are important in shaping futures. Four questions are *prophetic questions* (what will be the future?) that are answered with a *Prediction*, and two of these are *envisioning questions* (what should be/could be the future?) that are answered with a *Vision*.

When we shape the future with others it is important to be sure that we are asking precisely the same question and that we are all considering the same future, not different ones. The six futures are the *plausible* future, the *particular* future, the *probable* future, the *prospective* future, the *preferred* future and the *possible* future (FUTK41). All too often we are not precise enough in the questions we ask when we seek to shape the future. And we often ask these questions without being as conscious as we could be of whether we are asking the same or different questions. We should discuss and agree upon which of the six alternative futures we are currently exploring. This way we can avoid many misunderstandings and disagreements, and probably shared failure as well.

The first four of these questions are based on our Futurist as *prophet and manager* and result in *predictions*. These are:

1. *What might occur in the future?*
   There can be many answers to this question and each time we ask this question we will imagine a different scenario, scenarios I call different *plausible futures*. Scenario planners usually call these *alternative futures* or *alternative scenarios*. There can be an almost unlimited number of *plausible futures*. I recommend a *Destination dialogue* with a consideration of *plausible futures* but then moving on to more precise questions about future trends, the future self, and future options, threats, and opportunities.

2. *What if...? What will be our future if a particular situation or event occurs?*
   As we look forward to exploring many different plausible futures, there will be several or even many *specific and foreseeable* situations or predictable events, and if we are wise we can prepare ourselves for them. Those who fail to do this will be more likely to be disrupted by change. For example, oil companies are spending US $5 trillion over the next 10 years on searching for more oil, an activity most people outside the industry would see as foolish and even suicidal. The industry clearly believes that they are powerful enough to shape the future to benefit themselves, even if these activities cause severe collateral damage to our planet's climate. They are in for a rude shock. Gary Lew gives us his warning on how to be resilient to disruption when he said: *this is your world, shape it or somebody else will*. This is a *particular future* question. The answer will be a *particular prediction*.

3. *What will be our future if we continue to pursue our current course and do not change?*

Our answer will be a *probable future, a probable prediction.* When they consider their future, too many people do not sufficiently consider the consequences of continuing with *business-as-usual.* These *predictions* will often offer a much less promising prognosis than that offered by initiating a conscious program of structured change. In the example just discussed relating to oil companies, these companies are seeking to carry on with business-as-usual. If they continue on this trajectory, they will hit a wall. Many people are comfortable operating on an *if it isn't broken don't fix it* strategy. They carry on with more of the same until something really goes wrong. Two decades ago, this strategy might have worked reasonably well when our world was changing more slowly. Now such attitudes are completely unwise. Those who continue going on the same track with *business-as-usual* can be disrupted by the sudden emergence of an alternative product or service or a new mode of production that makes what they do obsolete.

4 *Now that circumstances have changed what will now be our future?*

Our answer will be a *prospective future, a prospective prediction.* Whether or not we are well or badly prepared for a predictable or unpredictable future event occurring, many of these events are likely to cause at least some degree of disruption. The degree of disruption we experience will be determined by how well we ask and answer Question 2, the *Particular future* question.

In such cases, we will often need to consider making contingency plans to minimise potential threat and disadvantage and maximise potential opportunity and advantage. And the consequences of any disruption will not be a *probable future* that we might have previously expected, but an alternative future that we call the *prospective future* (a scenario we can describe as a *prospective prediction).* If a specific particular foreseeable event occurs, and if we have not consciously prepared for such an event, and not sought to be resilient to its impact, this disruption is likely to be more severe. But we might get lucky and gain advantage from this change. Then such a *prospective future* will permit us to reset our trajectory as a new *probable future.*

The remaining two questions are based on our Futurist as *leader* and *visionary*. Answers to these two questions we call *visions*, and they are *preferred visions and possible visions*. These last two questions are:

5   What future do I/we wish to realise? What future is my/our dream?
    Our answer will be our *preferred future, our preferred vision*. In G.B Shaw's play, *Back to Methuselah*, the Serpent says: *I dream things that never were, and I say why not!* Throughout history, it has been the visionaries and the dreamers who have said *why not* who have been the great change agents. There are many futurists who refuse to recognise the role vision can play in shaping the future. Some of them do not believe that envisioning a preferred future scenario is a legitimate component of a futurist's toolkit. They believe that imagining and then seeking to realise an inspirational aspiration is not a legitimate component of scenario planning. Needless to say, I do not agree with them.

6   What future can we realistically realise?
    Our answer will be our *possible future, a possible vision*. Sometimes we don't have sufficient knowledge, resources, determination or political power to realise a *preferred future* destination, so we need to settle for less, at least in the interim. But it is also important to recognise that such an interim destination can be turned into a *preferred vision* in the future when changed circumstances permit this. Such changed circumstances could result from improving our *resource capacities* and our *knowledge and skill capabilities* so that we can realise a *possible future destination* that is as close to our preferred *future destination* as we can make it.

We will all need quite a bit of practice to be able to comfortably use the *Six Future Questions and the Six Futures* as a holistic and interactive toolkit. Below are two exercises to help you start.

4.3. Integrating the Six Futures into a Unified Toolkit
Exercise 1

1.   Think of as many *plausible futures* as possible. Imagine and describe a *preferred future destination (a preferred vision)*. Then explore.

2. What will be your *probable prediction* (probable future destination) if you don't change direction and you continue with your current journey? This will inform you about the consequences and cost of not changing.
3. Are there any *particular predictions*, foreseeable disruptive threats or potential opportunities? Will you need more intelligence, surveillance and vigilance, followed by contingency planning and strategic action to ensure you can be more future successful?
4. If you change course from a *probable future destination (probable prediction)* to a *preferred future destination (preferred vision)*, what *preferred pathway* would you chart and what strategy should you adopt to change from your *probable pathway* to your *preferred pathway*?
5. Are there are any external environmental changes and limitations or internal limitations such as a lack of political power, financial resources, skills and knowledge (which we can explore as *plausible predictions* or anticipate as *particular predictions*) that might necessitate changing course to a *possible future*?
6. If this is the case, what is the *possible vision, or possible future destination* that can be realised under current circumstances? And what could be your *possible pathway* to reaching this destination?

A table summarising these six futures (FUTK38) is below. All of these 'futures' can be used to assist us become more resilient future takers (managerial excellence) and more purposeful future makers (leadership excellence).

Future question	Future	Search process	Realisation process
What might be the future? What future scenarios are plausible?	Plausible Future	Prophecy leading to several/many Plausible Predictions	Plausible Pathways
What if I am concerned about being disrupted by a particular event and I want to prepare for this event?	Particular Future	Prophecy leading to a Particular prediction	Particular pathways

What will be the future if I do not initiate significant change?	Probable Future	Prophecy leading to a Probable Prediction	Probable pathways
What will be the future with changed circumstances?	Prospective Future	Prophecy leading to a Prospective Prediction	Prospective pathways
What future is my aspiration?	Preferred Future	Envisioning leading to a Preferred vision	Preferred pathways
What future could we realistically achieve?	Possible Future	Envisioning leading to a Possible vision	Possible pathways

Exercise 2

Imagine yourself skippering a sailing boat in a three-knot tide/current and a six-knot wind. You are on a voyage to a destination you have consciously chosen to initiate, a *preferred future*. It is perhaps a voyage you have made many times before and you know the environment you are operating in very well, so it might also to be a *probable future* as well, provided 'normal' conditions prevail. The current and the wind are metaphors that describe the environment in which you are seeking to realise your aspirations. This environment might include changing market demand, competition, finance and investment availability and limitations, relationship commitments, new investor partners, new knowledge, an economic crisis, laws and regulations, illnesses or pandemics, skills shortages and resource limitations.

If your voyage is based on a pre-planned course to reach your *preferred future* and the environmental conditions are either deteriorating or improving, how might you respond?

If deteriorating conditions prevail, you can seek to make landfall at a *prospective future* destination that also might be a *possible future* as well, the best outcome you can realise for the time being until conditions improve. When this occurs, it might subsequently be feasible for you to set sail for a *preferred future* again.

In the interim, the more you know about the environment and its behaviour, the better will be your chances of successfully navigating your way in any challenging situation to a *prospective future destination* or even the best *possible future destination* in these conditions. This will be the least disrupted outcome you can manage.

But over a longer time, what is 'normal' might also change. The *climate* might be changing and with it the *weather,* with extreme weather events becoming more common or severe. It would be useful if you have some understanding of the long-term changes as well as the short-term changes occurring in your environment that might influence your long-term plans.

Most sailors commence a sailing boat voyage with a purpose in their mind: a *preferred future* such as winning a race or going to an offshore island for a picnic. If you wish to win a race, you might seek to position yourself at the start of the race on the windward side of the fleet: 'winning' here means *getting to the future first*. *Getting to the future first* is a concept developed by Gary Hamel and C.H. Prahalad in their book *Competing for the Future*. But whether favourable or unfavourable, changing circumstances will affect us differently depending upon our mindsets, our local environmental and sailing knowledge, and our degree of preparation.

We humans are genetically programmed to fear and be vigilant to change. *Homo sapiens* evolved with genes that informed us change was a potential threat and we reacted to change as future takers. To Palaeolithic humanity, change was rare and usually a threat: the main change agents in Palaeolithic times were floods, droughts, and other natural disasters, epidemics, and wars.

The wind shifts faced by a sailor will come and go. Some will be threats. Some will be opportunities. However, if the sailor has already decided to chart a course to a *preferred future* destination it then becomes clear which wind shift will provide an *opportunity* and which will pose a *threat*. If a sailor does not envision and plan his/her future journey by charting an appropriate course by asking him/herself enough appropriate future questions any wind shift will be perceived to be an ill wind shift by a sailor who has no course. We will disempower ourselves and become more vulnerable to disruption if we do not envision our preferred future.

As we saw in the first two chapters, when we looked at Modernist populism, there are some Modernist populists who regard pretty much all change as a threat and they fear they will be severely disrupted by change. What most of these people have in common is they have not set a course for themselves other than carrying on with business-as-usual. The concept of *future proofing* has been created to give them reassurance. But this is a false reassurance. The concept of *future proofing* is not the same as being *future ready* or *future prepared*.

The use of the word 'proof' implies perceiving all change and even the future itself as a potential negative and disruptive threat. This is the mindset of Palaeolithic people to whom all change was a threat, a mindset which is baggage from humanity's past. People who seek *future proofing* are like sailors who have not chartered a course for themselves, and they are less likely to identify whether a change is an emerging threat or an emerging opportunity. There is insufficient vision and aspiration in their mindsets. And many of them ask few, and even no, future shaping questions.

In a fast-changing 21st century, it is not enough to assume the future will be a *probable future*, or more of the same. *Future proofing* is an ultra-cautious mindset that emphasises fear of future change and the disruption that might be caused by it. It does not consider the role of aspiration or vision and of proactive action through the development of a *preferred or possible* vision and seeking to realise this vision.

It is important to be *future ready and future resilient* to *particular future* events that might offer either or both threats and opportunities. But stop for a moment and consider the limitations and implications of shaping the future within a culture that promotes *future proofing* as a mental crutch.

4.4. The Six Future Shaping Tools

The next component *of Future Shaping Knowledge* to look at are the *Six Future Shaping Tools* (FUTK40). They are:

- *Leadership*: being a purposeful change-maker/future-maker.
- *Management*: being a resilient change-taker/future-taker.
- *Planning*: combining and integrating physical and metaphysical resources to realise a future goal.
- *Design*: creating the form and function of an innovation, product, or process.
- *Innovation:* creating a new product or process to do old tasks better or quicker, or do new tasks first.
- *Learning:* growing our knowledge and capabilities and renewing our mindsets and beliefs so we can become more effective and successful in the future.

These six future-shaping tools are all forms of *metaphysical wealth*. And as Buckminster Fuller told us, this form of wealth can only grow. The creation of new *future shaping ways and wares*, new future shaping innovations, has already contributed massively to humanity's wealth building capacity. I believe that effective shapers of the future, whether operating as individuals or part of a collaborative team, will have the capability to combine and use all six of these tools.

The first two future shaping tools are Management and Leadership. We will discuss these two tools now.

4.5. Shaping Futures: Rethinking Management and Leadership

We all need to be both competent managers and leaders in order to be effective shapers of the future. And despite the belief of many, we can all learn to become competent managers and leaders. But we should seek to become competent managers and leaders of self before we seek to become competent managers and leaders of others. Many of us have experienced leaders and managers in our workplaces or communities who disappoint us. They might be poor management and leadership role models because they are making a mess of their personal or professional lives, because they abuse their position for personal gain, or because they undermine or damage collaborative working environments.

Management and leadership are not abilities that should belong only to people who are designated to be managers and leaders. They should belong to all of us. We also need for the balance between management and leadership in ourselves and our society to be proportionate. At present in many working and collaborative environments we tend to have too much management and not enough leadership; we are over-managed and under-led. We too often place managers in positions where leaders are needed, and we too often witness competent managers performing poorly as leaders. The role of the *manager in each of us is to run the enterprise.* The role of the *leader in each of us is needed to change the enterprise.*

What follows is a discussion about the important differences between management and leadership. When asked how management and leadership differ, many people say they recognise they are different, but they have trouble detailing more precisely what these core differences are. The differences between management and leadership are detailed in the table below.

The Ten Complementary Capabilities of Managers and Leaders (FUTK39):

Manager	Leader
Responds to change: reactive	Creates and shapes change: proactive
Future taker, path taker, change taker	Future maker, path maker, change maker
Cautious about risk	Careful about risk
Does the thing right	Does the right thing
Guided by fate	Guided by destiny
Controls actions and events	Facilitates actions and events
Works in the organisation	Works on the organisation
Prophet	Visionary
Probable futurist, particular futurist, prospective futurist	Preferred futurist, possible futurist
Problem centred strategist	Mission directed strategist

All of us can be and should be good managers and leaders of self. And all of us can become, when needed, effective managers and leaders of others as well. Management and leadership have core responsibilities to ensure that the other four future shaping tools (planning, design, innovation, and learning) are collectively and productively used in shaping the future, in shaping projects and events and reshaping and transforming organisations

The skills required to be effective manager and leader may be different, but they are also complementary. A simple way to express the key difference between the manager and leader in each of us is: *Management perfection is the Resilient Future Taker. Leadership perfection is the Purposeful Future Maker (FUTK26).* Every decision maker should recognise why they should be and when they should be operating in either *management mode or leadership mode.*

Several of these capabilities have already been discussed, but others haven't. In order, these are:

1. Taker and maker:

A taker is reactive. They respond to change that is already under way. A maker is proactive and initiates change.

2. Cautious versus careful:

Cautious means we are more future fearful than we need to be, and that we have as our major objective the protection of ourselves and avoidance of significant risk. Careful means we can plan positively to accomplish an aspiration while we also minimise risk and endangerment. We can be simultaneously careful and bold. We can act this way and still minimise risk. Imagine yourself on the edge of a minefield. On the other side of the minefield is paradise. How might a cautious person and a careful person respectively behave in this situation? Which of these is more likely to find a way to get to paradise?

3. Doing the thing right and doing the right thing:

What a difference the word order makes! The first involves doing the thing properly and correctly. The second involves doing what is both appropriate in terms of the time, place, and circumstances, and what is ethically appropriate.

4. Guided by fate versus guided by destiny:

Fate is change in the external world that might impact on us. We operate as change takers and future takers in responding to fate. Destiny involves becoming aware about what is embedded inside ourselves. The Destiny Duet tells as that Destiny = aptitude + passion. The recognition of our destiny can activate the change maker and the future maker within each of us, and initiate new actions to realise change in the outside world.

5. Control and facilitation:

Control involves acting to prevent or discourage bad outcomes from being realised. Facilitation involves acting to promote or encourage good and desired outcomes to be realised.

6. Prophet and visionary:

The prophet in us makes predictions of what will happen. The visionary in us creates visions of what could or should happen.

7. Problem centred (managerial) and mission directed (leadership) strategists:

The problem centred strategist focuses on eliminating negatives (undesirables) from the future. They solve problems. The mission directed strategist focuses on adding positives (desirables) to the future. They determine and build strategies. These are *the two strategic modes* (FUTK36).

We can use both strategic modes together, for they are complementary skill sets and are best used this way. However, in many cultures there is a dominance of management over leadership, where most future aspirations are focussed on removing undesirables from the future. Removing undesirables from our future world is of course a legitimate part of the shaping the future toolkit. However, we also need to put into the future world elements that are desirable and will make our future better not just less awful! Or to put it another way:

- Ending war does not create peace
- Ending poverty does not create prosperity
- Ending illness does not create wellness
- Ending cruelty does not create kindness

Management is important to any future shaping activity, but we are seldom inspired by the work of managers. However, leadership can be, and often is, inspirational. In the real world we need both, but in most management–leadership environments we need relatively more leadership and relatively less management: more visionary people who proactively envision the new and initiate their own change, and fewer who respond only when change is upon them or expected to happen.

Some people believe that problem solving is a critical and even heroic skill. But if we solve a problem, we finish up no worse off. We will seldom be better off. Mostly we can do much better than this. Without sufficient leadership, a vision to build a better or even a magnificent future will not even be on the table for discussion. To create a heroic or magnificent future, we first need to imagine a better or magnificent *preferred future* and then set out to realise it through a leadership-moulded mission directed strategy.

4.6. From Visualisation to Realisation

The first stage of operating in *Foresight Mode* is the *Visualisation Stage* that is based on the *Two Modes of Visualisation, Prophecy and Vision* (FUTK18). The second stage of operating in *Foresight Mode* is the *Realisation* or *Strategic Action Stage*, in which the visualisation is realised *(FUTK49)*.

Obviously, the key purpose of *The Six Future Shaping Tools* (Management, Leadership, Planning, Design, Innovation and Learning) is to turn *Visualisation* (as both *Prophecy and Vision)* into *Reality*. These Tools (FUTK40) have just been discussed. However, they need to be implemented within a *Coherent and Effective Strategic Action Framework* or template. There is no point in having heroic or even modest *Visualisations* if there is no coherent and effective *Strategic Action Program* in place to realise a visualisation on the ground. As the ancient Japanese saying goes, *Vision without action is a daydream. Action without vision is a nightmare.*

There is one more concept to be introduced before proceeding further with the *Six Future Shaping Tools*. This is the concept of Utopian Realism.

4.7. Optimism, Pessimism and Utopian Realism

As discussed above, when we seek to imagine and to realise our visualisations, our mindsets and kind of commitment to world can make a big difference to what we achieve. We can be bold or timid. We can be committed or cautious. When we enter leadership mode we can, and should, bring out the purposeful future maker in each of us. And we will shape the future most effectively if we can combine imaginative visualisation with bold but careful realisation.

We can also be either optimistic or pessimistic. Some readers will have already concluded that I am an optimist. For some, I might be too optimistic, to the point of being regarded as unrealistic. That I am unabashedly optimistic should not really surprise anybody. After all, there is not much of a market for pessimistic futurists!

I believe the best concept about being constructively optimistic in the 21st century is to introduce readers to the concept of *Utopian Realism. Utopian Realism* is a concept developed by British sociologist and public policy authority Tony Giddens which I wish to include in the Future Shaping concept bank and toolkit. Giddens believes we can and should use a combination of *Utopian Visualisations* of the destinations we seek and *Realistic* strategies to realise these ends or destinations. In other words, we should have Utopian Ends but Realistic means to achieve them.

I believe *Utopian Realism* is an important mindset for people who want to be effective at shaping the future. *Preferred future Visions* are often more achievable than many people recognise. When one sets out to realise an aspiration that might initially seem somewhat *Utopian* it is often surprising how realisable such an aspiration can become. The Apollo Program is one such example. Nobody knew how a journey to the moon might be accomplished when President John Kennedy envisioned the USA going to the moon by the end of the 1960s and returning safely to Earth. He established NASA and the Apollo Program to realise his vision. NASA invented its way to the moon because it was asked and empowered by Kennedy to do this.

The Third Way politics discussed earlier uses capitalism informed by Planetist values to construct change. Blair's politics followed the trailblazing work of the Hawke and Keating governments in Australia, and were in turn followed by the Clinton administration in the USA. All of these were politically highly successful. However, I believe that they could have sought more Utopian ends than they did. A fourth proponent of *The Third Way*, Emmanuel Macron, who is still in power at this time of writing, might succeed even better if he seeks to be less pragmatic in his visualisations and switches to becoming more inspiring, more unabashedly *Utopian Realistic*. The Biden Administration is showing many promising signs of embedding *Utopian Realism* into its aspirations, but Biden is being held back by Modernist politicians in the US Congress.

I believe that a second coming of *The Third Way* type politics based on more overtly Utopian Realistic politics will emerge in time. Such a second wave can be directed towards creating a liveable global village informed by *Planetist Values*, using *cosmonaut capitalism* and *cosmonaut globalisation* as its realisation tools. The world is ready now for a blossoming of Planetist values based political movements such as The Third Way and its descendants. Over time this values-driven politics will eliminate the remnants of the 19th and 20th century ideological politics of both the far left and the far right.

4.8. The Visualising and Realising Mind: Cerebral Intelligence

We use our *cerebral intelligence* first to understand more about our world and our own situation in it, and second to realise our aspirations and our visualisations in the world. However, we are unequally skilled in being able to use our minds in this way.

The *Four Philosophical Tools for Future Makers (FUTK25)* could help us become equally skilled with both.

4.8.1. Four Philosophical Tools for Future Makers (FUTK25)

As suggested by ethicist Simon Longstaff, some key philosophical domains of knowledge should be added to the future shaper's curriculum. The four core branches of philosophy most relevant to shaping futures are:

- *Metaphysics*: which asks and answers the questions *What do we know? What are the facts?*
- *Epistemology*: which asks and answers the questions *How do we know? Are our sources of knowledge good and reliable?*
- *Reason*: which asks and answers the questions *What can we conclude? What sense can we make from what and how we know?*

- *Ethics*: which asks and answers the question, *What should we do? What is the right thing to do?*

Everybody should become acquainted from an early age with some basic philosophical tools just as Kate Kennedy White is doing with primary school students (www.kinderphilosophy.com). We will then be well placed to succeed in an increasingly knowledge-rich future society where most of 21st century wealth will be derived from our ability to be critical and creative thinkers. Richard Buckminster Fuller (or Bucky Fuller as he is known to his millions of admirers, including this writer) has reminded us that 'wealth comes from two resources, the *physical* (resources and ecosystems) that must be conserved, and the *metaphysical* (ideas, knowledge and wisdom) that can only grow.' This is *Bucky Fuller's Wealth Duet (FUTK10)*.

4.8.2. Rumsfeld's Knowledge Quartet

If we want to be systematic when we assemble what we know and don't know, we can use what I call *Rumsfeld's Knowledge Quartet (FUTK38)* after its originator, Donald Rumsfeld. He suggested that there are four categories of knowledge:

- *Known Knowns*: what we know we know
- *Known Unknowns*: what we know we don't know
- *Unknown Knowns:* what we don't know we know
- *Unknown Unknowns*: what we don't know we don't know

4.8.3. The Two Stages of Foresight

Let us examine the use of cerebral intelligence when it is in *foresight mode*. There are two stages of *foresight: Visualisation* and *Realisation* (FUTK49). As discussed above, there are also two *Modes of Visualisation* used when visualising our destinations, prophecy, and vision, which I have called the *Destination Duet (FUTK2)*

Both the visualisation and realisation stages of foresight are somewhat complex. However, the realisation stage of foresight is more complex and harder to accomplish because it requires a higher level of collaboration and cooperation than the visualisation stage. And, as Japanese saying 'Vision without action is a daydream, action without vision is a nightmare' warned, visualising without acting or acting without visualising do not provide an effective means to shape futures because this can lead to ineffective or destructive outcomes. Therefore, I decided to embed both these visualisation and realisation stages into a single integrated framework. I suggest that when we are in *Foresight Mode,* we use our cerebral intelligence to enable us to effectively turn our visualisations (both as predictions and visions) into reality. I call this integrated tool the *Future Shaper's Quintet, the 5Vs*. This consists of a combination of Visualisation plus Values plus Venturers plus Voyages plus Vehicles (FUTK40). These are explained below.

1. *Visualisation* involves imagining future destinations that will motivate our subsequent actions. Visualisation has two modes. These are Prophecy plus Vision. I call this the Destination duet (FUTK18). Realisation involves turning our visualisation into reality.

The manager in each of us asks one of four questions about *what will happen*? These are

What might be the future? What future scenarios are plausible?
What if I am concerned about being disrupted by a particular event and I want to prepare for this event?
What will be the future if I do not initiate significant change?
What will be the future with changed circumstances?

Each of these four manager's prophetic questions leads to one of four predictions. What is our *plausible, particular, probable, and prospective, prediction?*

The leader in each of us asks what should be/could be the future? These two leader's questions will lead to one of two visions. What is our *preferred vision* or our *possible vision*?

These need to be *agreed upon* and precise to ensure that all members of a team are asking and answering precisely the same questions as they shape the future together. If this is not done well and carefully, conflict might arise from misunderstandings about what future destination the team is seeking to realise. Such misunderstandings and consequent disagreements can endanger our whole future shaping effort.

2. *Values* describes the core ethics embedded in us, the values that we believe in. They are also the first part of the second stage of foresight, the Realization Stage. The remaining three stages of Foresight are all realization stages. In my work on values I distinguish between *values* and *virtues*, a difference I call *The Moral Compass Duet*. This duet consists of *Values*, which are values embodied, plus *Virtues*, which are values that we put into practice when we act. *(FUTK44).*

I make this point because when we work together to shape the future we may or may not put all our values into practice. But as we shape the future it is wise to ask, *What values do members of the group have?* And *do they hold different values that are likely to cause disagreement or conflict?* For example, do all members of the group have *Planetist* or *Modernist* values, or some of each? Having a dialogue using these *values* as a checklist to assess whether everybody on the team has these or other values is probably the most effective means to proceed. If all participants hold similar values, they are more likely to be able to collaborate. But if there are significant differences we will have to discuss and agree on what *values* we will put into practice.

The dialogue can commence around whether there is support for the nine Planetist values. Those who strongly hold different Values, such as modernist values, will need either to temporarily suspend their values and practice *planetist values as virtues* while they are collaborating with others, or to withdraw. But whether we adopt planetist values as virtues or not, it is important that there be an understanding of the values held by those involved in any collaboration and what *values* should be promoted as *virtues* during any collaborative future shaping process.

3. *Venturers* are the people who are going to shape the future with you. We will often work in teams and with others to shape the future. Changing our world and shaping the future can be a difficult thing to achieve, often because there are those threatened by the changes we wish to make and who will resist our endeavours. There are also those who have a vested interest in keeping the status quo. Therefore, a wise future maker will try to have a person in place to intervene on our behalf and support our endeavours when the going gets tough. There will also be others who have an equally strong commitment to our venture who will try to ensure

our voyage into the future reaches its destination. Some of these might provide us with resources of one kind or another. Others will support us because their own moral compass tells them that what we are seeking to do will bring positive outcomes and that are on the right side of history. I suggest that careful attention be given both to those involved in working with us to shape the future, and those supporting our future-shaping journey. I call these two groups *Seafarers* and *Supporters* respectively. *Seafarers* are the members of the team involved with you in shaping the future. *Supporters* are external supporters of the venture who can be engaged to actively support our endeavours and/or provide additional stimulus and resources to our venture. I call these two critical supporters of the venture *The Venturer's Duet (FUTK54)*.

4. *Voyages* involves identifying and facilitating appropriate strategic actions to realise our destination successfully. These tools are critical for success in the realisation stage of any collaborative shaping of the future. What kinds of strategic actions should we identify and take? There are three core strategic actions, which I call The Strategic Action Trio (FUTK50). These are:

- *Impediments removal:* actions to remove barriers and overcome problems currently preventing our forward progress
- *Improvements*: actions to improve our current practices and actions. This improvement can and should be continuous
- *Initiatives:* new actions that we should take now if we want to be successful. Some but by no means all of these will be those that are components of the two twin-pair categories identified below as *Vehicles*.

5. *Vehicles* comprises exploring and using the additional resources, innovations and experiences needed to realise our goals/destinations. There are two categories of Vehicles: *Capacities and Capabilities* or the *Resources Duet (FUTK51)*, and *Ways and Wares* or the *Innovation Duet (FUTK53)*.

Capacities and Capabilities involve uplifting physical and human resources. Looking at *Capacities* means asking firstly what additional financial and physical resources we need to realise our *visualisation* and secondly how we obtain and use this additional capacity. Looking at *Capabilities* means assessing what additional skills and knowledge we need to accomplish our visualisation and how we build them.

Ways and Wares involves developing and introducing innovations to enable us to realise our goals better. I introduced the concept of *Ways and Wares* at the very beginning of this book. Here we are placing *Ways and Wares,* the two components of Future Knowledge's *Innovation Duet,* into our collective future shaping toolkit.

Ways are social innovations or innovations to what we *do*. These might include changes to public policies and laws, changes to activities and behaviours, changes to methodologies, changes to how we learn, and changes to how we conduct relationships.

Wares are physical innovations or innovations to what we *use*. These include new designs and plans, new patterns, new learning curricula, new algorithms, new infrastructures, and new technologies.

To illustrate *Ways and Wares*, consider the following examples:

- A *Water Conservation Way*: shortening your time in the shower
- A *Water Conservation Ware*: a low volume showerhead

Together, they enhance water conservation. How many other water conservation ways and wares can you imagine?

- *Pandemic Protection Ways:* social distancing, wearing a mask, not consuming wild animals that are sources of Zoonotic pandemics
- *Pandemic Protection Wares*: a face mask, a vaccine

Many *Ways and Wares* which need to be invented to supply our emerging planetist global village marketplace will be listed in the remainder of this Compendium.

The Future Shapers Quintet, or *the Five Vs, (FUTK43)* provides a framework to enable us to best use our *cerebral intelligence* to shape the future.

Let us now turn to considering *emotional intelligence*. I call the framework enabling us to engage our *emotional intelligence* to shape the future and realise our visualisations both as prophecy and as vision *The Six Emotional Pillars of Future Shaping, the Six Cs (FUTK45)*. In his book *Frames of Mind* Howard Gardner described his theory of multiple intelligences: he ultimately described nine intelligences in all. Of these, two are emotional intelligences that he respectively called *Intrapersonal and Interpersonal intelligences.*

Intrapersonal emotional intelligence involves being able to access and understand, and appropriately and wisely respond to, one's own emotional status. This ability enables us to gain more insight into our overall wellness and our relationship with others and the world around us. *Interpersonal emotional intelligence* involves being able to access and understand the emotional status of others, so that we can relate to them more effectively. We will be better shapers of futures in many ways if we are able to access and understand both forms of emotional intelligence.

When we begin to shape the future, we are often driven not only by a cerebral aspiration to improve what we are seeking to do to get better outcomes, but also by many emotional drivers, both positive and negative. It is important to recognise the power of these emotional drivers, for they can assist us to more effectively realise our aspirations or they can and undermine our capacity to achieve our aspirations. Here, there several emotional twin pairs which tend to play a major role. These emotional twin pairs include hope and fear, kind and cruel, respect and disrespect, love and hate, and selfish and generous. I have called the five twin pairs that matter *The Motivational Pairs Quintet* (FUTK67). They are hope/fear, kind/cruel, respect/disrespect, love/hate and generous/selfish

What are the emotions we can use to support us so that we become the most effective shaper of futures we can be? When we are in Foresight Mode, there are six core emotions critical for successful shaping of futures. Three of these emotions are associated with masculinity. Karl Jung identified these as male principles that he called 'Animus', while Taoists call them 'Yang'. The other three are associated with femininity. Karl Jung called these female principles 'Anima' while Taoists call them 'Yin'.

These six emotions, which can also be seen as attitudes, are *The Six Emotional Pillars of Future Shaping, the Six Cs (FUTK45)*. They are:

- *Confident*: having self-belief in one's abilities without hubris (masculine, animus, yang)

- *Courageous:* going where some dare not, overcoming self-interested opposition (masculine, animus, yang)
- *Committed:* doing what must be done, acting purposefully and assertively not aggressively (masculine, animus, yang)
- *Considerate:* listening and responding to the opinions and the interests of others (feminine, anima, yin)
- *Courteous:* showing respect in conversation and negotiation (feminine, anima, yin)
- *Compassionate:* responding with empathy to victims and the disadvantaged, and equally to crises within oneself (feminine, anima, yin)

Great political, community and corporate leaders such as Nelson Mandela, Martin Luther King Jnr, Angela Merkel, and Jacinta Ardern embody and can access all six of these key emotions or attitudes.

4.9. Futures Narratives: Scenario Building for Shaping Futures

- *We cannot create a future unless we first imagine it*
- *Vision without action is a daydream. Action without vision is a nightmare*

Over millennia, humanity has embedded deep and precious knowledge into narratives. We are so deeply conditioned to stories and narratives that if somebody says to us *'Let me tell you a story'* we lift ourselves into a mode of high attentiveness and anticipation. Many of these narratives we called *Myths*. We tell these stories to our children and to others to share with them the knowledge they should and even must have if they are to become successful. We tell many of them in *Rite of Passage* periods, such as at adolescence. And we tell stories of heroes and villains to inspire us and to serve as sources of wisdom to guide our own behaviour.

In Joseph Campbell's *The Hero with a Thousand Faces* and his other extraordinary works, Campbell reminded us of the critical importance of mythical stories. Narratives, stories and myths provide a huge repository of insight and wisdom in all cultures to ensure that what really matters is passed on from one generation to the next. Narratives have been told around countless campfires and at cultural events throughout the ages. They have informed, delighted, warned, moved, frightened and inspired us. If we are seeking to shape the future, we can similarly make and tell future narratives to inspire and motivate us, to ensure we are all on the same page, asking and answering the same questions, and building truly shared visualisations of our future self. Myths and narratives are important motivators for building purposeful collaboration.

We have already discussed *The Six Future Questions and The Six Futures (FUTK41)* and how we can create different alternative scenarios from each of these *Six Questions and Six Futures*. We have also described the *Three Selves (past self, present self and future self) (FUTK21), The Three Sights (Hindsight, Insight and Foresight), (FUTK1)*. We all want to be successful in the future. However, most of us, even after a decade and a half of formal education, have not entrenched sufficient *shaping the future knowledge* in ourselves to ensure we are able to accomplish this as well as we wish to do.

Many readers will be familiar with the concept of alternative future scenarios. I believe the tool of scenario building has an important role to play in any Shaping the Future toolkit. In this section, we are going to explore the role narrative making can play in successful future taking and making. If we wish our visualisations of the future to include rich detail, we should write them down and, where appropriate, tell them. Here are some suggestions for how to create this narrative.

First, put yourself into *Utopian Realistic Mode*. This might include putting an alternative scenario, a *Probable prediction* that describes the consequences of changing nothing, into our narrative. This could include a grim prognosis of endangerment and failure. If we are concerned about a particular threat or opportunity we might want to include them as *Particular predictions* that might take us to a *Prospective future* that we can prepare ourselves for. You could also ask (and answer) one or more of the *Six Future Questions,* so the narrative can include strategies enabling us to realise, to adapt to, or to mitigate, these visualised future scenarios.

Second, I suggest imagining you are *Astral Traveller* visiting the future. Or you might prefer visiting the future in a time machine. Either way, once you are imaginatively in this future, I suggest you engage in the *Future Narrative Duet (FUTK59)*. This consists of *future present* and *future history*.

The *future present* means describing your status, your situation, and your activities, *at a future time in the present tense*. You are describing yourself and the future world around you in the *present tense* as you are surrounded by, and experiencing, it. The time frame you use can be whatever you choose. Future fiction (or science fiction) has played a very significant future-shaping role. For example, William Gibson's book *Neuromancer* (1984) introduced three fictional concepts that subsequently became reality: cyberspace, virtual reality, and the World Wide Web. Our world was shaped by Gibson's *future present* imagination.

Imagining in the present tense as if you were a character in a science fiction novel can be very powerful. Be as Utopian as you are comfortable being. Unfortunately, too much science (or future) fiction is dystopian rather than utopian. While this is obviously necessary for the plot, it is an imbalance I believe could and should be rebalanced. You can use the *future tense* if you are referring to events even further into the future beyond the time you are currently visualising, and you can use the *past tense* when you describe events occurring between now and your imagined future time.

This then brings us to *future history*.

Future history, in contrast to the future present, is a tool we use in the *realisation stage* of the *Two Stages of Foresight* (FUTK49). When we seek to imagine the strategic actions that might contribute to our realising our future present vision, we need to switch our attention from imagining a Utopian Preferred/Possible future Vision to imagining and constructing Realistic strategies to realise our Vision.

We will do this best if we remain 'living' in that future time while we tell our narrative. This process is called 'backcasting' by futurists, as distinct from forecasting. Past tense is used to describe how we achieved what we have in this imagined future time. If this imagined future time is 20 years hence, we need to describe the events and actions over a 20-year period. We can even give precise dates and as much detail as we wish to these imagined events and strategic actions. But remember that as this is the *realisation stage* of the Utopian Realistic forecasting process, all our events and actions need to be realistic.

When you imagine your future self in a *future present* scenario, you can be as Utopian and heroic as you feel comfortable with. When you describe the *future history* of how you realised this preferred/possible future, you should be realistic, but you can also be bold. Timidity should never be a part of any Future Knowledge process even if the scenario itself is intimidating.

Some of our plans to shape the future are small and short term. We don't usually need to create narratives of substance to activate these. But future narratives can make a big difference if we are seeking to initiate bigger planned future shaping processes, such as charting individual career paths, collaboratively exploring organisational or community futures, or investing in projects, programs, or businesses. Here we usually will be charting *preferred or possible futures* while we are acting in *leadership mode*, as *purposeful future makers*.

In his *The Hero with a Thousand Faces,* Joseph Campbell showed us that many traditional myths from different cultures are variations of a basic generic form. Most myths contain some or all of the following events: expression of an aspiration to go to a particular place or meet a particular person; beginning the journey; meeting and dealing with many different kinds of people who both inform and inspire us or threaten us on the journey; learning from these experiences, navigating ourselves through difficult circumstances; arriving at forks in the road and having to make difficult and critical choices about which path to follow or option to take; persisting through thick and thin; and arriving at one's destination a changed, more mature, more knowledgeable, and wiser person. A major theme of any myth is the transformation of the person, group or entity making the journey.

Each future narrative can be given highly individual, even poetic names, or uplifting or threatening titles. This will clearly distinguish each of these from other future narratives. I encourage all would-be futurists to dedicate sufficient time to growing their future narrative making capabilities, using some of the concepts described here. Collective narrative making can be great fun and is an excellent way to build core relationships and future-making teams.

And now we will go into the future of relationships more generally. We turn now to the issue of the future of relationships in our emerging global village.

Chapter 5: Relationships in 21st Century Society

As I often seek to shape the future with others, what can I do to ensure our relationships in these circumstances are as productive and harmonious as they can be?

5.1. Two Capabilities That Really Matter

Two most important capabilities required for future success are being able to effectively shape the future and to initiate, nurture and support, and where necessary, amicably end, relationships. Astonishingly, we usually don't learn to do either of these at school. We discussed the first of these, shaping the future, in Chapter 4. Now in Chapter 5, we will consider how we might grow our capacity to build and manage thriving 21st century appropriate relationships.

5.2. The Century of Interdependence

As humanity moves further into the 21st century, our emerging interconnected global society is becoming ever more interdependent. We are facing many daunting global challenges: a planet that is warming because we are releasing too much carbon into the atmosphere; endangering our health by infecting and reinfecting ourselves with zoonotic diseases such as COVID-19; planet wide economic recessions; and bringing peace to planetary war zones. We know we have no choice but to collaborate to deal with such issues. We also recognise this interdependence is increasing. We are becoming more cognisant that, living as we do on a shared planetary home, collaterally harming others will become increasingly less acceptable. Moreover, those who seek to be a winner-take-all will increasingly be designated as pariahs in this emerging global village.

In this ever more interdependent world, having the skills to build relationships that are effective, harmonious, and mutually beneficial will be critical for our long-term success. And the reality is that many of us recognise that we cannot accomplish this as well as we would like to. Additionally, some of us are beginning to recognize that if our behaviour is guided by Modernist values, we will be ever more likely to alienate ourselves from an emerging Planetist majority. Although *Homo sapiens* has cohabited on this planet with both friends and enemies for the whole of human history, an increasing number of people are beginning to realise we must reinvent ourselves if we want to thrive in our emerging global village culture. Unfortunately, many of us do not yet recognise we have a problem in this regard. Most identity unadaptable Modernist populists and autocrats fall into this category.

When we seek to shape the future with others, it is critical we do not undermine but instead seek to continuously improve our relationships while we are doing so. Most of us will have experienced circumstances when an attempt to shape the future with others has resulted in conflict and sometimes significant, even terminal, damage to our relationships.

So, one question we can ask ourselves is what must we know and be able to do in order to ensure we are able to conduct successful interdependent relationships, whether these relationships be interpersonal, organisational, community or international in nature.

Here are some concepts and tools that can maximise our chances of ensuring collective success when involved in shaping our personal or collective future in our emerging interdependent global village.

5.3. The Three Relationships

There are *Three Relationships (FUTK06)* important to those who want to shape futures:

- Dependent
- Independent
- Interdependent

International relationships have changed considerably over three centuries:

- *The 19th century was a century of dependence*: Much of humanity lived in colonies or under other forms of subjugation. Many of these entities were even called *dependencies.*
- *The 20th century was the century of independence:* Most of humanity became independent during the 20th century.

- *The 21st century is the century of interdependence:* Ever more of us, but unfortunately not yet all of us, now recognise that we share a planetary home and we have a shared future. In order to flourish we should collaborate with each other and we should respect those who are different.

We experience these three relationships (FUTK06) during the process of maturation: we mature from *dependent child* to *independent adolescent* to *interdependent adult.* Two of these relationships are well understood and require little additional information here. We will now focus on the third of these relationships.

5.4. The Interdependent Relationship in the 21st Century

We cannot prosper in emerging 21st century society unless we become competent managers of interdependent relationships. The *Interdependent Relationship* is characterised by three core principles, which I call *the Interdependence Trio (FUTK08)*. They are:

- The Golden Rule: treat others as you would like them to treat you.
- Commit to shared aspirations and outcomes.
- Seek Win/Win, or mutually beneficial outcomes from any collaboration or interaction.

In the first two chapters, I described the global social transformation of our world from a 20th century built on Modernist values to a 21st century built on Planetist values. The 21st century is not just an extension of the 20th century with a few minor differences. When from the perspective of the year 2050 we compare the global cultures of the mid-20th century with those of the mid-21st century a yawning difference will be observed. We can already see many of these differences emerging. Ideals-based Planetist politics are already evident, as is the decline of ideologically based Modernist politics. Humanity is already transforming Modernist neoliberalism into a Planetist form of neoliberalism. We will discuss this issue further in in Chapter 12.

Modernist populist and Modernist autocratic political leaders behave as they do because they still see our world through lenses shaped by their independence-retaining mindsets rather than interdependence-building mindsets. These politicians, those such as Trump, Bolsonaro, Orban, Putin, Salvini, and many of the Brexiters, will be on the wrong side of history. Bolsonaro's electoral defeat in late 2022 already indicates this.

International politics in the 21st century will be shaped by the need to innovate the means, *the Ways and Wares,* that can enable humanity to flourish together in the 21st century. Those who do not work to this end or who even seek to consciously undermine our collective efforts to thrive together, people such as Trump and Putin, will be designated as unfit planetary citizens and increasingly will be subject to *Planetary Pariah Punishments.*

This transformation of our global culture into one that seeks to uplift global interdependence and not undermine it, is challenging and changing personal, community, organisational, national, and international relationships in the 21st century.

In the 21st century world of business, there is a growing recognition that future success might be better guaranteed by constructing a loyalty scheme promoting greater interdependence with customers, suppliers, and employees, all of whom can benefit through reward-sharing, and by investing more in workplace harmony and employee work skilling and knowledge. This is just one adaptation the business community is already making as it seeks to adapt to our changing world by incorporating a 21st century culture of collaboration into a previously dominant 20th century business culture based solely on survival-of-the-fittest competition.

However, while this new culture of collaboration is emerging it is not yet consolidated. When businesses and economies are threatened by global danger such as by a COVID-19 pandemic they often retreat to trying to isolate themselves and face the threat alone: they seek to return to a form of individual defence rather than moving forward into new collective form of security. As we have seen with COVID-19, different nations have achieved different levels of success and failure, and generally the more individualistic cultures such as the USA and the UK have been less successful than more communitarian cultures such as China, Japan, and Germany.

We cannot solve problems in communitarian and interdependent environments with individualistic and independence-based solutions. The solution must be based on the recognition that the solution and the problem must inhabit the same cultural milieu.

In the 21st century, resilience will come not from separation and isolation, from walking out alone into the cold, but through strengthening the bonds of interdependence and collaboration.

In his essay *The Tragedy of the Commons*, Garret Hardin described how we might achieve this interdependence: we should seek *mutual coercion mutually agreed upon*. This reality will inform negotiations of every kind from now on. The world will learn much from the debacle that was its response to COVID-19.

Interdependence also requires mutual trust: trust in turn is built upon what I call *The Trust Trio (FUTK09)*.

5.5. Trust in Relationships

We cannot shape an interdependent future with others, or indeed any future in our emerging global village, unless there is trust between the parties in these relationships. And as most of us know from experience, trust is easy to destroy and difficult to build or rebuild. My *Trust Trio (FUTK09)* is based on a conversation with Buddhist psychologist, Teresa Milton.

We learn to *trust* another if we ask and can satisfactorily answer three questions:

- Is the other *Honest?*
- Is the other *Reliable?*
- Is the other *Competent?*

If the answer to all three questions is yes, we will be more willing to enter into a trusting interdependent relationship.

If the answer is *no* to any of these questions, then the relationship is at risk. However, it is possible that a negotiation could be held to remove this barrier to building a relationship. Many of us have experiences where we have needed to deal with one element of the *Trust Trio* to repair or rebuild an endangered relationship. If two are a problem but the relationship is a critical one, we might be willing to make the effort to work on two of these barriers. Obviously if all three are a problem we probably won't bother to repair or initiate the relationship.

Due Diligence is the process used by would-be investors when they are considering whether they will enter an interdependent relationship. *Due Diligence* is based on the *Trust Trio* even if this not fully recognised by most of those who undertake due diligence.

Imagine new *Trust Assessment Ways and Wares* based on *assessing and uplifting Honesty, Reliability and Competence*. Imagine innovating *Trust Building Ways and Wares* to enable trust to be established and built, including in on-line relationships. Before we seek to buy a product or service on-line, we need to know that we will not be scammed. Those who innovate these *Trust Assessment and Building ways and wares* will find many buyers in emerging global markets. Imagine the *Pandemic Collaboration Ways and Wares* we could innovate to ensure that when one nation is infected by a virus originating in a third nation it can still trust this nation and others sufficiently to work together effectively to ensure we all become more pandemic resilient and adaptable together.

Consider the interdependent relationship of marriage in terms of the *Interdependence Trio and the Trust Trio*. Are these useful in considering why some marriages succeed and some fail?

5.6. Committing Ourselves to a Relationship

The prosperity of our emerging Global Village will be advanced or held back by humanity's ability to initiate, maintain, and amicably end relationships. We need to understand the core purposes of all three relationships and why we commit ourselves to them, particularly to interdependent relationships. The interdependent relationship is critically important in the 21st century and all of us need to be as able as we can be at developing and maintaining trust and harmony within them. If trust is lost in a relationship and we want to restore it, we need to know why and where trust has been lost and what we need to do to restore trust. We also need to be as fully cognisant as we can be about why we want to form a particular relationship in the first place, and why we might want to either maintain and nurture a relationship or terminate it.

There are three forms of commitment we can make to each of the three relationships. First of all, we commit to some relationships because of who the other is: we love them, we want to be friends or intimate with them, we want to support them for *who they are*. These people are special to us: this is the *unconditional relationship*. Second, we commit to a relationship based on what the other does: we continue this relationship based on *what the other does or doesn't do*. This is the *conditional relationship*. Third, we commit to a relationship based on a desire to trade knowledge, goods, and services with them. This is the *transactional relationship*.

I call these reasons why we commit ourselves to relationships the *Commitment Trio (FUTK62)*.

It is important for parties to a relationship to fully understand the nature of the mutual commitment being created in each of their relationships. If there is ambiguity in this understanding the relationship is more likely to be jeopardised. These three forms of commitment apply to all the three relationships: dependent, independent, and interdependent. However, here for the most part we are considering the development of interdependent relationships in these three terms, for it is the interdependent relationship that growing in importance and status in emerging 21st century society.

In the 21st century, all three of these kinds of relationship commitments are growing. We can have, in theory, nine permutations and combinations of these two just described relationship-based Trios, *The Three Relationships* and *The Commitment Trio*. Imagine the difference between the independent transactional relationship and the interdependent transactional relationship or between the independent unconditional relationship and the interdependent unconditional relationship. Many relationships—personal, organisational, and international—seek to ambiguously combine interdependent unconditional and interdependent conditional relationships, and this can cause difficulties and even trauma because each party is confused by what the operating purpose of the relationship is at any one time.

The third relationship, the transactional relationship, is based on trade and exchange. Some of these will be transactional independent relationships without mutual obligations and some will be transactional interdependent relationships with mutual obligations. And one kind can be converted to another: a loyalty scheme or program is designed to convert an independent transactional relationship into an interdependent transactional relationship. As the world becomes ever more interdependent in the 21st century and as a planetist global village further emerges, loyalty programs and transactional interdependence more generally will grow.

In the future, many new *Interdependent Transactional Ways and Wares* and *Interdependent Conditional Ways and Wares* will be innovated. All three relationship purposes are based on Trust. The Trust Trio is required for all of these to different extents, with both dependent and interdependent relationships requiring a higher level of trust for their ongoing success than independent relationships.

Many relationships are currently limited by our capacity to trust the other. Over time humanity will be able develop new *Trust Assessment Ways and Wares* and *Trust Uplifting Ways and Wares* that can be based on the *Trust Trio*, and these can remove many of these barriers to our being able to trust others. However, at a personal level, most of us will still wish to continue to be intimate with only about 15 others and friendly with about 500. Our genes tell us that these numbers are what we are comfortable with. Our innovations also need to recognise this reality.

5.7. Collaboration to Shape the Future

When we shape the future, we often collaborate with others. When we collaborate to shape the future, we should be very clear in our minds about which of the *Six Future Questions and The Six Futures (FUTK38)* we are using to shape the future, so that we can minimise the chances of failure. And to be successful we need to be the best initiator and nurturer of relationships possible. Our outcomes can be regarded as successful if the net outcome is a *sum* of our respective separate contributions, that is 2+2= 4. Sometimes we can do better and produce a *synergistic* outcome, 2+2 =5. Or the outcomes of our collaboration might be negative. The outcome can be *antagonistic,* 2+2=3. I call this combination of three possible outcomes the *Collaboration Trio*. To sum up, *The Collaboration Trio = synergism + sum + antagonism. (FUTK29)*

Imagine new *Ways and Wares* based on the *Collaboration Trio* that we might invent to maximise synergistic outcomes and minimise antagonistic outcomes in all our collaborative endeavours.

5.8. Seeking Win/Win

Our emerging Planetist global village will be a communitarian village based on interdependence. In 1968, when Garret Hardin wrote his *Tragedy of the Commons* where he discussed *mutual coercion mutually agreed upon*, the global culture was dominated by national self-interest. Today, most of us want to cooperate in order to solve the problems of our global village, such as pandemics, climate change and peace building. Mutual coercion mutually agreed upon is now the last resort rather than the first resort, as it was in 1968.

The fear of a loss of national self-interest is driving the *Modernist populism movement* described in detail in Chapter 2. At the beginning of the third decade of the 21st century, there are political *Modernist populists* everywhere who feel that they have lost from increasing global integration and global trade. Many of these will seek to redress this situation by working to reinstate yesteryear in one form or another. A Trump or a Putin will seek to do this. They will include many who have moved to the extremist old ideological right and some to the ideological left where the true believers of Modernist populism or Modernist autocracy still find refuge. They will continue to try to undo successful collaborative interdependent multilateral arrangements such as the European Union, NAFTA, or the Transpacific Partnership (TPP).

Excepting for these remaining Modernists, who are members of a declining minority, most of us are becoming more aware that we live in a shared planetary home and we have a shared future. We all have a vested interest in decreasing our shared vulnerability to global danger of all kinds, including from those bent on bullying others to get their own way. If we do not collectively stand up against those who want to carry on with Modernist autocratic behaviours in the 21st century, we might harvest not only win/loss in economic terms but also loss/loss and collateral harm to our growing global interdependence. More global pandemics and increased global heating, as well as Modernist political bullying, can deliver universal loss/loss unless we collaborate more completely to negate these threats.

At the beginning of the third decade of the 21st century, *Modernist populists* in democracies and *Modernist autocrats* in places such as Russia are still trying to mount a concerted resistance to collaborative globalisation. Those who know some history might like to consider attempts by Metternich and others who tried to bring back yesteryear at the Congress of Vienna after Napoleon's defeat. They acted as if they wanted Europe to believe that Napoleon never existed, to re-establish the Pre-Napoleonic status quo. They failed because some change is irreversible. The world does move on.

We have already discussed those in *the Identity Renovation Movement* who are moving with, rather than against, global integration and who are seeking to shape their own relationships so that they can thrive in this new emerging world. These include secessionists in Scotland and Catalonia and the 36 million Kurds in Iran, Turkey, Iraq, and Syria who want to create Kurdistan, a nation for themselves, and who deserve global support for their struggle. *Identity renovation movements* will thrive in the 21st century. They are on the right side of history.

Individualism will always be a major part of our 21st century world and independence will be as well. Humanity has fought for a long time for our precious individual freedoms. However, in a world that is becoming increasingly communitarian and interdependent we will need to rethink individualism and independence for the 21st century. I therefore suggest a new concept, *Sustainable Individualism (FUTK29)*. This will be discussed further in Chapter 7, but for now note that while we will keep many of the key tenets of individualism in an ever more communitarian future in the 21st century, we will be most successful if we can work effectively in interdependent teams. Interdependence is the most important relationship in the 21st century: between mature people, between businesses and their suppliers and customers, between investors and investees, between traders in markets, between Nation States in global politics, and between people and the environment. To have an ability to collaborate with others to achieve successful collective outcomes is becoming ever more essential for 21st century success.

We have hardly begun creating what we can call the *collaboration ways and wares* and *global accord building ways and wares* that will be increasingly demanded in our emerging global village. New collaboration building software such as *Zoom* and *Teams* are now appearing in global markets. This is the beginning of a *collaboration ways and wares innovation revolution*. I believe that many of these new *collaboration ways and wares* will be based on the *Interdependence trio* and the *Trust trio*. I also recommend the work on team building and team roles of both Will Schutz and Meredith Belbin. Schutz and Belbin have provided excellent processes to enable people to become the most effective collaborating team members they can be.

Most adults can be fully independent, self-reliant, and able to stand on their own two feet. They are also able to have productive relationships with those who are dependent on them, such as by being effective parents. However, too many of us are much less able to effectively manage interdependence in our relationships. I believe this inability to manage interdependent relationships is because they not have sufficient maturity.

5.9. Interdependence and Maturity

This chapter and earlier ones have described the increasing dominance of the interdependent relationship in emerging 21st century society. Without the further consolidation of interdependence our emerging global village will not realise its full potential. Interdependence characterises the third and adult stage of maturity after children leave childhood dependence behind them and move on to embrace independence in their adolescence. Of course, there will always be some dependence and independence present in our lives, but unless we are able to build and maintain successful interdependent relationships, we will not thrive in the 21st century. This means that humanity should be devoting more time and resources than it currently is to the promotion of global interdependence.

5.9.1. The challenge posed by global immaturity

As discussed, many of our current social problems are caused by a lack of maturity. Unlike other species, humans take a relatively long time to mature. This is essential for creating a competent adult, but there are many potentially negative consequences of this slow maturation that must also be addressed. In his book *Myths to Live By,* Joseph Campbell says:

An unfortunate but inevitable side effect of the long time human beings take to mature, and hence to stay at home with their parents, is an attitude of dependency that has to be left behind before psychological maturity can be attained. The young human being responds to the challenges of his environment by turning to its parents for advice, support, and protection, and before it can be trusted as an adult, this patterning must be altered. Accordingly, one of the first functions of puberty rites of primitive societies, indeed of education everywhere, has always been that of switching the response systems of adolescents from dependency to responsibility—which is no easy transformation to achieve. And with the extension of the period of dependency in our own civilisation into the middle and even late twenties, the challenge is today more threatening than ever, and our failures are increasingly apparent. (p. 46)

The world is still full of political leadership that does not yet understand the emerging 21st century global culture of interdependence. Sadly, many of these so-called leaders are too immature to be successful leaders in our emerging 21st century society. Many of them have Modernist values including, if they are men, not sufficiently respecting women. Some will seek to commence a trade war or try to bully another nation state, seeking win/lose rather than win/win. They are adolescents in adult bodies. Trump and Putin are just two spectacular examples of such leaders.

Many people in the formal education system already recognise that education systems should be making a more significant contribution to the building of a more mature humanity. They also recognise that the education system could accomplish this task much better. As Joseph Campbell says, our failures can be seen everywhere.

5.9.2. The costs of discarding initiation

Throughout human history, adolescent initiation has helped teach the young to understand their place and role in adult society and learn what they need to know so that they can be successful adults.

Most traditional societies seem to have regarded adolescence as an unstable period that needed to be transitioned through in the shortest possible time. They achieved this transition from dependent child to independent adult by introducing adolescent initiation. This taught the young how to become mature, responsible adults in the communities and cultures to which they belong. Initiation served brilliantly in helping humanity to create successful and responsible adulthood for more than 50,000 years. But with the rise of Modernity in the last 150 years initiation has been jettisoned as a primitive barrier to human progress and as cultural baggage. How the initiation process was treated varied. It ranged from benign neglect to conscious destruction as part of imperial colonisation and religious conversion, though sometimes it was simply replaced by much weaker religious initiation rituals.

Without initiation, our young mature physically but not emotionally or psychologically. They might leave childhood dependency on their parents behind, but often they then seek reassurance and security in a different form of dependency: in groups of their own kind and, in more extreme versions of this, in gangs. Too many of our young have not been given sufficient opportunity to learn how to become responsible adults. Immature people can be soldiers but not warriors. To be a warrior, one must be mature and understand responsibility. This difference is critical. Too many immature adults and adolescents are:

- Bullies and violent in families, schools, on the Internet and in workplaces
- Damagers of property
- Intolerant and aggressive towards those who are socially or culturally different

- Devoid of responsibility in their relationships, including in sexual relationships
- Participators in gangs, including criminal gangs
- Underminers of their own wellbeing because of practicing high-risk, self-initiated initiation processes: car speeding, drug taking, sexual violence, train surfing, and the like.

In effect, uninitiated males often remain functional boys living in men's bodies, continuing to do in adulthood what boys have always done. Of course uninitiated females and non-binary people can, if they put their minds to it, do just as much damage to themselves and others as uninitiated males, which is why they too need initiations specifically designed for them.

In Modernist times, traditional adolescent initiation was treated with disrespect and jettisoned. Modernists regarded adolescent initiation not as *heritage* but as *baggage*. In its rush into modernity, humanity threw out the baby with the bathwater. In Postmodern times, the value of traditional practices has become more appreciated and adolescent initiation is regaining its status as *heritage*.

5.9.3. The traditional role of adolescent initiation

Initiation traditionally accomplished two major outcomes:

- It reaffirmed and explained the core ingredients of one's own culture. It gave people the identity and security that comes from belonging to a larger group so that they could become safely independent from their own parents.
- It taught the young how to become successful and responsible participants in the communities they would be entering as adults. This involved the acceptance by initiates that they had now arrived at a point in their lives where they, and not their parents, must from this point on be responsible for their actions. It also taught them that they had a responsibility to contribute to the society in which they lived to ensure it functioned well and harmoniously. This concept of adult responsibility is at the core of all adolescent initiation.

In his essay *The Age of Endarkenment*, Michael Ventura described adolescence as a *cruel world*. He described traditional initiation thus:

> *Tribal people everywhere greet the onset of puberty, especially in males, with elaborate and excruciating initiations, a practice which would not be as necessary unless their young were as extreme as ours are. They would assault their adolescents with, quite literally, holy terror, rituals that had been kept secret from the young until that moment, rituals that focussed upon the young all the light and darkness of their identity's collective psyche, all its sense of mystery, all its questions and all the stories told both to harbour and answer these questions…The crucial word is focus. The adults had something to teach them: stories, skills, magic, dances, visions, and rituals. In fact, if all these things were not learned well and completely, the tribe would not survive. This practice was so effective that usually by the age of 15, a tribal youth was able to take his or her place as a fully responsible adult.*

The world is now a very different place, in that our young will be entering a multicultural global village. While many young people like Greta Thunberg show impressive maturity, many lack this level of awareness and maturity. They need a different kind of initiation.

5.9.4. Reinventing adolescent initiation for the 21st Century

The time is right to go back to yesteryear to retrieve, and then re-imagine and update a process that should never have been allowed to wither. We can implement a universal program in the middle years of secondary school to reintroduce a 21st century version of traditional initiation. This new initiation could be both customised for the different needs of different cultures and identities and promote mutual cultural respect, thereby emphasising and celebrating both cultural difference and human unity. Much of our youth already understands the core message embodied in *Earthrise*, that in the 21st century planet must come first. A universal program of adolescent initiation would, however, ensure that the whole of global youth thinks similarly.

We could set aside the entire traditional curriculum for one year in middle secondary school and introduce initiation as a one-year-long program. Any secondary school teacher will tell you that years 8 and 9, as it is currently constructed, tends to be disappointment. Young people at puberty are less interested in mathematics and history than they are in learning how to become successful in the adult world they are just about to inherit. We should let biology rule and grant young people their wish!

There are already many programs which are promising starts, (e.g www.theritejourney.com) and there are many successful programs in individual schools and in a few nations, all of which are directed at the middle years of secondary school.

5.9.5. Ten capabilities for responsible adulthood

If we seek to grow maturity, we need to ask what the key elements of a responsible adulthood are. Initiation programs to develop maturity could include consideration of the *Ten Capabilities for Responsible adulthood (FUTK30)*. These are:

- Having a realistic understanding of one's destiny and being able to continuously develop one's capabilities
- Building career paths that can provide long-term economic security
- Being a leader of self
- Being able to build, maintain and amicably end interdependent relationships
- Respecting others who are different
- Recognising that there must be reciprocity between individual and community rights
- Practising healthy and sustainable behaviours
- Being capable parents and carers
- Being lifelong, learner-driven learners
- Valuing and avoiding collaterally harming the environment and other species

5.9.6. Building preparation for adulthood ways and wares

If a young person develops these *Ten Capabilities for Responsible Adulthood (FUTK30)*, their chances of having successful 21st century lives, and careers, would be significantly enhanced.

Imagine the *Learning Curricula* and the *Ways and Wares* that might be created to realise such a *Preparation for Adulthood* Program. Many of these

Ways and Wares and *Learning Curricula* could utilise the following components of the Future Knowledge curriculum:

- The nine values of planetism (FUTK05)
- The six pillars of liveability (FUTK46))
- The three sights (FUTK19) and the three dialogues (FUTK20)
- The interdependence trio (FUTK08)
- The trust trio (FUTK09)
- The six future questions and the six futures (FUTK41)
- The six future shaping tools (FUTK40)
- Four philosophical future shaping tools (FUTK25)
- The future shapers quintet (FUTK43)
- The moral compass duet (FUTK44)
- The six emotional pillars of future shaping (FUTK45)

5.10. Communicating in a Global Village

5.10.1. The elephant in the room

We cannot have effective relationships without effective communication. A relationship can only be as sophisticated as the communication between the participants in that relationship. In the 21st century, we should be able to communicate in a global village as effectively as we did in a small village 100 years go. There is no doubt humanity would love to be able to do this. Social media, the public media and the Internet have all played an enormous role in assisting humanity to effectively communicate but there are obvious limitations.

There is an elephant in the room when we discuss communicating across our emerging global village. It is language. In terms of language humanity is still constrained by its tribal and cultural past. Each culture rightly treasures its language as a core component of its culture. But in our emerging multicultural global village we need to do a lot better than that. And whatever solution we propose we should not advantage, disadvantage or offend any culture on our planet. If we are to achieve a workable and harmonious global village and society, we must all be able to communicate effectively with one another across cultures.

Right now, we just can't do this. As Arthur Koestler wrote in *Janus: A Summing Up*, 'It seems odd that, except for a few valiant Esperantists, no international body has as yet discovered that the simplest way to promote understanding would be to promote a language that is understood by all.' Imagine any village in which a different language was spoken in each street or precinct. We would all agree that this would most likely not be an effective or harmonious community!

In the next twenty years, the proportion of products and services traded across international boundaries will at least treble. And this is only one of the drivers increasing the need for more effective communication between different cultural groups, including those within new regional groups such as ASEAN and the European Union. It is ironic that an event such as the Eurovision Song Contest is conducted largely in English, the language of a nation that has seceded from the European Union. The French or Italians had significant misgivings about an arrangement that facilitated the increased domination of Europe by the English language. They will feel this even more strongly now that Great Britain has departed from the EU.

The rapid development of a global village makes it essential that we find a better way to communicate than translation devices, no matter how good these become. It is astonishing that for the most part we don't even discuss this matter. This is possibly because there is a low expectation that there could ever be effective communication between peoples and cultures. It just looks too hard. As global interdependence, trade and travel increase, this problem worsens every year.

The birth of a planetary culture requires us to solve the difficulty of language communication by finding a planetary wide language solution acceptable and available to all, a win-win solution for all, and delivered at a price humanity can afford.

5.10.2. Choosing a global language

The choice the world needs to make is whether this global language should be an existing national language that is given a new global job, or a new language designed specifically for the purpose. And this language should be easy to learn so it can quickly become a universal language. There are many who believe that the world has already 'decided' and that the international lingua franca should be (or will be) English. Clearly, English is showing signs of establishing itself as a world lingua franca and is favoured as the priority language for people to learn if they want to be successful on the global stage.

But if a national language such as English becomes a universal lingua franca, will this lead to cultural imperialism by the English-speaking world? The French and many others as well certainly think so. They have taken steps to protect French language and culture from the cultural imperialism they believe is associated with the English-speaking world by attempting to ban the importation of English words into the French language. And now that Great Britain has left the European Union, English is unlikely to be promoted as a European lingua franca.

In leaving the EU, Great Britain has totally surrendered any bargaining power it had in any decision making about what should be a future global lingua franca. And a post-Trump USA will need to do some heavy lifting before it will be listened to in any international conversations about cultural and economic relationships. Both nations by their own self-isolating actions have lost much of the bargaining power they might have had. English gained a head start through British imperialism and colonisation. Now it will be interesting to see whether English will maintain this hegemony.

More generally, cultural imperialism will ride (or at least be seen to ride) on the coattails of the use of any national language upgraded to do global duties. A better solution would be adopting a new easy-to-learn language that belongs to nobody but can be accepted by everybody as a global language and used as a *universal second language* by all. This would simultaneously show a respect for both cultural difference and human unity, and would not threaten any culture, weak or strong.

5.10.3. L.L Zamenhof's vision

A Polish ophthalmologist, L.L. Zamenhof, created Esperanto in the 1873, while he was still at school. He intended it to be an international language that would promote the development of internationalist values. He spoke twelve languages and created an artificial language containing the best elements of each. Esperanto is artificial in that it is not a language tied to a national or tribal culture because it was created to be a language to be used in international affairs, for the very global village that is now emerging 150 years after Esperanto was created.

Esperanto has a mixture of linguistic roots derived from Romantic, Germanic, and Slavic languages so it will be widely accepted as a trans-European language. Some of its strongest adherents are Esperanto clubs in Poland, Hungary, and Bulgaria. Interestingly, China and the Republic of Korea have significant Esperanto movements and these cultures find Esperanto very easy to learn. Most people can use it effectively after studying it for six months to a year. Around our planet there are about 2 million active Esperantists.

Esperanto would not threaten any culture as would English or any other national language if it were officially adopted as an international lingua franca. It would solve the problem of international communication in a practical, low-cost, and culturally non-threatening way. Esperanto was nearly adopted by The League of Nations in 1922 as an official working language. But trenchant opposition led by the French Government, that wanted the only working languages of the League of Nations to be French and English, defeated it. At the same time the French Government even banned Esperanto from French schools.

The US is still a huge economic and cultural global power even if this is declining relative to other nations. This reality and the domination of English in social media and digital technology has certainly promoted a belief among many people that English should be the natural lingua franca for the 21st century. However, we should remember as we watch the rise of China in the early 21st century, including in its technological prowess, that there are more people on the planet who speak Mandarin than who speak English, and that Spanish rivals English as a widely spoken language. Bengali and Hindi are not far behind. What would happen if the Chinese used their emerging global political power to promote Mandarin as a world language? Or if all the Spanish-speaking world insisted it be Spanish?

We will soon reach a tipping point where the world will finally be forced to recognise that the issue of language and the need for effective planetary wide communication can no longer be swept under the carpet in the halls of international dialogue. It would be so much better if a global conversation could commence now about the issue of a global language so that humanity could make a clear collective decision about how we should proceed to fix this emerging communication problem without it being made by default.

A global language that belongs both to everybody and nobody should be a part of humanity's collective industrial and cultural future. A century after the attempt to promote the use of Esperanto at the League of Nations, the United Nations should commit itself to the task of initiating at ten-year programme to introduce and consolidate a global second universal language.

Thus far, we have explored in two chapters 21st century global trends and social and political change. This was followed by three chapters on how we might better prepare ourselves so that we are capable as we can be of thriving together in our emerging global village. In the next two chapters, we will discuss some curriculum items that that can assist humanity to shape and develop our 21st century global village so it is worthy of our best selves, and the planet can handed on to our children and grandchildren in the best condition it can be.

Chapter 6: Imagining and Building a Liveable Planet

What are the key ingredients of a future global liveable society that is worthy of the best of humanity, and how might we ensure that such a society emerges from our collective work?

6.1. A Liveable Future

In Chapter 1, I described the birth and emergence of the global paradigm of Planetism. This paradigm shift, now well under way and likely to be fully in place by the year 2050, will shape the coming decades of the 21st century. So how might the birth and spread of Planetism shape our emerging global society in coming decades? The answer to this question will depend on whether we are asking and seeking to answer a proactive leadership future-making question or a reactive management future-taking question. If we decide we want to be the best future-makers we can be, what *Utopian Realistic* preferred vision might we seek to realise and leave as a legacy to those who follow us?

Another question is, *what kind of future global society might human kind seek to build in coming generations, a global society that is worthy of humanity's best self?* As discussed, we cannot seek to build any future that we do not first imagine. So let us proceed to imagine and discuss what the human race might reasonably seek to realise in the next thirty years.

The UN system has already explored this territory to a certain degree. It has introduced two major initiatives of this kind so far. These are the Millennial Development Goals (for the years 2000-2015) and the Sustainable Development Goals (for the years 2015-2030). These initiatives are a brave start, seeking as they do for everybody to agree to adopt a shared agenda for shaping our collective future and creating a better world. However, some of the goals in these UN global strategies are expressed in problem-centred terms, and I believe these goals should be expressed as mission-directed terms not problem-centred ones. Mindset Number 5 recommends describing our goals in terms of building positive outcomes (mission-directed strategies) rather than reducing and eliminating negative outcomes (problem-centred strategies).

We already have an incredibly powerful prosperity-uplifting machine operating on our planet in the form of globalisation. Imperfect though it currently is, we can use it to fulfil any global vision humanity might visualise. This is not a machine we have to build. It is already in place. However, thus far we have not done nearly enough to develop a shared vision we could then seek to realise. We might have done this within a few national jurisdictions but, except for the two UN sets of goals mentioned above, we have not conceived what shared goals humanity might set for our shared planetary home.

What is really needed is a single unifying concept that can become a central catalyst for all our global conversations from here on. If we put ourselves into *Utopian Realistic mode,* we might choose to follow G.B Shaw's advice and explore *what 'never was' and say, 'why not'*. What follows might be the first steps of such a journey of collective planetary future shaping.

There will be many elements in such a vision and some words that might repeatedly reappear in our conversations. Peace alone is not enough. Prosperity alone is not enough. Sustainability, and equality alone or even together are not enough, important as all of these are. It becomes clear that a concept that is more encompassing than all these concepts is needed, although of course these are all components of what humanity might seek. And it would also be best if the word we use to describe this concept is not a totally new word or concept, but one already known to most of humanity. I suggest the concept of *liveability*. This concept could be used as a shared global holistic organising principle. We can discuss and visualise what might constitute a Utopian *liveability heaven*. We could then explore and invent the Realistic means to achieve such a *liveability heaven*.

In seeking to check out the potential of liveability as a universal organising concept, I asked people who had a planning background to describe their views of what might constitute *liveability heaven* and what ingredients might contribute to liveability. From what they told me, I concluded that liveability has six components: Prosperity, Harmony, Inclusion, Sustainability, Health and Security. I call these *the six pillars of liveability* (FUTK46).

6.2. Defining Liveability: The Six Pillars of Liveability

I called these *The Six Pillars of Liveability (FUTK46)* because if one were absent the whole house of liveability might collapse, these six pillars are:

Liveable = Prosperous + Harmonious + Inclusive + Sustainable + Healthy + Secure (FK42)

These six aspirations summarise most of what most of us want in abundance in our lives and in our communities both today and tomorrow. I would like to propose that humanity initiate a new planet-wide Apollo Type Program built around the concept of universal liveability. It is a concept that can unite governments, commercial corporations, and civil society in imagining, building, and realising ever more liveable future outcomes. If we wish to realise this aspiration we can use *The Six Future Shaping Tools* of leadership, management, planning, design, innovation and learning to build this liveable future. Then our global conversations can be focussed on this common theme and framework and all our actions can be integrated through the sharing of strategic action templates.

6.3. Building an Ever More Liveable Planetary Society

We can construct liveable places both at the local and the global level. We can construct more-liveable precincts to create exemplars, then liveable communities and cities, and finally a liveable Planet. The construction of an ever more liveable global village could be a work in progress throughout the entire 21st century. Liveability is like happiness. Can there ever be an end point to realising more liveability? Each of *The Six Pillars of Liveability* can be constantly raised. Our views of whatever constitutes each of the Six Pillars of Liveability will change as well. Creating an ever more liveable future can be a rolling *Utopian Realistic* vision for our planetary home.

If we wish to measure human progress more effectively in the 21st century, these six pillars of liveability would be a worthy replacement to the utterly inadequate measure we currently use to measure human progress, namely the Gross Domestic Product (GDP).

6.4. The Liveability Economy: Our Industrial Future?

Here are some of the reasons why liveability can be a major driver of social, economic and community development and advancement in the coming decades:

- All people want to live in places that are as liveable as they can afford. This is true for the booming educated middle class and many if not most of those who aspire to join it. All the *Six Pillars of Liveability* matter to this cohort of global society in the 21st century. Indeed, if we revisit the modernist aspiration of *continuing progress* and seek to define it in Planetist rather than *Modernist* terms, we could redefine *progress* as innovating and implementing the means we use to uplift liveability.
- The rising global educated middle class, which will number 5 billion in 2030 and that already treasures all the six pillars of liveability, will increasingly demand and be willing to pay for the raising of liveability for both themselves and their communities. They will then seek to acquire the *liveability uplifting ways and wares* humanity will collectively innovate.
- Because there is already a growing demand for increased liveability, the goal of uplifting liveability can become an engine for increasing and spreading global prosperity. It will not need to be significantly subsidised. The prosperity-uplifting machine that is globalisation can be given the job to assist humanity to realise this aspiration.
- Every real estate agents and urban developer knows that the more liveable a place, precinct or community is, the greater will be its market value. Aspirations that uplift liveability will attract increased investment because every year there are more people being raised out of poverty by globalisation and there will be more people who can invest an increased amount of their income in building ever more liveable places for themselves and others.
- We just can't create liveability with a mindset based on narrow self-interest. We will not want to live in a gated liveable fortress in an unliveable precinct. Nelson Mandela said, we *cannot have islands of plenty in seas of poverty*. Or, to put this another way, we *cannot have islands that are liveable in seas that are unliveable.* That might have been the view of the well-off in the mid-20th century who could happily live in a world that accepted exclusion, but in the 21st century, those with

Planetist values will want to contribute to building an inclusive planetary society that is liveable for all.
- If we uplift liveability, we will raise the market value of all places and precincts, all communities, towns, and cities. Liveability is both a sought reward for present wealth and a generator of future wealth. Exemplars of liveability are admired by those who live in less liveable circumstances, and they become exemplars for the rest of us.
- People in democracies are always pressing their national and local governments to invest more in liveability in their communities. In fact, uplifting the Six Pillars of Liveability, separately and collectively, can be regarded as the main motivator and purpose of government public policy and expenditure everywhere.
- Global markets are already demanding *liveability ways and wares*: products, services and technologies that improve liveability. We can all do economically well by doing liveability good.

In the next decade, an entire liveability industry will be born because the market for liveability is already here and will grow further.

6.5. Exploring the Six Pillars of Liveability

Let us now consider each of the six pillars of liveability.

Prosperity is not just an absence of poverty. It is a state where wealth is being generated by the invention and marketing of products, services, and technologies relevant to the 21st century. Economic prosperity built from metaphysical resources, from our knowledge, can be unlimited. Many if not most of the job categories and products, services, and technologies, what I call *liveability ways and wares* have yet to be invented.

In Chapter 7 we will have a detailed discussion about prosperity and poverty where we will see that we can define prosperity in each of four forms: economic, ecological, social, and cultural prosperity. Humanity is now learning how it can do economically well while simultaneously doing ecological, social, and cultural good, not bad. Chapter 12 will discuss *cosmonaut globalisation, cosmonaut capitalism,* and *cosmonaut economics*, or planetist-informed globalisation, capitalism and economics, and the role these will play in building 21st century prosperity.

Harmony is more than just an absence of hostility, just as prosperity is more than just an absence of poverty, peace is more than an absence of war, wellness is more than an absence of illness, and kindness is more than an absence of cruelty. Harmony is a key ingredient of interdependence. Because human interdependence is growing, a yearning for harmony will grow with it. After all, an increasing number of us are recognising the reality that we share a planetary home and that we have a common future. To improve harmony, we can use the *Interdependence Trio (FUTK08): practicing the Golden Rule; making mutual obligations to achieve shared aspirations; and seeking win-win outcomes in everything we do.*

Harmony will only be possible if there is trust between individuals, groups, and cultures. Therefore, the components of the *Trust Trio (FUTK09), Honesty, Reliability and Competence,* will need to be promoted and embedded in all our behaviours. Harmony will grow when we simultaneously respect and treasure both difference of every kind and human unity. Imagine the *ways and wares* that could be innovated and marketed to uplift *harmony* based on the *Interdependence Trio* and the *Trust Trio* alone!

We have already described how some people such as Modernist populists and autocrats, fundamentalists, and terrorists of all kinds are still seeking to grow their power and influence by promoting division that undermines or crashes harmony. Our success in increasing harmony therefore will be dependent on the simultaneous uplifting of the other pillars of liveability, especially prosperity and security.

Inclusion is more than an absence of exclusion. It focuses on both minimising disadvantage and disability and maximising advantage and ability for all. Everybody should have the opportunity to reach their full potential. Additionally, other species should also be able to thrive alongside humanity. The *Circle of Identity (FUTK35)* and *Singer's Circle of Concern (FUTK34)*, which are discussed elsewhere, can help us understand how much each of us is open to including in our lives those who are different or disadvantaged.

Sustainable is more than just an absence of *unsustainable*. It means what we, both individually and collectively, should act and behave so that we avoid causing net collateral harm to life (both our own and other species), place and social and cultural systems *(FUTK29)*. We have yet to invent many if not most of the new means, the *sustainability ways and wares*, to achieve this. Sustainability will be discussed more fully in Chapter 7.

Health or Wellness (health status) is not just an absence of illness. It is made up of two components: *well-being*, which is being and remaining well both physically and mentally; and *well-becoming*, which is becoming well, both physically and mentally. *Sustainable behaviour* involves causing zero net collateral harm to *other*. On the other hand, *healthy behaviour* involves causing zero net collateral harm to *self*. Healthy behaviours both enhance wellness and avoid causing illness. Creating wellness requires that we plan, design, and build environments that are health promoting not illness inducing. It also involves encouraging all of us to live a consciously healthy lifestyle, including regularly consulting one's doctor.

This is already happening because educated people are seeking to live more consciously healthy lifestyles. An example of the changing health trends is that in 1900, the rich were more likely to be fat and the poor were more likely to be thin. Today, the opposite is true. Obesity is now more often associated with poverty than with prosperity. In Chapter 10 we will explore another aspect of healthy behaviour, namely Stephen Boyden's concept of *Meliors*.

Finally, there is much we need to learn from the trauma that has been the COVID-19 pandemic. We will discuss this matter more fully in Chapter 8. Here, it is sufficient to say that we need innovations such as *pandemic surveillance ways and wares, pandemic protection ways and wares,* and *pandemic abatement ways and wares* in abundance.

Security is not just an absence of insecurity. Firstly, prosperous, harmonious, inclusive, sustainable and healthy environments are likely to be more secure environments. If we improve the five other *pillars of liveability* and include those who are living lives with disadvantage or disability there will be fewer people within our communities who feel excluded, and who are motivated by their anger, disappointment, or desperation to threaten and disrupt others.

Many Modernists regard the words *defence* and *security* as virtual synonyms. Most defence planners tell their governments that competition between nations will always be present, and we need to arm ourselves to the teeth to stay secure. Their thinking has not changed for 100 years. These people have not expanded their *circles of identity* beyond that of first allegiance to nation, and they are unwilling or unable to see differently and to put planet first. Many defence planners seek to keep their budgets growing by dreaming up new enemies and new existential threats based on predicting future combat between nation states or with religious or cultural extremists. Defence operates on the premise that danger comes from outside our national boundaries and from people who are different from us. In our emerging multicultural global village this is archaic and dangerous thinking. Security is based on the concept that danger can come from anywhere, including from within our national boundaries and people who are (or seem) the same as us. Yes, we will need some smart weapons to remove such people. But to create a more secure future we need a whole toolkit of responses, most of which are not military in nature. Our allies and enemies are no longer geographically separated by national boundaries so we must ensure that our responses cause zero net collateral harm. We will need many different strategies other than the standard military and diplomatic strategies.

We can significantly diminish what we spend on armaments and we can invest instead in making our world more secure without relying on the military. For example, we can punish the *planetary wicked* through using the *Planetary Pariah Punishments*. We can plan and design communities so that they become safer and more reassuring, and less threatening and anxiety creating. And we can grow our interdependence through trade and investment, as is the case in 21st century Europe where European nations have become so interdependent that they can no longer afford to go to war again.

A 21st century war between France and Germany is now hard to imagine. We can spread this European interdependence route to increased security to the rest of the planet. Imagine the designs, plans and innovations (ways and wares), and the learning curricula we could create to build more secure precincts, places, and communities. The 21st century security industry will be based on uplifting liveability while we implement public policies and public works and develop and market new *ways and wares* to protect us from danger. Security is the concern of all of us, not just the police and defence bureaucrats and their political masters. The best way to secure us from being endangered by others is by investing in building a liveable and an ever more peaceful global village through innovating and marketing more *liveability ways and wares* and *peace building and peace keeping ways and wares*.

We can also improve security by three different activities. These involve increasing our intelligence, surveillance, and vigilance capabilities. I call these three capabilities *The Security Trio (FUTK48)*. Imagine the *intelligence, surveillance and vigilance ways and wares* that could in turn be embedded into many new *security ways and wares*.

6.6. Mindsets for Building a Liveable Future

Now we are going to move into future-making mode. Most of us would agree that a worthy aspiration of the parent in each of us would be to leave a legacy for our descendants of a world that is more liveable than the one we inherited.

I propose that a global conversation should begin now about creating a common framework for the actions of governments, politicians, industrialists, academics, innovators, entrepreneurs, and investors. These groups need to have a shared understanding of what needs to be done to create a liveable world. The concept of the Six Pillars of Liveability provides a future-making template to facilitate a convergence of imagination, ideas, and public policy and innovation for humanity to build a planet wide liveable future.

The demand for greater liveability will increase throughout the 21st century everywhere, and a major liveability industry will blossom as well. This industry will, amongst other things, need to customise liveability for different cultures and different environments. There will be different perceptions and interpretations of *the six pillars of liveability* in different cultures. Liveability is not a one-size-fits-all concept.

We have already discussed the interactive relationship between increasing liveability and raising the market value of homes, precincts, and urban districts. The increasing demand for greater liveability will in turn generate a liveability-based industrial future, driven and funded by a growing global market demand for liveability.

If you doubt this, here is some evidence that planetist values and liveability are already shaping economic and industrial futures in the 21st century:

- Socially Responsible Investment (SRI) organisations (or ethical investment organisations) and mutual funds sourcing investment funds from people holding planetist values usually perform better than other investment organisations. Their moral compasses for the most part are already informed by planetist values, even if they do not recognise this fact. Their actions mostly involve investment in economic activities contributing to a more liveable future. They will divest themselves of investments that lessen liveability in the next decade.
- More than $100 trillion will be transferred between generations and for the most part this will accrue to people who are informed by Planetist Values.

- An increasing number of banks and other investors won't invest in energy projects based on fossil fuels. More of them are becoming Planetists. These investors don't want to face condemnation from their own children at the breakfast table for investing in projects that will collaterally damage our planetary home and undermine their future. Think Greta Thunberg sharing your own breakfast table! And increasingly if not already, your own children will be embedding Greta Thunberg type views in themselves.
- In the past, those who thought we could derive all our energy from the sun were ridiculed. Ralph Nader told us in the 1970s that that solar energy would never get off the ground because the corporate producers of hydrocarbon-sourced energy, including oil companies, didn't own the sun. That he has been proven so wrong is due to the shifting global moral compass and this illustrates how much has our world is changing. This change is already under way because the arrival on the investment centre stage of what Future Knowledge calls planetism-informed *Cosmonaut Capitalism.*
- On the other hand, those organisations undertaking actions, including making investments, that reduce future liveability are increasingly likely to fail because they face a future of declining market share and stranded assets. In more extreme cases they will face the *planetary pariah punishments* of trade sanctions, frozen bank accounts, customer boycotts and investments strikes, or prosecution in national courts, the international criminal court, or the soon to be created anti-corruption court.
- The 2017 Nobel Peace Prize was awarded to ICAN, the *International Campaign to Abolish Nuclear Weapons.* Those who work for ICAN have Planetist mindsets, while those who favour the retention of nuclear weapons adhere to nationalist-dominated Modernist mindsets. Which of these two alternative viewpoints is on the right side of history?
- We are already being shaped by Planetist values. Just consider how social media organisations are being asked by planetary global public opinion to remove from their sites opinions and assertions that conflict with planetist values. These include statements that promote interreligious or racial intolerance and conflict, threaten women and women's rights, or threaten our future by promoting actions that increase

global heating. The gap is closing between what we might aspire for as a *preferred vision* of a liveable future and a *probable prediction* for our future that is already being realised by long-term global trends.

I believe that the time is right for humanity to articulate a new 21st century-relevant and Utopian Realistic goal for its own future on its shared home, a goal that is worthy of humanity's best self. The concept of universal liveability is such a goal.

Chapter 7: Reimagining Sustainability: Sustainable Behaviour, Sustainable Prosperity

7.1. Sustainability: Do We Need to Reinvent It?

Chapter 1 outlined how the concept of sustainability was born in the 20th century with the birth of Postmodernism in the two decades after Earthrise. It was born as the concept of Sustainable Development. It formally became a mainstream concept with the 1987 publication by the United Nations through Oxford University Press of *Our Common Future*, the report of the Brundtland Commission, The World Commission on Environment and Development. Since then, the concept of Sustainable Development has become a core mainstream concept. It was conceived to encourage those who undertake development of any kind to be fully aware of the environmental impact of their development activities and to encourage them to design their developments so that they avoid or at least minimise collateral environmental harm.

Over thirty years later, unfortunately we have to conclude that this concept has been at best only a partial success in protecting the global environment. *Homo sapiens* is still polluting the planetary public domains of atmosphere and oceans and overusing and polluting its freshwater resources. It is continuing with the mass extermination of much of the planet's plants and animals either by eating them or by destroying their habitats. Scientists are talking openly about the Sixth Mass Extinction. Though some progress is being made in many spheres and places, we are not yet accomplishing enough to turn the two challenges of global heating and loss of biodiversity around. I believe that a major part of this problem is the yesteryear Modernist mindsets embedded in too many people, along with greed in some of them.

I have asked many people *What is sustainability?* Most believe it is a concept designed to better protect our environment. However, most people cannot take it much further than that. Our concept of sustainability is not precise enough and is not well understood enough. We should review the concept of sustainability so that it can provide a bigger contribution towards designing and building a 21st century global village that it is more liveable for all life.

I believe a new concept of sustainability could be built around two concepts: sustainable *behaviour* and sustainable *prosperity*.

As discussed earlier, sustainable behaviour consists of achieving *zero net collateral harm to life* plus *zero net collateral damage to place (FUTK29)*.

Assessing damage brings us back to the issue that was fully discussed in Chapter 2: that we still have too many people with Modernist mindsets. They think that protecting the global environment is not an issue they should give any significant priority to. They also think we must make a choice between economy and ecology. This declining number of people still assert that economic issues must always prevail and that ecological, social, or cultural harm and damage is the price we must pay for economic development. They cannot conceive that win/win outcomes might be realistic options. Thus would-be beef and soy producers are continuing to destroy the Amazon rainforests, undoing much of the progress made by Brazil after the 1992 Earth Summit. This is despite the reality that beef (and meat in general) and dairy products will soon be produced in abundance by bioreactors/factories using cloned cells, microorganisms and plant protein in solar powered processes that will cause zero net global heating.

Like all tropical soils, the soils of the Amazon rainforests become infertile when their organic matter is removed by fire, development, and agriculture. The indigenous people of the Amazon basin knew this and invented a way of restoring Amazonian soil fertility by adding a mixture of charcoal, compost, bones, broken pottery and manure to the soil, creating what are called *terra preta* soils, which are enormously rich. In this way they lived and fed themselves for centuries in the rainforest without destroying their rainforest habitat.

Humanity would be better off if it learned from the foresight and wisdom of these First Nations peoples of the Amazon Basin rather than trashing our world with Modernist yesteryear development practices. This behaviour puts on full show the self-interest and short-sightedness of the deforesters pillaging of the Amazon rainforest.

After this large-scale clearing of the rainforest commenced the world demanded that Brazil reverse these destructive activities; but Brazil's *Modernist populist* former president, Jair Bolsonaro, mercifully removed from office in late 2022, believes nation must come first over planet and facilitated this destruction. The newly elected administration of incoming president Luiz Inácio Lula da

Silva, universally known as Lula, is committed to reversing Bolsonaro's rainforest trashing policies and to beginning the restoration of the ecological integrity of the Amazon rainforest. The future of the Amazon rainforest was a major issue in the Brazilian election. A planetary-conscious Lula does not want to be cast as *global pariah* and he has both global and majority Brazilian public opinion on his side.

The deforesters believed they would create economic prosperity by levelling the Amazon rainforest. They acted with embedded 20th century cowboy win/lose Modernist mindsets. Like mid-20th century economists, the deforesters and Bolsonaro and his supporters see the Amazon Basin in its natural state as *worthless*. Planetists both in the rest of the world and the nearly 100 million of them in Brazil regard the Amazon Basin as *priceless*, believing it should remain as the biggest carbon sink and the richest biodiversity hot spot on the planet. Tragically, thanks to Bolsonaro's facilitation of the bulldozing and destruction of the Amazon forest, an exhaustive examination by scientists in July 2021 demonstrated that the Amazon Basin had been damaged to the point that it had totally lost its capacity to be a net carbon sink and had instead become a net carbon emitter. In late 2019, the European Union stopped work on an almost fully negotiated free trade agreement between the EU and the Mercosur Group (Brazil, Argentina, Paraguay and Uruguay), something which would land a new component of the global economic prosperity uplifting machine in South America. Brazil's fellow members will be ecstatic that this process can now recommence.

Finally, in a significant sign of the shifting values in the global financial sector, many financial institutions had already indicated they would not invest in any organisation that contributed in any way to deforestation in the Amazon, or that was a beneficiary of that deforestation.

To people with Planetist mindsets and sensibilities, the recent history of the Amazon was an imminent spectacular failure that an election suddenly changed into an emerging beacon of Planetary hope. However, Bolsonaro and his *Modernist populist* friends elsewhere are unlikely to change their environmental destructive practices. They continue to believe that the only possible option on the public policy table is a win/lose choice between economy and ecology.

But for those with 21st century values, there is of course a win/win solution. With the introduction of carbon trading, Brazil can gain more wealth using the Amazon Basin as a carbon sink by simply leaving the remaining rainforest undeveloped and restoring what has been destroyed. In this way, the rest of the planet will be willing to pay Brazil to keep the Amazon in its natural state, thereby nurturing its biodiversity and protecting the lives and communities of the indigenous peoples living there. Moreover, if the beef and soy producers had Planetist mindsets, they would seek to enter the carbon trading market and use the income derived from this to invest in the bioreactor/factory food production of meat and milk and other food products, or other environmentally benign agricultural alternatives. By 2035, world markets will be flooded by artificial meat and milk that will make much of the beef and milk production everywhere obsolete.

The split in global opinion is stark. Planetists everywhere support the retention of the Amazon rainforest and nationalists everywhere are unconcerned if it is destroyed. But the choice is no longer economy *or* ecology, win/loss, but economy *and* ecology, a win/win. With global carbon trading in place, many ecosystems, from rangelands to rainforests, can be used to sequester carbon, a rewilding measure that will simultaneously benefit landowners and our planet's climate and biodiversity.

Interestingly, the words ecology and economics are both derived from the Greek word *Ecos* meaning home. Ecology means understanding the home and economics means managing the home. We need to create a new concept of sustainability that reminds everybody that words like worthless and priceless are not just about value in economic terms. Prosperity can exist in many forms. Prosperity can be described in ecological, social, and cultural terms as well as in economic terms. I have sought to create a template for sustainability that shows how we can more thoroughly assess and know how we can do economically well by simultaneously doing ecological, social, and cultural good rather than bad.

Can sustainable development be reimagined and reconceived so that it always delivers win/win solutions between economy and ecology, economy and society, and economy and culture? I believe that we can create such win/win outcomes by thinking differently. We can show Modernist environmental vandals how even they could both prosper economically and become planetary heroes at the same time rather than planetary pariahs! However, to do this they will need to acquire some new 21st century mindsets and put planet first.

7.2 Sustainable Prosperity

People with Modernist development mindsets believe that economic development and economic prosperity must come from exploiting environments: for economies to prosper ecosystems needed to be impoverished. The Amazon case history just described provides a good illustration of the continuation of this mindset into the 21st century. And of course, whole cultures and social systems were sometimes also impoverished in the name of building economic prosperity. In Modernist times, the value of a natural environment was not even considered part of any evaluation process used by economists. Modernist economists in the mid-20th century used to talk about what they called *externalities*, meaning that it was not possible in the 1960s to include concerns such as environmental or cultural protection into their Modernist economic frameworks.

I believe we can bring the words *sustainable* and *prosperous* into a single concept in a way that enables us to *internalise* these former *externalities* into a single framework. This concept could become a central integrating concept that can be used to guide the building and management of our 21st century global village. *Sustainable Prosperity* involves seeking to become sustainably prosperous: uplifting economic prosperity while *simultaneously* elevating ecological, social, and cultural prosperity instead of simultaneously impoverishing ecosystems, societies, and cultures *(FUTK15)*. Here *impoverishment* means causing net collateral harm to people (life) or to place and degrading the effective functioning and complexity of economies, ecosystems, societies, and cultures.

We don't yet know how to accomplish this, but this is where humanity must seek to go in the coming decades. It will need to innovate its way there. I believe we will find we know more about how to accomplish this than we think. However, the innovation journey there will be more successful if would-be innovators are informed by these core concepts:

- *A Planetist moral compass.*
- *The Six Pillars of Liveability.*
- *Sustainable Prosperity as it is being described in this chapter.*

We have already discussed the other key concept in this discussion, namely sustainable behaviour, which involves inventing the means to act while *causing simultaneous zero net harm or damage* to economies, ecosystems, societies, or cultures. Innovating the means to achieve this outcome requires creating new *ways and wares* (which we can call *sustainable behaviour ways and wares*) to enable us to accomplish this. We can judge whether our behaviour is sustainable or not by using a *quadruple bottom line*, based on assessing our prosperity-uplifting outcomes in economic, ecological, social, and cultural terms. This is a reinterpretation of the *triple bottom line* first suggested by John Elkington in his book *Cannibals with Forks,* in which he suggests that sustainable businesses need to measure their performances via profits and their effect on people and the planet.

We can innovate many more *sustainable behaviour ways and wares* to enable humanity to do economically well by doing ecological, social, and cultural good. This is a challenge to see how smart we can be! Sustainable prosperity is realised when our knowledge (our metaphysical wealth) is used to maintain or grow economies, ecosystems, societies or cultures without causing net collateral net harm or damage to any of these. We will now discuss each of *The Four Domains of Sustainable Prosperity* (FUTK15) in sequence.

7.3. Economic Prosperity and Economic Poverty

In the 1970 book, *Approaching the Benign Environment*, Richard Buckminster Fuller told us that our wealth comes from a combination of the *physical* (materials and ecosystems) that we should conserve, and the *metaphysical* (ideas, knowledge, and wisdom) that can only grow (*Bucky Fuller's Wealth Duet FUTK10)*. The emergence of what we now call *the creative industries* over the last 20 years is an excellent example of the expansion of the sources of metaphysical wealth in the 21st century.

In the past, we thought prosperity was limited because physical resources were limited. We were willing to accept poverty as part of the natural order. We often operated as pirates and exploiters of both natural and human resources, particularly when we operated outside our national borders, and where we regarded it as acceptable to steal from or exploit those different from us. Political or military power and inherited power enabled people to enrich themselves at others' expense, or to acquire disproportionate amounts of wealth for themselves.

Additionally, 50 years ago most people thought all real wealth came from using resources we derived from beneath the ground, from the land, and from the sea. We believed we primarily became wealthy by 'exploiting' (and exploiting was the word we usually used), and then adding value to, natural resources. And we believed that because resources were limited, wealth would always be limited. The idea that prosperity could ever be universal would have been regarded as Utopian. We could not have imagined a future world where wealth might be unlimited because we can all create ever more metaphysical resources for ourselves, most of which does not involve adding any value to physical resources. Many people who thought this way could not see what Buckminster Fuller, amongst others, saw: that universal prosperity could be created by further growing the metaphysical, the knowledge-based component of wealth. Education in the past was for the fortunate few so any metaphysical-resourced wealth was held by those privileged enough to be able to tap into metaphysical sources of wealth. Because most people thought that wealth originated in the physical world many even claimed that too much economic growth itself could also endanger our planet. For example, in the 1970s the prestigious Club of Rome promoted the idea that there were *limits to growth*. Even today some environmentalists still tell us that humanity will have to limit economic growth and development if humanity is to save our planetary home.

In the 21st century, this is archaic thinking. We now know that there are some forms of economic activity and growth that collaterally harm people and planet and some forms that do not. The issue was not economic growth itself but the kind of economic growth we undertook or permitted. In the 21st century, we will need to eliminate the kinds that cause net collateral harm and grow the forms that do not. This is precisely what the concept of *sustainable prosperity* can offer us.

Many people claim that the world is still becoming more unequal even though overall poverty is steadily decreasing and globalisation is expected to create 5 billion educated middle-class people by 2030. As indicated earlier, globalisation is the biggest prosperity-uplifting machine ever invented and when it is transformed into a Planetist form it will uplift prosperity for all, even more so.

There are currently more extremely rich people than ever before. But the important issue to note is that most of these rich people are not becoming rich because they are stealing from others but because they are increasing overall wealth, including their own wealth. There are still too many poor people but there are also more people who are prospering economically. The rich are getting richer, but the poor are not necessarily becoming poorer. Admittedly, some of the rich are now so wealthy that the differential between rich and poor has widened. However, the poor are becoming more prosperous as well, even if for many of us this is not happening fast enough.

For the most part, the people who have become very wealthy have done so because they created new products and services drawn from their own and other's metaphysical resources, such as through planetary interconnectivity ways and wares such as digital technology, telecommunications, and social media. Unlike many of their predecessors, these wealthy people have not stolen from others or unreasonably exploited physical resources to become rich. They have created wealth through their own brainpower. They are providing products and services to service the needs of our growing and increasingly complex global village. We now know that all of humanity can potentially follow the same metaphysical route to wealth and that all humanity can potentially economically prosper. The only limits to our future metaphysically-based prosperity are the limitations we place on our mindsets, on our critical and creative thinking, on our willingness to learn and grow our knowledge, and on our willingness to invest time and money in new ideas and initiatives. And we will do this better if we are dedicated to the shared benefits that can come from of the *Interdependence Trio* of the Golden Rule, shared envisioned aspirations and win/win outcomes.

Management can encourage us to create smarter means to do old tasks faster and better and to make our future world more productive through the innovation of new *ways or wares* to raise productivity. *Leadership* can chart new courses to fulfil new goals that facilitate the opening-up of many new possibilities and destinations. *Planning* can assist us to better organise ourselves, embed our values into new projects and better accomplish new tasks or accomplish new projects that reflect these values. This includes being informed by *planetist values* and seeking to make our future world ever more *liveable* through uplifting *the six pillars of liveability*. *Design* can encourage us to accomplish a new or old task with a new form or function that will inspire and satisfy our psychological, spiritual, and material needs.

Innovation can create the many *ways and wares* that are mentioned in this book, or are not yet imagined by anybody. As well we can innovate many *ways and wares* to uplift the other three domains of sustainable prosperity, namely ecological prosperity, social prosperity, and cultural prosperity. *Learning* can include research and development to better understand our world, our aspirations, and our basic human needs, so we can live successfully in our emerging global village and make it ever more liveable.

In this way, we can all uplift and grow our metaphysical resources so we can climb a ladder into universal sustainable prosperity. As Buckminster Fuller reminded us, our metaphysical resources can only increase. The contribution of education and learning, and research and development, to the creation of a world that is capable of being universally prosperous cannot be overstated.

All this this can be done as well in impoverished communities as in already prosperous communities. Poor communities usually contain few new innovative start-up enterprises, but poor communities are also becoming better educated and in the coming two decades the doors to metaphysical-based future prosperity will open to the world's poorest and most disadvantaged people. This pathway to prosperity is already being promoted by governments and community development banks/microcredit banks such as the Grameen Bank.

However, the opportunities that are offered must be taken up and realised in ventures and enterprises established in these communities. This will require that future making and resilient future taking mindsets, and planetist moral compasses, be incorporated by those who are building these enterprises. These emerging entrepreneurs should also be able to expand their *circles of identity* and to build an ever more liveable and sustainably prosperous future for themselves, their communities, and our planet. In short, they first need to become the kind of people who can be uplifted by the prosperity-uplifting machine of globalisation.

Nations such as Singapore and Japan have known all of this is for a long time. These nations had very few or no natural resources, so they have used their human resources to create wealth from metaphysical resources, from their brainpower. This is the route being taken by them and many other once poor nations such as the Republic of Korea, China, Vietnam, and India. These nations have all built their future prosperity on an investment in mass education up to tertiary level and the use of their metaphysical resources to create wealth. It is now possible for the first time in human history to totally decouple ourselves from resourced-based wealth and prosper economically.

Nelson Mandela said in 2000 that in the 21st century we should not create *islands of plenty in seas of poverty.* He told us that we needed to ensure globalisation would benefit all of us and not just some of us; that we need to *globalise responsibility.* We now have the tools to create universal plenty. Globalising responsibility means that the planet must come first and we should accept we have a responsibility not only for our own personal futures but also for our planet and all its inhabitants.

Here are the key points that relate to the uplifting of global economic prosperity so far:

- 21st century economic prosperity will be increasingly generated from the innovation and marketing of products and services derived from our metaphysical resources: our knowledge. While wealth derived from physical resources is limited by resource availability there are no limits to the wealth that can be derived from our metaphysical resources. The higher our investments in education and learning, and research and development, the wealthier we can become.
- 21st century economic success will be generated and shaped by the knowledgeable and creative minds of largely Planetist-informed 21st century people, who will use their metaphysical resources to build future economic prosperity. They can use *The Six Future Shaping Tools* (FUTK37) to build this future economic prosperity. However these people will not thrive under autocratic regimes of governance.
- Much economic prosperity in the 21st century will come from increasing, maintaining and, where necessary, restoring ecological, social, and cultural prosperity and reducing ecological, social, and cultural poverty. Future economic prosperity will also come from uplifting the other *Five Pillars of Liveability*: harmony, inclusion, sustainability, health and security.
- Those entrepreneurs and investors who place individual, identity or nation before planet will, in the future, face resistance and even trade sanctions, customer boycotts, and investment strikes and frozen bank accounts from Planetist governments, consumers and investors (*the planetary pariah punishments*).
- Most of the industries, products and services that will dominate global markets in year 2050 have yet to be invented.

7.4. Ecological Prosperity and Ecological Poverty

We have already noted that the words *economics* and *ecology* come from the same Greek root: Ecos, meaning 'home', and that *economics* means *managing the home* while *ecology* means *understanding the home*. Most of the world's environmental problems have occurred because we have tried to manage, develop, exploit, and reconstruct a 'home' that we don't sufficiently understand, don't care enough about, or are too greedy and blinkered to want to know about. In the past we trashed nature out of ignorance, stupidity, or greed. Of course all these behaviours persist but the values system that approves of or tolerates this behaviour is withering. In several parts of this book, I have also suggested that most of our environmental problems come from behaving in ways informed by yesteryear Modernist mindsets.

Unfortunately, even now, economists rarely learn any ecology (a natural science) and most ecologists rarely learn any economics (a social science). It is only in the last three decades or so that *ecological economics* has been born and is now seeking to bring these two sciences into a single interactive framework. Concepts such as sustainable prosperity and liveability are offered to enable a convergence of economics and ecology. And the emergence of new cohorts of decision makers who have planetist values will ensure the conceptual gap that characterised and dominated our modernist past will close in the 21st century. Regrettably, it will most likely take a generation for the yesteryear attitudes to completely vanish.

Meanwhile, an increasing number of businesses and philanthropies are adopting Planetist-informed visions and strategic aspirations. They want to create new innovations to develop, trade, produce, and consume without causing net collateral harm. Humanity will invent many more *ways and wares* to achieve these outcomes and restore ecological prosperity where ecological harm and impoverishment has previously occurred, such as through what we can call an emerging *ecosystem restoration industrial future.*

There are five other design principles/rules/innovation/practices we can use to guide our innovation of *ecological prosperity ways and wares.* I call these five principles *The Ecological Prosperity Quintet (FUTK16).* These principles are:

- Live solely on perpetual solar income
- Learn from nature
- Create circular economies
- Use resources JEPAT (just enough in place and time)
- Protect and nurture biodiversity).

These are the positive design rules to enable us to prosper economically while avoiding net collateral harm to ecosystems and to humanity, simultaneously creating 21st century economic prosperity and ecological prosperity. Imagine developing *ways and wares* to enable us to:

- *Live solely on perpetual solar income.* Buckminster Fuller told us in *Cosmic Costing* (1970) that we should live within perpetual solar income. Total solar income is 10,000 times current global energy use. There is absolutely no danger that our use of energy will ever exceed total solar income.
- *Learn from nature and be inspired by and/or mimic nature.* As Leonardo Da Vinci said, *Nature is the source of all true knowledge. She has her own logic, her own laws; she has neither effect without cause nor invention without necessity.* From our very beginnings, our observation of nature has influenced human behaviour. Hence physician and economist Francois Quesnay, a court physician to Louis XV, founded a school of economic thinking called *The Physiocrats*, a school of economics based on the principles of physiology. He created the theory of economic cycles after being inspired by William Harvey's discovery of the circulation of the blood and after he himself described the circulation of the blood in detail. The innovation consultant and natural sciences writer Janine Benyus, who coined the term biomimicry to describe problem-solving design inspired by the natural world, has pointed out that what lives today are nature's success stories: nature's failures are fossils.
- *Create circular economies: turn waste into food.* Sustainability Architect William McDonough suggested these words. He too was inspired by nature and possibly by the work of François Quesnay. He pointed out that in nature there is no such thing as 'waste': one species' waste is another species' food. Unfortunately, at present many of the things we make and throw out are toxic to life and cannot be successfully recycled. The challenge is to innovate *ways and wares* to build *circular economies*, where toxicity in waste is reduced to zero so that when it degrades it will not poison the environment. And one of the most important cycles we need to recreate and rebuild is a circular economy

for carbon. We need to innovate the *ways and wares* to, reduce, reuse, and recycle all carbon waste, and thereby create future zero net waste.

- *Use resources JEPAT (just enough in place and time).* This is one of my own ideas. Most of us know what Just-in-Time (JIT) is as it is used in manufacturing. JEPAT means that at any and every time and place, we need just the right amount of material or resources for nature and humanity to use, neither too much nor too little: the *Goldilocks* amount if you like. Using too little or too much medicine in our body stops it from working as well as it can, and this can also cause collateral harm to us. Too much water-soluble chemical fertiliser added to the soil means it washes out in heavy rain and causes water pollution because it delivers excessive nutrients in the wrong place. We call this form of pollution by excessive nutrition *eutrophication.* Eutrophication is very damaging to coral reefs in offshore tropical waters.
- *Protect and nurture biodiversity.* Keep as much nature and biodiversity as you can. Restore what you can't and rebuild it when it is damaged. The planet's priceless biodiversity is under assault and much of it is severely threatened by development, habitat destruction, and global heating. Global collaboration to protect biodiversity began with the adoption of a Framework Convention on Biodiversity at the 1992 Earth Summit. This is now being followed up by annual global meetings to continue this global collaboration. Much of this biodiversity destruction is being driven by organised crime, which is illegally trafficking endangered species and logging valuable trees. And there are many modernist governments who do too little to stop this.

7.5. Exploring Social and Cultural Prosperity and Poverty

Prosperous societies and cultures are ones that function well and are resilient. In postmodern times, social or cultural prosperity are now less likely to be destroyed or impoverished in the interests of economic prosperity. But *what are the essential ingredients of social prosperity and cultural prosperity?* If we know the key elements of these, we can then assess their level of prosperity and implement programs of strategic action to improve or repair them.

7.6. Social Prosperity and Social Poverty

I believe there are five building blocks for uplifting social prosperity. I call these *The Social Prosperity Quintet, or the Social CHOIR* (FUTK17). It can be used to both build and assess the level of social prosperity. The Social Prosperity Quintet's five building blocks are **C**ohesion plus **H**armony plus **O**pportunity plus **I**nclusion plus **R**esilience (CHOIR). These building blocks consist of:

•*Cohesion*: possessing a high commitment to work and act collaboratively to manage and lead change. We must recognise our social interdependence: that if we all do not seek to win together, we all will be more likely to lose together.

•*Harmony*: ensuring that conflict is prevented and abated and a culture of harmony between interest groups, classes, religions, and cultures is nurtured, through shared aspirations and delivering universal win-win outcomes from economic and social development. And harmony will be maximised if respect for those who are different, and *circles of identity* are enlarged to the maximum. Harmony will also be maximised if the three elements of the *Interdependence Trio* are promoted.

•*Opportunity*: maximising access to opportunity and providing the pathways that enable the fulfilment of the aspirations of all members of the community.

•*Inclusion*: supporting and including those who are excluded from opportunity because they suffer from prejudice, disadvantage, or disability. Creating social environments that welcomes those who are excluded.

•*Resilience*: preparing communities to be resilient to, and able to prevent and abate hostile and endangering behaviours and threats, while promoting social cohesiveness.

Imagine the social prosperity-uplifting ways and wares we could innovate to improve social prosperity.

7.7. Cultural Prosperity and Cultural Poverty

There are five components of Cultural Prosperity, which I call The Cultural Prosperity Quintet: Cultural POWER (FUTK18). They are *Participation* plus *Originality* plus *Wealth* plus *Esteem* plus *Resilience*. These five components of Cultural POWER can be used to assess cultural prosperity and cultural poverty so that we can uplift the former and reduce the latter. These five components are:

•*Participation*: this indicates the proportion of the culture that participates in cultural events, programs, and rituals, and that contributes to the creation of new cultural knowledge, artefacts, products, and services. The higher the proportion and the total number of participants the more likely it will be that cultural prosperity will be high.

•*Originality*: refers to the original product being added regularly over time to the culture, thereby contributing to its further development of the culture. Such 'products' include language, literature, music, visual images, the performing and digital arts, and the sciences and technologies. Many cultures both large and small are withering because insufficient new material is being added to maintain the culture's vitality and adaptability. Consequently, these cultures are becoming more vulnerable to social, cultural, and technological disruption.

•*Wealth*: is the contribution to economic prosperity derived from concepts embedded in a culture, in its ideas, language, literature, the visual, performing arts, digital arts, and the sciences. Culture can provide an immense metaphysical source of future economic wealth and prosperity.

•*Esteem*: refers to the degree of respect for a culture shown by other cultures. Modernism carried with it a disrespect for difference, and this led to the massive cultural impoverishment in the past. In Post Modern/emerging Planetist times intercultural esteem is increasing, but not equally for all cultures. Some cultures are still being assaulted, impoverished and left behind because there is insufficient respect for this culture.

•*Resilience*: is the resilience shown by a culture when it faces endangerment or discrimination.

7.8. Sustainable Prosperity

We have outlined the fact that sustainable prosperity is realised when prosperity is uplifted in each of its four domains. It is not realised if, when we shape the future, we create prosperity in one domain while increasing poverty in another domain. In an earlier discussion on sustainability, the concept of sustainable behaviour, of avoiding causing net collateral harm and damage, has also been introduced. Provided collateral harm and damage is repaired or restored, and the cost of doing this is borne by those who caused the harm or damage, some short-term impoverishment can be accepted as within the concept of remaining sustainable provided arrangements are in place to repair, regenerate, and restore past harm and damage.

Change to each of the four prosperities (FUTK15) can collectively interact synergistically or antagonistically. If all four prosperities are simultaneously increasing, the net result will be *synergistic* (2+2=5). If in one or more domain poverty is increasing, the outcomes will be *antagonistic* (2+2=3).

7.9. Sustainable Individualism

Before we leave sustainability behind us, there is one more concept I would like to suggest. Garrett Hardin wrote in *The Tragedy of the Commons* that successful negotiation would increasingly require that the parties negotiate *mutual coercion mutually agreed upon*. He accepted the view that was current in 1967 that in most circumstances development could not occur without causing net collateral damage. We simply did not know how to avoid causing collateral harm, and many also did not even care enough to seek to do this. The concept of *sustainability* (defined as causing zero net collateral damage/harm) was born in the 1980s. Hardin could not have imagined we could ever develop, produce, or consume anything without causing some net collateral harm to our planet.

In Modernist times endless economic growth accompanied by an endless loss of nature and more net damage to ecosystems, societies, and cultures was assumed to be inevitable. However, we are now on our way to produce all the power we need without causing collateral damage and live our lives solely from solar income.

Hardin's belief that coercion of some kind would usually be necessary was reflected in most environmental legislation of the late modern and early postmodern era. Now we are beginning to see that, increasingly, we will be able reach win/win voluntarily and without any need for coercion. This is because enough of us now recognise that whether we like it or not, we have a shared planetary home and a shared future. From now on we will only need *mutual coercion mutually agreed upon* if there is going to be some degree of win/loss. We might then have to negotiate outcomes that produce, at worst, modest and minimal shared loss/loss.

What does individualism need to become if it is to thrive in a 21st century global society that is becoming ever more interdependent and communitarian? I suggest it needs to become a new sort of individualism: *sustainable individualism*. This can be defined as *individual behaviour that causes zero net collateral harm to life and zero net collateral harm to place (FUTK64)*.

We can then aspire to imagine and build innovations, *sustainable behaviour ways and wares,* that would promote and facilitate individual behaviours that cause zero net harm/collateral harm to life and zero net collateral damage to ecosystems, society, or culture. And we can discourage those behaviours that do not. *Sustainable Individualism* can become a behavioural option in the third decade of the 21st century. With this concept in our minds we can imagine, innovate, and build a future that is both less susceptible to, and more resilient to, collateral harm/damage by either individual or collective action. What we will do in future or be prevented from doing will increasingly depend on whether our actions improve, maintain, or reduce sustainable prosperity.

Increasing both liveability and ever more uplifted economic, ecological, social, and cultural prosperity, will be what humanity will be seeking to achieve as the century as the 21st century proceeds. However, right now humanity is now being forced to face and deal with some more urgent matters currently undermining our capacity to focus on these just discussed important matters. We will address these urgent matters in the next chapter.

Chapter 8: Abating and Adapting to Three Global Challenges: Global Pandemics, Global heating and Demographic Ageing

8.1. Three 21st Century Global Challenges

There have been many times throughout human history when human beings have been so endangered that they have had no choice but to collaborate to save themselves. This genetic capacity to respond collaboratively to shared danger is a very important ability which will become increasingly important as we innovate the means to live and flourish together in our emerging 21st century global village. If we perceive we are facing a shared threat such as an invasion, flood, fire, epidemic, or tsunami, we will collaborate, for suddenly what is urgent dominates our thinking. Humanity is genetically programmed to collaborate in such existential emergencies in the single culture communities where it has lived for millennia. But now we are collectively endangered in our emerging multicultural global village. Our history of collaborating in multicultural communities is far from good, but it is improving. Planetists most likely will willingly collaborate, but Modernists may not. We are now facing shared global perils that requires us to act together and thus far humanity is not doing this as well as it might or could.

In this chapter, we are going to deal with three challenges currently facing humanity. Unfortunately, each of these challenges highlight the deep division between those who have 21st century Planetist values and who put planet first, and those with 20th century Modernist mindsets who put nation or tribe first. These Modernists will often go to great lengths to avoid collaborating with those who are different from them or who they do not like, to the point of denying that these threats exist at all.

The first threat we will discuss exposed this division only briefly before, because of its overwhelming magnitude and urgency, we were forced to collaborate at least to a degree. This is, of course, the COVID-19 pandemic. This pandemic is the latest and most severe of several challenges caused by zoonotic diseases, diseases transferred to humans from animals. It has had a major impact on both global human health and global economic prosperity, to the extent that the processes of global integration described in this book have been significantly slowed though not stalled. Our collective response performance was so poor that the result has been not win/lose or win/win but lose/lose for all of us.

In this event, everybody on the planet lost. And of course everybody was on the same side. Even nations such as the DPRK (North Korea) and Myanmar who are not integrated into an ever more globalising interdependent world were threatened and damaged by COVID-19. In this case, there was simply no opting out available to anybody.

There will also be no opting out either with the second issue, which is global heating, a true existential threat! We already know what we must do to first stop and then reverse it. Our knowledge is based on a scientific understanding of its root causes. However, humanity is struggling to collaborate sufficiently to remove this threat before the collateral harm caused by it becomes unstoppable.

In the first two of these challenges, there are powerful vested interests that combine with those carrying obstinate 20th century Modernist mindsets to resist global collaboration and even actively work to undermine it. These include oil and coal companies, conservative politicians, and religious fundamentalists, who act out of self-interest and because they carry frozen *circles of identity*.

The third challenge is demographic ageing. This third threat seems a much more benign issue than global heating or the COVID-19 pandemic. But demographic ageing is challenging humanity now even if many of us do not yet see this challenge as urgent.

We have to perform better in dealing with these three issues. We also need permanent collaborative arrangements to deal with autocrats who bully and oppress their own or other people without starting a war. Our goal must be a collaborative infrastructure and future readiness that ensures these kinds of crises seldom occur again.

So how should we respond to such crises? *The Future Shaper's Quintet (FUTK43)* contains a framework to organise an effective and appropriate global response. *The Four Philosophical Future Shaping Tools (FUTK25)* can also assist us to ask and answer the right questions to help us make wise decisions.

In approaching these global challenges we should also operate as much as we can in future making (leadership) mode rather than future–taking (management) mode. And as well we should use mission-directed strategic modes rather than problem-centred strategic modes. *The Two Strategic Modes* are *Problem-Centred Strategies* and *Mission-Directed Strategies* (FUTK39).

Problem-Centred Strategies involve seeking to remove a threat, a hazard, or a problem, and all too often this means fighting head on the vested interests that are supporters of the existing reality. Bucky Fuller reminds us that this approach is both unwise and enervating. This approach, however, is still used by many NGOs, such as environment groups facing vested coal and gas interests. Seeking to build a new model that makes the old obsolete is the approach of great leadership. The sooner these vested interests realise that an innovation apocalypse is coming at them that will leave them with stranded assets, the better. They will give up themselves.

We will now discuss these three issues of global pandemics, global heating, and demographic ageing, and examine what is the most appropriate way to respond to each of them based on what we have already discussed. These three issues are all, to a significant degree, consequences of humanity's past successes. We became complacent about zoonotic disease pandemics because we believed humanity was on top of the threats posed by infectious diseases, and now we are finding out that bats alone have at least 15,000 Corona viruses, all of which might threaten us. Without fossil fuels the current industrial world would not exist.

8.2. Creating a Pandemic-Safe Planet

The COVID-19 pandemic began in Hubei Province in China, when somebody ate a wild animal obtained in a so-called wet market. COVID-19 is a *zoonotic disease*, which is a disease that has evolved so that it can pass from animal to humans. The causal virus COVID 2 was mostly known only to a few animal virologists. We knew that the COVID 2 virus was the causal agents of another less global damaging pandemic, SARS. Unfortunately, we did not have the foresight to prepare for a second pandemic caused by another strain of the same Corona virus. Some of this was because too many of us were thinking nation first and therefore thought this was somebody else's problem. We changed our minds when we faced the magnitude of the COVID-19 planetary pandemic. Also, with the exception of many scientists and public health experts, we had become complacent about contagious diseases, believing we had for the most part conquered them. Yes, we recognised that some zoonotic diseases could come to us from pets, such as rabies from dogs, or from Creutzfeldt-Jacob

Disease from cows, or Hendra Disease from horses. But there was no serious recognition and preparation for the possibility that the diseases of wild animals could become such a mega threat to human health.

However, humans were entering many more wild places around the planet to mine resources or grow food there. These included many species-rich tropical environments. For example, mining companies were building new operations and building significant human settlements for their workers in ever more remote places, meaning an increasing number of people were coming into closer contact with wild nature and its associated pathogens.

A whole range of new zoonotic diseases began to appear and spread around the world: HIV, Zika, SARS, several forms of encephalitis, and human haemorrhagic fevers such as Ebola and Marburg disease. Many of these diseases originated in Africa, where a number of zoonotic diseases were transferred to humans by consumption of bush meat, in the main the flesh of primates such as monkeys and chimpanzees, and that of fruit bats. And they often spread further either by inter-human contact such as for HIV and COVID-19 or by insects such as the Aedes mosquito as in the case of Zika and Dengue fever and several forms of encephalitis.

The long-term trends of our ever developing and more interconnected interdependent global village and our simultaneously intruding into ecologies we have never or rarely been in before are now combining to endanger the health of all of humanity.

The good news is that compared with the other two challenges discussed in this chapter, the global response needed to stop these pandemics is relatively simple. After the most extraordinary collaborative research project in human history, the first generation of vaccines already exists and is playing an essential role in assisting humanity to stem this pandemic. Coming generations of vaccines could engender immunity to all 15,000+ Corona viruses, possibly including the common cold Corona virus. This will become a model for all research on zoonotic disease threats from now on. This temporary collaboration against a shared existential threat will certainly be transformed into a permanent global health research infrastructure. In this response both virus-specific vaccines will be created and many new antiviral products as well. Some of the measures that need to put in place to deal with this increased zoonotic disease threat include:

- The building of complete databases as a shared global information resource of all potential zoonotic viruses. This would include details of their genomes and relevant antibodies and the building of a permanent global capability to rapidly mass produce vaccines and other antiviral agents on demand from these shared databases and genome banks.
- The development of pandemic protection plans for the whole planet and for each nation and human settlement, and for each major industrial sector.
- The total banning/severe limitation of the consumption of the flesh of all wild animals likely to endanger humanity through zoonotic epidemics or pandemics.
- The accepting of the responsibility by all industries, such as the mining industry, that undertake development projects in remote biodiversity-rich regions, that they must give priority to planet-wide zoonotic disease protection.

8.3. Innovating and Building a Climate-Safe Planet

The biggest single threat to humanity is global heating. This is so serious that our current level of collective endangerment has only been rivalled once before, by the threat of collective nuclear annihilation at the height of the Cold War. The 12th UN Environment Program (UNEP) Global Emissions Gap Report (October 2021) warned that continuing on the current carbon emissions path will lift global temperature by 2.7° Celsius by 2100. It contends that to keep temperatures below 1.5° Celsius above pre-industrial levels would require humanity to halve its current carbon emissions by 2030. The Glasgow Climate Summit's major purpose was to develop and agree upon an adequate response to this UNEP challenging scenario. While it did not achieve all of its goals it was far from a failure. It still progressed the global response agenda enough to give all of us reasons to hope that humanity can successfully meet this challenge. The Glasgow Summit was a good example of *utopian realism* in action, as is the whole global response.

However, the challenge is considerably more complex than just seeking to create a future of net zero carbon emissions, critical as this is. To create a truly climate-safe future humanity will have to innovate and implement the means to simultaneously *decarbonise the atmosphere and the economy,* and *recarbonize the soil and the* land. We also need to accomplish this by 2050 at the latest. If humanity continues to emit carbon dioxide and methane emissions levels at current levels beyond 2030, only 8 years away, it will destabilise our planet's climate by creating an accelerating pathway to ever more extreme weather events and to elevating sea levels, to the point that coral atolls, coastal human settlements and low-lying regions all over the planet will be terminally endangered.

Imagine the *climate safe ways and wares* needed to accomplish this global mission. Those who can assist humanity to accomplish this global mission will do economically well by doing climate good.

The planet began to warm because of human activity at the birth of the industrial revolution in the late 18th century. This was primarily driven by the massive increase in the production and use of fossil fuels, first coal and later oil and then natural gas. This increased use of fossil fuels has been accompanied by major changes in land use. Much the world's forests have been cleared for food and fibre production. And some of this food we are producing is causing other problems as well. Cattle and sheep, for example, generate the climate changing gas methane in their rumens, one of their four stomachs. Methane is 28 times more deleterious, molecule for molecule, for global heating than carbon dioxide. And of course, the high rate of land clearing of the rainforests and rangelands that sequester massive amounts of atmospheric carbon continues.

Humanity has become so powerful it has significantly disturbed our planetary environment. In recognition of this new sobering capability, our current epoch has been given a new name, the *Anthropocene*, which was born just 250 years ago. It replaced 12,000 years of stable climate, *the Holocene*, which facilitated the birth and evolution of human civilization. Just some of the consequences of humanity's increased carbon emissions since the birth of the *Anthropocene* are worsening extreme weather events such as longer droughts and bigger floods, rising sea levels, melting polar, oceanic, and alpine ice, the last of which that will reduce and destabilise the flow of many of the world's major rivers, the decimation of coral reefs and extinction of many more species of flora and fauna.

These changes could collectively generate large numbers of environmental refugees, disrupt food production patterns, and make some urban habitats less liveable and even unliveable. Humanity has about two decades to turn these global heating trends around and redirect the trajectory back towards a cooling planet and a stable global climate, a climate safe planet.

Despite their small size, the island nations of the Pacific are highly visible on the planetary stage in global warming discussions. They are already thinking planet first. They have no choice other than to do so. Unfortunately, others are not so ready. For example, this appears to be the case for those nations living on the plain beneath what has been called the Roof of the World. This is an expression used for the ice and snow covered high region also known as High Asia, which covers the Tibetan plateau, the Himalayas, the Pamirs, the Tian Shan and the Altai Mountains. Throughout history this has been a barrier to collaboration and a cause of separateness, not togetherness. This separation suited a nation-first 20th century world, but this is not enough for a planet-first 21st century world. High Asia is the common water source for the many mighty rivers that flow through the plains of North, East, South-East, South, and North-West Asia. They include the Yangtze Kiang, Hwang Ho, Si Kiang, Brahmaputra, Ganges, Indus, Mekong, Amur, Yenisei, Ob, Amu Darya and the Syr Darya rivers. Global warming is endangering the stability of the flow of all these rivers, thereby threatening massive economic and ecological dislocation in many places including China, Bangladesh, India, and Pakistan, and much of SE Asia, a total of 2.5 billion people in all. Yet the fate of The Roof of the World is presently absent from global climate change discussions. For the most part these nations are still thinking nation first and seem unwilling to discuss their need for regional collaboration on global heating. They need to begin to collaborate as the Pacific Islanders do. From now on they could see the Roof of the World not as their history as plain dwellers have seen it, but as a planetary treasure and shared heritage, a reason for future purposeful 21st century Planetist ecological restoration and climate protection collaboration. It is in their shared interest, and in the planet's interest as well. Unfortunately, there are still many places where the planetary consciousness is not where it needs to be to meet this global heating challenge.

8.3.1 Decarbonizing the Atmosphere

To create a climate-safe future. Humanity should seek to restore the carbon levels and distribution patterns that prevailed during the Holocene. To achieve this, it will need to reduce atmospheric carbon levels from 420 ppm (parts per million) carbon dioxide equivalents today to approximately 300 ppm. This current atmospheric level of 420 ppm is the highest it has been for 800,000 years. If we can restore the *Holocene* atmospheric carbon levels, we can recreate the climate of the *Holocene*. If humanity can achieve and maintain an atmospheric carbon of level 300–350 ppm level, it will be able to thrive on a climate-safe planet indefinitely.

Because we have burned so much fossil fuel, we have released additional carbon into the atmosphere, carbon that was sequestered beneath the Earth's surface for millions of years. We must now remove this extra carbon by transferring it back to the land. We must now recarbonize the soil and the oceans with biological carbon, carbon stored in organic matter, plants, animals, and microbes. We will need to innovate over time other *ways and wares* to both reduce carbon levels in the atmosphere and transfer this carbon into carbon sequestered in the soil.

The greatest means we can use to lower atmospheric carbon is through photosynthesis. If humanity doubled the photosynthetic capacity of the planet through elevating forest, rangeland and oceanic photosynthesis, this could be accomplished. This additional photosynthetic capacity is equivalent to adding 3 trillion trees to the planet, double the current number of trees. Eight of the geographically largest nations on the planet are Russia, China, Canada, Brazil, the USA, Australia, India, and Argentina. These eight nations could possibly achieve this goal among themselves. All of them are members of the G20, so the G20 could unilaterally take on this global responsibility, thereby setting an example to other nations, including those in the equatorial belt. Hopefully, this would encourage them to restore and regenerate rainforest ecosystems and benefit financially through carbon trading by sequestering more atmospheric carbon in rainforests. As these developed nations caused most of the current climate crisis, it is appropriate that the G20 leads the way in reducing atmospheric carbon.

This is what I call *mining the sky* for carbon, the direct removal of carbon from the atmosphere. We can accomplish this by placing a price on atmospheric carbon sufficient to achieve this outcome. Landholders, First Nations people and rural populations everywhere could then generate income for themselves by providing this atmospheric decarbonization service for the planet. And if, as I expect, meat and milk will increasingly be manufactured in factories most of the rangelands and other land currently used for cattle and sheep production could be regenerated to increase global photosynthesis and biodiversity.

We can add to this by developing other industrial *atmospheric decarbonisation ways and wares*. As well as utilizing photosynthesis (see below), humanity can innovate what we can call *atmospheric decarbonization ways and wares*, other new innovations to *mine the sky* for carbon. And we can store carbon mined from the sky into various places: into plant, microbial, or soil carbon; into minerals such as limestone; in carbon materials such as biochar or bio-graphene; and even industrial diamonds. Imagine a carbon rush into the sky, a 21st century equivalent of a gold rush. And like any gold rush, such a carbon rush could uplift prosperity wherever and whenever people mine carbon from the sky. As necessity is the mother of invention, I believe the human race will invent increasingly better means to mine the sky for carbon.

8.3.2 Decarbonizing economies

The Glasgow COP21 Climate Summit in October 2021 has set the decarbonizing challenge humanity must meet in the next generation: we must fully decarbonize the global economy by 2050 and achieve at least half of this by 2030. There are some nations, current high carbon intensive economies, that think they will not be able to accomplish this feat and want perhaps another 10 years to accomplish this outcome. China and India are two such nations. They are committed to zero net carbon emission future, but are seeking support from the rest of the world for their requiring another decade to accomplish this outcome. As discussed above, these two nations are very vulnerable to and endangered by the destabilization of their major rivers, so they will have to be as committed to achieving long-term climate security as any other nation will be.

I believe that the decarbonisation innovation and application challenge is now so urgent that humanity will develop the means to accomplish this in time, just as it did to meet the challenges posed by the COVID-19 pandemic, when it developed vaccines within 15 months, instead of taking the decade usually required. However, it is clear that humanity must do much of this work within the next decade. In order to do this, I suggest humanity needs to establish a new mission-directed, proactive narrative for realizing a positive energy scenario for our global future. We should not rely only on a problem-centred, reactive mission designed to remove a negative energy base.

A climate safe planet will be a reality when humanity achieves a goal first articulated by Richard Buckminster Fuller in *Cosmic Costing*. He said that humanity should seek to *live within perpetual solar income.* In the 21st century we will imagine and innovate large numbers of *ways and wares* to *live solely on perpetual solar income.* Global markets and investment patterns are already shifting towards building a liveable, climate and pandemic safe global village powered by the sun.

I also believe that emerging Planetist humanity is putting into practice another one of Buckminster Fuller's suggestions: that we should avoid fighting with the now rapidly diminishing numbers of recalcitrant Modernists who remain defenders of fossil fuels, and instead get on with innovating and building the *new* solar powered future, thereby making fossil fuels obsolete.

As we seek to decarbonize the economy, we will stop propping up the coal and oil industries with subsidies. Currently, in the G20 countries alone taxpayers subsidize the oil and coal industries by more than $500 billion per year. Regrettably, in October 2021 the G20 refused to remove government subsidisation of the fossil fuel industry. This was probably to buy some time to transform their current fossil-fuelled industrial bases. However, any government facing a budget deficit will begin to wind back these subsidies. And this will be supported by progressive public opinion, with its belief that we should be prioritising planet over nation Without subsidies these soon-to-be yesteryear industries will quickly disappear as an increasing amount of investment goes into decarbonizing economies.

This investment will not go into the nuclear power industry. It is, of course, carbon free but it is too dangerous to be a plausible alternative: we cannot risk another Chernobyl or Fukushima. It is also more differentially expensive to produce compared with solar power.

An increasing number of us know that we can now access all the energy we need from the sun, and store and transport this energy without polluting our planetary home. For another few years there will be a few modernist political and corporate leaders who will continue to believe that fossil fuels should play a continuing role in our energy futures. Carbon will continue to be used in other industrial futures, including becoming the material resource for a carbon materials future which we will discuss further in Chapter 9. We will soon learn that to burn carbon for any reason at all will be a gross waste of precious resources. From now on public attitudes will harden further against those who continue to offer us energy solutions based on a continuing role for fossil fuels.

We will also first discourage and then ban any activity in the economy that is climate endangering, such as those that enable the leakage of fugitive carbon, particularly as methane, into the atmosphere. This means we will soon need to abolish all these sites, such as natural gas production sites, urban landfill sites, peat production sites, and carbon waste to energy facilities. In October 2021 the COP26 Glasgow Climate Change Summit agreed to reduce global methane emissions by 30% by 2030. A number of high emitting methane nations refused to sign. However, this decision gives methane a new pariah status as a gas that is toxic to the planet's climate. By 2040 all methane emissions will be banned.

An increasing number of people will understand that still another reason why it is irresponsible to burn carbon into carbon dioxide or turn it into methane is because we should create a circular economy for all carbon to recarbonize our carbon starved soils. All industrial activity that releases carbon into the atmosphere will either disappear or be modified so it produces zero net carbon emissions by 2050 at the very latest.

Energy produced from solar sources is growing massively and it has very low recurrent costs of production. Coal is already uncompetitive as a source of electric power. Natural gas production for energy, an industry that is a major source of fugitive methane emissions, will decline and disappear by 2040. Petroleum-driven transport is dying and being replaced by hydrogen powered, ammonia powered, or electric powered vehicles. It is likely that after 2040 petroleum driven transport will be banned in most parts of the world.

We can already produce all the energy we need without using any form of carbon as a resource. We can store it as electrical energy in batteries such as lithium ion batteries, as hydro energy in water storages, or as zero carbon-containing gaseous and liquid fuels such as hydrogen or ammonia. We are now innovating *solar energy ways and wares* in many forms. These include *ways and wares* from the following solar sources: direct solar thermal, direct solar electric, wind-driven solar power, and terrestrial hydro and marine hydro (ocean currents). And to this we can perhaps add some lunar sources of energy such as *tidal and wave power ways and wares*.

To solar electrical energy and lunar electrical energy, we can add solar and lunar sourced hydrogen power and green hydrogen, produced by the electrolysis of water to become a transportable form of energy, both as hydrogen or converted into ammonia using new membrane or electro-chemical technology. Ammonia is a safer means of transporting energy than hydrogen and is a denser source of energy, so it can be used in creating a solar-resourced aviation and aerospace industrial future. As natural gas as an energy source declines there will be numerous former natural gas pipelines that can be used to transmit energy as hydrogen or ammonia. We should be seeking not to use carbon in any form of energy production, so we will not need to capture and store any carbon produced generation process but only from activities that directly seek to decarbonize the atmosphere. In turn, this means that *green hydrogen* (hydrogen sourced from solar powered electric water electrolysis) will make *blue hydrogen* (hydrogen sourced from fossil fuels) obsolete.

Innovators in research institutes, commercial corporations and governments everywhere are already imagining and building a low carbon future to replace the declining carbon dependent energy sector. Natural gas pipelines such as the Nord Stream 2 linking Russia and Germany continue to be built. However, public sentiment towards Nord Stream 2 between its commencement in 2011 and its completion in 2020-2022 has shifted so much that I believe the pipeline's developers will be left with a very expensive stranded asset. But perhaps there might be good news for its investors in that, as indicated above, their investment might be used to transport solar-sourced hydrogen or ammonia instead of natural gas.

The world oceans can also play a major role in sequestering atmospheric carbon. Sea grass and other forms of marine photosynthesis can fix much more carbon that the world's rainforests. The fact that the world's oceans are not so dominated by nations should mean that we will be able to come to a quicker global agreement on sea carbon sequestration.

There are other industrial sectors including the waste management and primary industries, and activities relating to land management more generally, where the global heating prognosis is less promising, and there is more work to do. It is in these sectors that new practices and innovations (*ways and wares respectively*) that can make a difference will be needed to create outcomes that are as significant as are many of the zero carbon innovations in the energy, transportation, manufacturing and mining industrial sectors.

When we seek to manage land and soil to ensure they are part of the global heating solution rather than part of the global heating problem, we are seeking to work with nature in ways that do not harm its complex systems, but instead enhance and uplift their functionality. We need to be very aware of this complexity as we innovate new *climate safe ways and wares.* To do this we need to recarbonize the land and the soil simultaneously as we decarbonise the atmosphere and the economy so that, over time, we can mimic the carbon distribution arrangements present in the Holocene.

8.3.3 Recarbonizing the land and the soil

While most people know the story of how fossil-fuelled energy is a significant cause of global heating many are not so aware of how humanity's exploitation of the soil during the Anthropocene has contributed to global heating. A consequence of this exploitation is that carbon that was in the soil in the Holocene is now in the atmosphere. In the Holocene it was mostly in the right places, the right forms, and in the right amounts to sustain a stable climate. There was then approximately 300 ppm of carbon dioxide equivalents in the atmosphere and up to 5% carbon in the soil. Now it is respectively 420 ppm and less than 1%. Now while much of this extra carbon has come from the fossil-fuelled energy, transportation, manufacturing, and mining sectors, much also comes from misuse of the soil.

Holocene farmers were carbon-conscious farmers. They kept and even increased carbon in the soil. Then Justus von Liebig invented chemical water-soluble fertilisers in 1840 and John Bennet Lawes invented superphosphate in 1842. These two innovative giants created a new era of high productivity food and fibre production, but these inventions collaterally harmed the natural biodynamic (organic) systems used until that time. Anthropocene farmers have virtually mined the soil of carbon, decarbonizing the soils through over-cultivation and other poor agricultural practices. These carbon poor soils are now more structurally brittle, less fertile, less water permeable, and less drought resilient.

The decarbonization trend can and must be reversed. The amount of carbon held in soils, forests, rangelands, mangroves, marine sea grass, marine phytoplankton and algae can be massively increased, and it is here that we can store the carbon that humanity recovers from the atmosphere. Plants and other photosynthetic organisms are both *atmospheric decarbonisation wares* and *land and soil recarbonisation wares*. But we also need more humans who are not only consciously developing more *atmospheric decarbonisation ways and wares* but also innovating new *soil and land recarbonisation ways* and wares such as reforesting, rewilding forests, rangelands, tropical and sub-tropical savannah, tundra, and alpine ecosystems all over the planet.

We can recarbonize the soils by such things as mimicking the practices of the indigenous peoples of the Amazon basin who invented *terra preta* soils by returning organic waste and burned carbon to the soil. We are already developing new *ways and wares* to recycle carbon derived from food green waste back in the soils, most desirably in carbon-rich biological fertilisers customized for that purpose, a 21st century form of *terra preta*. We could eliminate all carbon waste in landfill dumps all over the planet, which would have the additional advantage of reducing global methane emissions by more than 15%. We are already learning how to do this on an industrial scale sufficient to meet the planetary need.

Many new innovations will be needed to realize these aspirations. But the net outcome of these innovations will be a highly productive agriculture, horticulture and forestry that can continue forever. We will do this because we have no other choice. As more people live in cities the carbon and other waste generated in cities will continue to grow and will need to be met with ever larger and more efficient treatment facilities for turning waste into soil.

One sign that we are on the way is that in November 2021 the COP26 Glasgow Climate Change Summit signed and launched a major new program to end deforestation by 2030. This was signed by 124 nations. Most rainforest rich nations, including Brazil, Columbia, Ecuador, the two nations occupying the Congo Basin, Indonesia, and Papua New Guinea, are signatories. The world is changing faster and more positively than many Planetists would have dared to hope. This will be the first of many such agreements.

There are still recalcitrant conservative Modernist populists who believe it is beyond humanity's capability to innovate and build a solar powered global society and village. Solar energy sceptics, they want to continue with fossil fuelled and nuclear power deep into the 21st century. Many will go to their graves believing what they believe. But their more highly educated children will not follow them. I believe the wisest strategy to promote a climate safe future is to avoid fighting those seeking to keep alive the declining carbon-emitting industrial past and instead dedicate their time and energy to building the new solar-based industrial future that will render it obsolete.

The coal and oil industries and the politicians and people who still support them constitute the last stand for Modernity in an emerging Planetist society. Like the tobacco industry, they know their industrial death is imminent. They might try to buy time to postpone their extinction and make some quick money while doing it. They might continue to construct their own dishonest narratives and fund support groups denying that global heating is real. It is important to recognize that the issues of the three challenges mentioned in this chapter are the major political issues used by modernist populist politicians to grow their political bases. All these people will be shown to be on the wrong side of history, for they are actively seeking to undermine global and collaborative efforts on these critical issues.

8.4. Demographic Ageing in an Emerging Global Village

As the combination of globalisation and mass education lifts an increasing number of people out of poverty and into the educated middle classes, the number of children born to each woman is decreasing. More educated women are choosing to have fewer children for a number of reasons. Most of these educated women and their partners want to stop at two or three children and many prefer fewer or even no children. In most developed countries the number of children born to each woman is already below the replacement rate of 2.1 children. The principal determinant of whether a population is stabilising or declining, and thereby causing demographic ageing, is the status of and education levels of women. The higher the status and education levels of women in a culture the fewer children they will have.

Current projections are that the population of our planet will cease to grow around 2070 and stabilise at about 9-10 billion; that is, about 60% more than our current population of approximately 6 billion. There are some who believe that the peak will be reached a decade or two later, but I believe that, through the faster than anticipated spread of mass education and the spread of prosperity through globalisation, 2070 is a more likely peak date. After that the planet's population will begin to decline.

There are many consequences of this trend. First, there is an ageing of populations: the mean age of humanity is rising. Many developed countries are already ageing at significant rates. Many of these nations are investing in automation. Robotics is now a mainstream component of their industrial future. Much of this automation seeks to replace workers who are no longer there. Japan leads this field, as it was the first nation to begin to age. It did not choose to open its doors to an increased migrant intake. It now has a declining population, and Japan's pathway to a more automated future will be followed by many other nations.

Japan is a global leader in robotics and automation because necessity has been the mother of invention. First, robots are enabling high industrial productivity to continue with ever fewer human workers. Second, robots are enabling many older people and people with disability to enjoy more comfortable and fulfilled lives. Home robots are already assisting us to do chores such as cleaning our homes and supporting the aged in many other ways.

In the next ten years, robots will enter almost every sphere of our existence to make our lives more comfortable, to keep us free to choose how and where we live for longer, and to live more productive lives. In an ageing population people will be able to continue to work for longer because they will be assisted by ever-increasing levels of automation.

This ageing society will slowly abolish the concept of compulsory retirement. More people will choose to work for longer in terms of years but shorter in terms of days and hours per week. As work becomes smarter, wisdom will formally enter the 21st century workplace. Elderhood as a concept will be reborn both in terms of social participation such as through activities like maturing our youth in *Adolescent Initiation* programs and providing workplace mentoring. There will be a new generation of *Wisdom Workers* in workplaces everywhere. This has major implications for governments in terms of social welfare, incomes, and superannuation public policy.

8.4.1 Demographic ageing and migration

However, demographic ageing is also influencing a major global change most people do not normally associate with it. This demographic ageing is now occurring in an emerging global village where people no longer feel that their mobility needs to be restricted by the national borders that have constrained the movement of people in past eras. As astronaut Bill Anders said when he took his famous *Earthrise* photograph, 'Once-distant places appeared inseparably close. Borders that once rendered division vanished.'

Of course, these borders do still exist but people's attitude to them has changed and is continuing to do so. These borders are becoming ever more porous artifices in an emerging global village. Whether they can do so legally or not, more people are feeling more entitled to seek opportunity wherever they can find it. And the more highly educated they are, the more they will feel this and the more they will expect they will be welcomed when they seek to migrate to a new nation to live and work. An increasing number of people believe that they have a right to live anywhere they choose to live.

Two generations ago, very few people would have considered it possible to choose to live anywhere one liked. And most people were happy to live in their homeland and not seek opportunity elsewhere. This is a revolution that backpacker tourism has significantly contributed to and shaped. But in an emerging global village with ever more declining population growth rates, to be followed by increasingly declining populations in absolute terms, there will be growing workplace vacancies and ever-increasing labour mobility to fill these vacancies in coming decades. This will be slowed by the introduction of robots, but artificial intelligence will never be able to replace natural human intelligence. All workers will become more valuable. In Chapter 11, I will discuss a consequence of this change as it suggests that in the 21st century all work will become professionalised. We will discuss human and artificial intelligence in Chapter 9.

As our wealth comes increasingly from metaphysical resources, our universities and other tertiary learning institutions will provide increasingly powerful passports for future success in our emerging global village. Irrespective of where they were born, ambitious people will want to join a global mobile workforce by taking their skills, their intellectual property and their brainpower to anywhere these can be used. Within two decades, global integration will produce an ever-growing internationalised global workforce.

One consequence of this which has already been touched on is that this will increase the need for a global language, and so far Esperanto appears to be the best candidate for the job. The potential global economic benefit derived from all humanity gaining access to a shared global second language in a global economy increasingly based on metaphysical resources would be massive. Every university and vocational learning institute in our emerging global village could attach a core course in this global language in all professional and personal development programs. Over a longer time, this language could be taught in every primary school on the planet.

As population growth rates further decrease, labour mobility arrangements will be increasingly introduced into more international trade treaties. More people are seeking to move even if the legal regimes controlling migration still remain mostly in the hands of individual nation states. An increasing number of demographically ageing nation states will soon realise that automation cannot fully replace people and they will seek new arrangements enabling them to fulfil their workforce needs. I am certain that, provided these planetary migrants have Planetist values and they can communicate effectively because they have appropriate language capabilities, migrants will be increasingly welcomed by most cultures in most nation states.

Over time, the legal arrangements that facilitate the ever-freer movement of labour will be put in place. This is the only realistic means to enable a global village to function well. Trying to prevent the ever-freer movement of people in a world that is becoming ever more globally integrated will become increasingly futile.

Any member of the European Union can now live and work anywhere in the European Union. In Chapter 2, I related the collapse in populations in some of the nations of Eastern Europe as their educated young emigrate west because of the opportunities offered by European integration. And one of the reasons they are mostly welcomed there is because these Western European nations have stagnant or declining populations because they are demographically ageing, and these immigrants possess the skills they need to improve their prosperity.

Europe is showing the way to the rest of the world. Young well-educated people will seek to live and work in places that best support their aspirations, and more of them will be willing to expand their *circles of identity* to ensure they can succeed in cultures that are foreign to them but also offer a more promising future than they have at home. Increasingly better education in the next decades will raise more people into situations where what they know and are able to do can open new horizons of possibility for them.

As population growth further stagnates in more places, this movement of people will increase further in the decades ahead. And as the 21st century proceeds, metaphysically based wealth will increasingly grow and the demand for more skilled and knowledgeable people will further increase. Over the coming decades, the current European patterns of labour mobility will become more universal and this voluntary movement of people will continue to grow.

In the short term, many of these people will face opposition from Modernist populists, many of whom dislike those who are culturally, racially, or religiously different. The transition in some places will be challenging and even traumatic. The stresses of European migration have been eased by the fact that most of the people involved are European Christians, but in other places racial or religious based opposition from the less well-educated will most likely cause many confrontations. However, by approximately 2050, a global village will have evolved that is borderless to the movement of trade and people. The children of those who resist change will themselves become better educated and will want to participate in and benefit from these long-term trends.

Those with Planetist values will both make the most of these migratory moves and accept the arrival of foreign Planetists. However, if a would-be immigrant has Modernist values and is hostile to difference, recipient nations will see them as threats and oppose their entry. If these migrants are perceived by recipient nations to be likely to uplift the *six pillars of liveability* in their new home nations, they will be welcomed. If they threaten liveability by, for example, lessening national security or harmony, they will not be welcomed.

Many developing countries in Africa, the Middle East and Latin America have populations that are still growing. They will do so for at least a decade or two more until their populations begin to stabilise under the combined effects of globalisation and education. Many of these nations are still not doing enough, for a host of reasons, to entice educated people to remain at home and not emigrate. Eastern Europe has already lost a large part of its educated population to Western Europe. This is because some of their governments still carry frozen yesteryear modernist mindsets, are corrupt, or both, and because they do not implement 21st century public policies designed to entice their best and brightest young Planetists to stay at home.

8.4.2. Involuntary migration and refugee futures

Thus far, we have discussed the voluntary movement of people. But of course there are also involuntary movements, of people we usually call *refugees*. At the beginning of the third decade of the 21st century, much of the significant voluntary pattern of migration is being submerged and masked by the plight of refugees. The only thing these voluntary and involuntary movements have in common is that both involve the movement of people. The two processes are quite different.

In the case of the second form of people movement, namely refugee movement, Modernist populists in migrant recipient nations will, over time, begin to recognise that their Modernist abuse of those who are different will lead to them being cast as Planetary Pariahs, and in some cases this pariah status might accrue to their whole nation. They will also learn that any continuing confrontation based on race and cultural difference can also lead to a reduction of economic prosperity as those who are the sources of their metaphysical wealth will emigrate to live and work in more tolerant and less threatening places.

Importantly, refugees everywhere are usually driven to migrate from their homes by danger: by wars, natural disasters including global heating and its results, political oppression, ethnic cleansing and intolerance towards them by others. Governments can collaborate to seek removal of the circumstances that caused many refugees to involuntarily leave their original homes in the first place, and to create the conditions that will give these emigrants the opportunities and the quality of life they seek. So governments seeking to encourage their citizens to return (or stay) at home will need to work on uplifting *the six pillars of liveability* in their own nations, and build education systems and work cultures that nurtures metaphysical resourced prosperity.

Another potential major cause of future refugees is global heating. As a result of this, many developing nations have become subject to increased droughts (as in Kenya, Somalia, and Ethiopia), to rising sea levels and to extreme weather events (as in Bangladesh). These nations will need special attention to make them more resilient to these events. Many developing nations have a significant proportion of their populations living in climate vulnerable rural areas. Their agriculture is already more vulnerable to greater and longer droughts, less plentiful and reliable rainfall, sea rise, and extreme weather events, including more destructive cyclonic events and flooding.

There is a real danger that a global heating induced refugee crisis could be triggered in the next two decades if humanity's response to global heating is inadequate. Either these potential refugees will be supported in their own countries, or they will begin arriving at the borders of developed nations. Mikhail Gorbachev, a very far-sighted man, established the Environmental NGO *Green Cross* because he was particularly concerned about a possible future global heating generated refugee crisis.

Refugee crises, like all global crises, cannot be solved at the national level. It is a global issue that requires a global perspective and a global response. Under Donald Trump, the USA wanted to solve its refugee problems by putting a wall along the border with Mexico. Such approaches are totally yesteryear. These issues will not be solved by the USA alone or even through a collaboration between the USA and Mexico. It will require a continent-wide collaborative process involving most of the countries in the Americas. In future this approach will increasingly apply everywhere.

8.4.3 Moving people in a global village

Most of those who voluntarily seek to migrate are not fear-driven refugees. They are hope-filled ambitious people seeking economic and social opportunities not currently available to them at home but existing in nations whose populations have stagnated, or nations with economic and industrial structures that are seeking workers with the skills and knowledge they need.

This book has discussed the rise of *Modernist populism* that opposes the arrival of both voluntary immigrants and involuntary refugees. Clearly, both voluntary and involuntary migration have already triggered, and could make even worse, much political discord in many migrant recipient nations, particularly between Modernists and Planetists in those nations. Voluntary migrants who are seeking opportunities in other nations will go wherever they can find opportunities to realise their aspirations. They will test the increasingly archaic systems of nation-state-based immigration controls to their limits. However, in the next decade it will become easier to move around the world as more nations reach the stage of population stagnation. People and their brainpower will become ever more precious and increasingly welcomed by more recipient nations as the century progresses and as their populations decline further.

In the short term, the relative proportions of Modernists and Planetists in any recipient nation and the degree of demographic ageing will determine how welcoming its citizens will be to both high-knowledge, high-skilled migrants, and to refugees. Nations with stagnant or declining populations and a high proportion of Planetists are more likely to welcome both. Planetists in these nations recognise that global issues such as international migration and global heating need to be met by planetary-wide collaboration between nations. These people are *communitarians* in this regard. On the other hand, *Modernist populists* and ultra-nationalists are nationally individualistic in their approach. They believe that nation states should keep the primary control over the movement of people. They are more likely to be hostile to anybody arriving at their national borders and to lock out all or most of those seeking entry. And they will be willing to treat refugees as criminals and with cruelty and brutality.

From now on, an increasing number of international trade agreements will contain clauses enabling the free migration of people so that they can move to places where they can best create fruitful lives for themselves and contribute better to the uplifting of national and global prosperity and liveability in the coming decades. People movement everywhere will increasingly mimic the processes of the European Union. During the next three decades the mobility of people around our emerging global village will become as free and fair as the movement of goods, services and finance has become in the past two decades.

In an emerging 21st century, nations with stagnant and ageing populations will begin to recognise that metaphysical wealth, the brainpower and skills possessed by people, will become the most important route to increased prosperity. Those nations with the best education systems and the best research and development capabilities will be the ones that best prosper. The world is increasingly turning its back of the concept that wealth mostly comes out of the ground or from the soil. If the planet's national governments want to collectively create a future where sustainable prosperity and liveability are maximised, they must promote the most effective use of the talent and skill of all their people, and it is in their interests to facilitate all people living and working in places where they can best contribute to lifting overall global economic prosperity. Knowledgeable and capable would-be migrants should not be put into gulags because they are different but treated with the respect they deserve; they should be rewarded because they are bold and ambitious enough to choose to seek a more fulfilled life elsewhere. In an interdependent 21st century, migration can be win/win/win for recipient nations, the planetary economy, and the migrants who are seeking to migrate to a place that is better for them.

In coming decades voluntary migration will increase further, and involuntary migration (refugees) will decrease, hopefully to zero. At present, both voluntary and involuntary migration are part of 21st century reality. The crises and dramas caused by refugee migration and the resistance to this by holders of modernist populist values and by the political parties supporting them have masked and diverted attention from the massive global people movements currently occurring in voluntary migration. However, the world is also transforming itself from a culturally confronting and competitive win/lost modernist past into a more harmonious collaborative planetist, win/win future. As educational levels continue to rise, as wealth is increasingly drawn from metaphysical resources and as birth rates continue to decline realizing the best possible fit between any employment-seeking person and their optimal employment will be increasingly sought by individuals, communities, and whole nations. This will be irrespective of where both are currently geographically situated. However, Planetist attitudes will need to be embedded in everyone for this transformation to be successfully and completed. I believe this transformation will be complete by 2050, where we will witness a world with borders totally open to goods, services and people.

As for involuntary migration (refugees), there are reasons to believe this will first slow and then end in the mid 21st century. The rise in democracy will become unstoppable despite the attempts by the Putins and Trumps of the world to keep their hands on the steering wheels of political power. We have already discussed the shift to a democratic future in autocratic nations places such as China in Chapter 2. The world will see ever fewer political refugees as the century proceeds. This is because the world will also slowly create a climate safe future with climate safe food production. We will increasingly be producing food in factories, thereby breaking the highly climate-vulnerable nexus between food production and land and oceanic resources. More industries will develop in rural areas everywhere and these areas become less dependent on food production for their economic viability. Our food will be increasingly plant and microbe sourced. For these reasons there will be fewer and eventually no climate change generated refugees. Mining, naturally, will remain rural-based but it will be designed to cause zero net harm in a world seeking to become ever more liveable.

Over time, we can expect most of those who resist global integration, including the increasingly free movement of people, goods and services around the world, to give up. And if they don't, their children, who will more likely be better educated than their parents and will seek to live and work in another part of our emerging global village, will not carry such hostility to change. The integrative transformation of our global society will continue for decades. Some predicted that global challenges, such the COVID-19 pandemics, or Putin-initiated tribal wars, would stop this integration. They won't, although they might, for a while, slow it down.

The shared challenges posed by globalisation, demographic ageing, and voluntary and involuntary migration can only really be solved by global cooperation, just as global heating and zoonotic pandemics must be dealt with by global collaboration. There are still some recalcitrant Modernist nationalist governments guided by Modernist populist leaders and political parties that oppose collaboration being used to solve our shared global problems. However, their influence will first decline and then disappear in the next two decades.

Finally, there could be another significant consequence of demographic ageing: a potential peace dividend. Wars were once initiated by old men, who were quite happy to send young men, of which there were plenty, to war. And young men, particularly poorly educated young men, were once willing and even excited to go to war.

Now, all life is more precious. Mothers with two children are treasuring them more than mothers once treasured their six or seven children 100 years ago, and parents and governments are, as well, investing much more in educating their young than they were 100 years ago. The concept that young men can be used as cannon fodder and be sacrificed without question was senseless and callous then and is even more reprehensible today.

In fact, we have created automated and smart warfare because the numbers of young available to be sacrificed in war are both fewer and more valued. Even the most hawkish politician or general wants to maximise the chances of winning a war at minimal human cost. The bottom line is that an ageing society with a better-educated population makes war both less likely and less costly to human life if it occurs.

Will an ageing planet be a more risk adverse and less entrepreneurial planet? The traditional view is that older people are more risk adverse and less entrepreneurial and less adaptable than young people and, consequentially, ageing societies might stagnate economically. This book is dedicated to ensuring that as we demographically age our cultures do not become less adventurous, less adaptable, and less entrepreneurial. With the right mindsets, concepts, and tools we can all be much more effective shapers of our own and other's future than we are now! Just as we have automation to replace workers who are no longer there, we need mindsets, concepts, and tools to ensure we keep and even grow more vitality and entrepreneurship in people of all ages, as there will be fewer young people to refresh us with their vitality.

We will all thrive better if we learn to nurture our own vitality and entrepreneurship throughout our whole lives. Imagine *entrepreneurship development ways and wares,* including those based on *leadership development* (purposeful future making), and *adaptability uplifting ways and wares.* Such innovations can empower us to be 21st century successful irrespective of our age! We will discuss realising this outcome in the next three chapters.

Chapter 9: Renewing the Agents of Change: Innovation and Technology Futures

9.1. Renewing the Agents of Change

In every chapter of this book, one constant reality discussed has been that we are living in a world of continuing and relentless change. This means we must change as well. This is why this book offers a new curriculum to better comprehend the patterns of rapid change currently operating and to enable all of us to be our own futurist.

Three of these patterns are the birth of the paradigm of Planetism; the changing nature of globalisation from Modernist-informed cowboy globalisation to Planetist-informed cosmonaut globalisation; and humanity's imminent cohabitation in an interdependent global village. Once we become aware that these trends are real and continuing, we can consider what we can and even must do to ensure we can thrive rather than just survive in this emerging 21st century reality. In the next four chapters, we will examine what we can do to reimagine, renovate, and reconstruct some of our existing future-shaping processes to ensure we give ourselves our best shot at being successful in this emerging world. These four future shaping processes are:

- Innovation and technology
- Education and learning
- Work and careers
- Economic management and capital investment

9.2. Social and Technological Innovation: Which Drives Which?

Karl Marx argued that technological change was a big driver of social change. On the other hand, Max Weber, the founder of sociology, believed that society shapes technology. He argued that social change, driven by the emergence of new ideas and new thinking, was the main driver of technological change. Personally, I am more Weberist than Marxist.

There are many who assume Marx's viewpoint is correct and that technology drives change, who are fearful that technological change will decimate many current jobs and careers. I call this thinking *Negative Technological Determinism*. There are also many who hold the opposite view, who believe that emerging technology is a positive driver of change. I call this perspective *Positive Technological Determinism.*

Some futurists believe that future studies should primarily focus on observing emerging technological change and predicting its impacts on society. I am not one of these. I believe that if we see the world through Weberist rather Marxist lenses we will empower ourselves to deal with change much more effectively than if we don't.

It is true that technological change can be very disruptive to our lives. The industrial revolution beginning in the late 18th century dislocated countless families and friends. Human organisation previously based on the extended family has shifted to being based upon the much more vulnerable nuclear family. More recently, globalisation and voluntary and involuntary migration has steadily internationalised this kind of family disruption, often splitting nuclear families as well.

All technological change can cause both winners and losers. However, if we have a Marxist view of technological change rather than a Weberist view, and if we combine this with a change-taking/future-taking managerial mindset as well, our vulnerability to change will much greater. We will be like the sailor I mentioned in chapter 4 who has not charted a course for herself and so perceives every change of wind as a threat. If we think like Weber we will recognize we can be much more empowered in the face of any change. I will soon discuss this further when I discuss the *five social drivers of innovation*.

Before that, I want to formally introduce a new concept I call the *innovation arena* (FUTK69). I have already mentioned *innovation arenas* when I discussed block chain technology and digital currencies in Chapter 1 and factory food production in Chapter 8. Block chain technology is a component of what I call a *secure global finance innovation arena.* Factory Food production is a component of *a planetist food production innovation arena.* Humanity needs to produce sufficient high quality and culturally customised food to feed all the human race well without causing net collateral harm to our planet while doing so. Social media, which are *planetary interconnectivity ways and wares,* are in the *planetary interconnectivity innovation arena.*

We need more of these *planetary connectivity ways and wares* because we need to improve our ability to conduct our relationships in the same real time and with the same intimacy and completeness in a global village as we can in a small village. This *planetary interconnectivity innovation arena* will continue to blossom and many new ways and wares will be created. I have already described how society is finding new means, new inventions, to enable us to fulfil our genetic needs for friendship and intimacy. Social media such as Meta (Facebook), Alphabet (Google), FaceTime, TikTok, Instagram, Zoom, Teams, and Skype have been developed to enable us to do just this. They facilitate our ability to have relationships and work with others in our emerging global village.

Any *way or ware* that can assist the human race build a Planetist-informed global village as productive and harmonious as the small village that was humanity's home during the Holocene will be welcomed in global markets. But our 21st century global village is a multicultural global village while our previous villages were almost always monocultures. Imagine the *multicultural global village harmony ways and wares* we could innovate to accomplish this task!

9.3. Social Innovation: The Five Social Drivers of Innovation

Innovation, which is one of *The Six Future Shaping Tools (FUTK37),* has two roles. First, it provides us with the means to improve how we accomplish old tasks, tasks we have done before and continue to do. Second, innovation enables us to initiate and accomplish new tasks. Some of these we have previously sought to do but did not have the means to, and some we have not contemplated doing before now.

We have already explored two kinds of innovation. These are the two parts of the *Innovation Duet* (FUTK53). The first are *social or ways innovations,* that involve changing what we do and how we behave to accomplish a task. The second are *physical or wares innovations.* These involve changing what we use, or the tools we use, to accomplish a task.

The core purpose of all innovation is to fulfil five basic human needs and aspirations. These are *The Five Social Drivers of Innovation (FUTK56).* These are the need or drive to:

- *Be more productive.* This may involve becoming more knowledgeable or becoming physically stronger, healthier, and fitter so we can accomplish more. It also involves using the one resource we cannot make more of—time—better. So any innovations involving making human effort more productive will be snapped up.
- *Extend mental capability.* This involves enabling the mind to operate more effectively by improving our knowledge and understanding, our mental health and the physical health of our brains.
- *Build more fruitful and fulfilling relationships.* This entails improving how we conduct unconditional, conditional, and transactional relationships between individuals, organisations, communities, and nations.
- *Shape the future.* This involves the more effective use of *the six future shaping tools (FUTK37)* of management, leadership, planning, design, innovation and learning.
- *Uplift liveability.* This entails improving our ability to be more prosperous, harmonious, inclusive, sustainable, healthy, and secure.

All these five social drivers of innovation have been catalysing our imaginations for centuries. But now our ability to use technology to assist us to fulfil our social needs and aspirations has never been greater. As we innovate to fulfil the *Five Social Drivers of Innovation*, we will seek to embed four generic technologies into all the resulting *wares*.

9.4. Technological Innovation: Four Generic Technologies

The second part of the innovation story is our innovation of appropriate *wares*. Here we will discuss only how we might use *technological wares* to realise most of our social innovation aspirations. At the beginning of the third decade of the 21st century there are four basic (generic) technologies. These will almost certainly be added to as the 21st century progresses. These *Four Generic Technologies (FUTK63)* are:

- Digital technology
- Biotechnology and bioscience
- Nanotechnology and nanoscience

- Material technologies and materials science

We will discuss each of these in turn.

9.4.1 Digital technology

Digital technology involves the conversion into a common digital language and the subsequent manipulation and integration of all the products of human creativity: our ideas and calculations, writing and language, the visual arts, music and sound, the performing arts, film, and video. It already enables us to use four of our five senses to mimic reality and shape our real world. In the future, the sense of smell will be added to create a complete virtual experience.

There are many new kinds of digital technology. Each of these can be used to fulfil one or more of the *Five Social Drivers of Innovation* (FUTK56). They include:

- Artificial Intelligence (AI)
- Virtual Reality (VR)
- Augmented Reality (AR)
- Robotics
- Social Media (SM)
- The Internet of Things (IoT)
- Blockchain technology

All these digital technologies, and many more that will be created in the future, will assist those who shape the future as managers, leaders, planners, innovators, teachers and learners to do their work more effectively and productively.

Digital technologies will also enable us to fulfil our second social driver of innovation, to extend the capability of our mind. This will include comprehending our past self and learning from our past; understanding our present self and our situation in the present world; and imagining and then eventually realising our future self in a future world. We can collect and use metaphysical resources of data, information, knowledge, and wisdom to better accomplish these tasks. We have already mentioned the *hierarchy of knowing* (FUTK31), and the development of KT (Knowledge technology) and WT

(Wisdom technology) as successors to DT (Data technology) and IT (Information technology), to extend the mind's ability to achieve all of this.

We will be using all these technologies to innovate all the ways and wares outlined in this book. The Metaverse, which is the next emerging version of virtual reality, will enable artificial reality to better mimic reality. Another new digital technology, blockchain technology, will enable many to communicate, collaborate and trade securely without being endangered by hackers and other types of digital raiders and without requiring much of the current financial services industries. Blockchain and other digital technologies will improve our ability to trust others, and uplift security, privacy and intimacy across all our global village.

Future digital technology of various kinds is already creating collaborative and collective environments such as virtual conferences, where we can work together, share ideas, play games, and collectively shape the future. And it can ensure greater security, privacy, and intimacy in our relationships. Social media provides a major means for building, nurturing, and ending relationships whether these relationships are personal, community or transactional. New *ways and wares* are already being innovated to enable humanity to achieve the same privacy, intimacy, friendship, and security in our emerging global village that we were able to achieve in a village of 500 people two centuries ago.

We cannot have a successfully functioning global village until we can have relationships like those of a small village on a global scale. In fact, humanity is well on its way to achieving this outcome. We can imagine the future of digital technology by asking and answering these questions: *What were the conditions that made our traditional village work well? How can we create these same conditions in a global village while protecting ourselves and not harming others?*

And finally, we need to imagine the role that digital technology can play in shaping the future through *the six future shaping tools (FUTK40)* and building a *liveable planet (FUTK46)* over the next 30 years.

By 2040 digital technology will be based on the more versatile carbon atom rather than the silicon atom and will therefore become more brain and living tissue compatible. Carbon and silicon are in the same column in the periodic table, and they have similar properties. However, everything the silicon atom can do, the carbon atom can do better. Carbon nanotube transistors are now being developed to replace silicon transistors on which digital technology has been based until now. This will be discussed again shortly.

9.4.2. Biotechnology and bioscience

The biotechnology and bioscience revolution are a result of our increased understanding of the human genome and the genomes of other species. The main two components of biotechnology are:

- *Genomics*: which involves understanding the structure of genes and the DNA and RNA that constitute our genetic structures, and the consequences of their activity in living things. This includes both gene mapping and gene editing, which is designed to alter the functioning of genes.
- *Proteomics*: this is a combination of the words *proteins* and *genomics*. It involves understanding and, when needed, transcribing the genetic information contained in DNA and in RNA into proteins. These proteins are responsible both for realising the encoded information in our DNA and RNA in the building and maintenance of biological structures and systems, and guiding and managing the physiological functioning of the bodies of living things. Genomics and proteomics combine to significantly contribute to advancing several sciences such as regenerative medicine, immunology, immunotherapy and neuroscience, all of which are important 21st century health research areas that will play major roles in the treatment of cancer, autoimmune diseases, and mental illness.

Genomics and proteomics will play a major role in assisting humanity to effectively manage global threats to our health such as COVID-19 pandemics. This will occur through mechanisms such as using reprogrammed T Cells or B cells to fight disease. Biotechnology will enable us to prepare better for fighting new epidemics and pandemics. As has been pointed out in the introduction to this book, we can assemble data bases of genomic knowledge and use this knowledge when we need to deal urgently with zoonotic diseases. Bioscience and biotechnology will also play a major role in assisting the creation of a sustainable world in areas as such as in biodiversity management, assisting the survival and revival of endangered species, and creating regenerative and sustainable agriculture.

9.4.3. Nanotechnology and nanoscience

The nanotechnology revolution is in its infancy. Nanotechnology and nanoscience involve the miniaturisation of processes down to molecular levels. A nanometre is a billionth of a meter. At this scale, nanotechnology can operate on molecules and atoms directly, for the tools it uses are the same scale as the molecules and atoms being manipulated. Scientists are already using nanotechnology to increase the strength of materials, and to make them more chemically reactive and lighter in weight. At this level of miniaturisation, systems also behave in a different way from the way they do when their scale is larger. Here they behave according to the principles of quantum physics rather than Newtonian physics.

Nanorobotics will be at the core of nanotechnology over the next decades. This involves inventing robots that work at the nano scale to reshape and change molecules. The door is opening to extraordinary possibilities such as repairing malfunctioning organs in the body, where it could operate in a complementary fashion to biotechnologically driven regeneration therapy using stem cells.

Nanotechnology can be used to create many new materials and devices and has a vast range of applications in fields as diverse as medicine, agriculture, electronics, environmental remediation, and energy production. Biotechnology is in fact an organic nanotechnology that utilises natural biological agents such as enzymes and hormones to manipulate molecules. Nanotechnology itself can be organic or non-organic or a combination of both, and it can be combined with other technologies such as ceramic materials technology to be used in developing products such as medical implants. It is also one of the three generic technologies converging to create carbon-based digital technology.

9.4.4. New materials technology

Scholars have labelled previous eras according to their use of one material: we talk about the stone age, the bronze age, the iron age and so on. We are now on the threshold of a carbon materials age.

The future of carbon materials will be immense. Graphene alone will play a major role in many industries including health and environmental management. Graphene is one hundred times stronger than steel and is ultra-light in weight.

And it can be made ultra-thin as well and built into structures that are just one molecule thick. It is compatible with living tissues and can be incorporated into medical devices. It can conduct electricity, and its molecular architecture enables it to become an amazing filter, creating for example pure water from seawater or sewage in a single step. This carbon materials revolution is just beginning and there will be many other equally amazing carbon materials created in coming decades. We are already learning how to decarbonise the atmosphere, mine the sky for carbon, and use this captured carbon to make new carbon materials such as graphene and even diamonds. We can now take carbon from where it is in the wrong places, where it can be a current global warming threat, to making it into a versatile material in the right places.

In the early 21st century, we will also have many other industrial materials based on various combinations of ceramic materials, metals, and carbon-based materials. These will include polymers, biomaterials, semiconductor materials, metallic alloys, silicon materials (as in chip technology), magnetic materials and medical implant materials. Other non-carbon materials, such as ceramic material and metals, will of course persist, but all of these will be changed by the arrival of an industrial future based on carbon materials.

9.5. Technological Convergence

These four generic technologies will converge in many yet unimagined ways in the coming decades. And this in turn will create many new exciting 21st century possibilities. For example, a combination of digital technology, laser technology and materials technology is creating another revolution: additive manufacturing or 3D printing. This is a manufacturing process that produces three-dimensional objects from a digital file. It does so by extruding or 'printing' carbon-based materials such as nylon or a metal or glass powder in layers from a nozzle under the guidance of the computer-controlled lasers at the heart of the 'printer' until the object is finished.

Another future for 3D printing is its potential for use in organics: to make, for example, new body components of increasing complexity. We can already make new blood vessels for ourselves from our own tissues. It is only a matter of time before we will not require a transplant for an ailing body part because we can construct another one for ourselves from our own tissues through either or both stem cell biotechnology or additive manufacturing.

An even bigger convergence between three of these four generic technologies is now commencing. These three converging generic technologies are digital technology, nano technology, and materials technology. In a decade or so digital technology will be largely based on carbon nanotube transistors that will replace silicon transistors. This will massively increase the capacity, performance and versatility of digital technology, producing digital technologies that will be much smarter and more miniaturised.

9.6. Embedding Technology into 21st Century Innovation

There is an ever-increasing amount of technology available to any would-be innovator. The four generic technologies listed above will all play a major role in 21st century innovation. An innovator or entrepreneur will be able to combine an appropriate blend of these four generic technologies into their inventions. Imagine a person whose work is that of *technology embedder/ware designer*. This person's work would involve knowing enough about all the four generic technologies and how each of them might interact with each other to be able to contribute to creating a successful and 21st century appropriate innovation. An entrepreneur or innovator who wants to build a new way or ware for a particular purpose could ask the technology embedder/ware designer to develop a technology solution to enable the ware to accomplish its stated purpose.

What possibilities can technology offer to an entrepreneur or technology embedder/ware designer? The only limit is one's imagination. Twenty-first century products and services will use digital technologies such as artificial intelligence, augmented intelligence, robotics (which is a combination of AI and mechatronics), social media, Internet of Things (IoT) and blockchain technology. They will also use biotechnologies and biosciences such as genomics.

For starters, imagine what a future *mind augmentation industry* might look like and what *mind augmentation ways and wares* might be invented in the coming decades. Those who seek to avoid or are concerned about being disrupted by artificial intelligence could have the option to augment their own biological minds.

People who have deep knowledge of one or more of the four generic technologies will be able to imagine and build almost unlimited 21st century career paths for themselves.

9.7. Social and Technological Disruption and Resilience

At the beginning of this third decade of the 21st century, there are some people who fear being dislocated by social and technological change, by such things as losing their jobs to robots or to refugees. Some of these seek to resist globalisation by joining modernist populist political movements. Many of them work in industries such as coal and oil that are already, or soon will be, in decline. Some want to 'future proof' themselves against change. For those who are fearful about being disrupted by change Gary Lew has the perfect response: *This is your world, shape it or somebody else will.* If we follow his advice, we should not seek to keep the old alive. We will fail if we try to resist change, just as all of those who have resisted change, from Ned Ludd and his Luddites onwards, have failed

Technology will not be a threat to anybody who acts in leadership mode. The best way to flourish in a rapidly changing environment dominated by high levels of social and technological change is to ensure that one consciously shapes the future both as:

- Manager, as a resilient future taker
- Leader, as a purposeful future maker

This is *The Exemplar Manager and Leader* duet *(FUTK26)*

The fact that our world was so easily disrupted by the COVID-19 pandemic is a good illustration of the silliness of the concept of *future proofing*. The only way to *'future proof'* our response to pandemics is to do what Gary Lew suggests: shape the future so we are better prepared for the next pandemic than we were for the last one.

Those who hold a Marxist view of technological change are more likely to be reactive and even fatalistic in such a situation. Those who hold a Weberist view will promote the idea that society can decide what role technology should or should not play in human, economic and social development, and whether we let technological change cause economic, social, cultural, or ecological trauma. We can also consciously introduce technology in a sustainable way, thereby creating zero net collateral harm/damage to our ecosystems, societies, and cultures. Social and economic public policy with a passive and fatalistic future-taking attitude to emerging technology is also often a primary reason why people are concerned that technology can decimate both jobs and job markets. Much potential disruption will be avoided if government public policy is based on mission-directed future-making leadership rather than problem-centred future-taking management.

Chapter 8 discussed demographic aging and the response to it by the introduction into the workplace of more robots and higher levels of automation. As demographic aging continues we can expect that public attitudes to social and technological change will become more positive and new technology will become more welcomed and less feared.

In both initiating and reacting to change we should always seek to become the most purposeful future/change makers as well as most resilient future/change takers we can be. And to do this, we must never stop *learning and seeking to continuously grow our capabilities.* We will now examine the important role of the huge change agents that is education and learning in the 21st century.

Chapter 10: Renewing the Agents of Change: Education and Learning Futures

10.1. Learning for 21st Century Success

If we are to become the most 21st century successful people we can be, we must also become the best learners we can be: *we should live to learn so we can learn to live.* Nothing is more important for ensuring we become future-successful than committing ourselves to continuous and life-long learning.

As already said, the two major drivers shaping the 21st century are:

- Globalisation, which is increasing interconnection, communication, and trade between the planet's peoples, and that is moulding the formation of an emerging global village.
- The growth of universal education, in terms both of its breadth and depth. An increasing number of people are being educated, and a growing number of them are being educated for longer.

Learning is now available to pretty much everyone. For most of us, if we want to learn, we can learn. For centuries this was not possible. Most learning came from one's elders, who had an exclusive right to teach you what they thought you would need to know to be future successful. Learning was also exclusive, in that it was not for everybody but for the chosen ones. Now nearly all of us can learn anything, from anyone, and from anywhere. This is our 21st century world of learning

The number of people who have completed secondary and tertiary education has massively increased and continues to do so. The proportion of tertiary educated 25 to 34-year-olds is now double the proportion of tertiary-educated 55 to 64-year-olds in most countries and this differential is increasing further. There are still too many poorer countries that are seriously lagging and where more investment in education is needed. But even in these countries there is a serious commitment to creating universal education and to the uplifting of educational levels. Most parents everywhere know that an investment in education is the best way to ensure that their children have the best chance of being successful in the future.

As discussed, as people become more educated, they become more likely to look beyond giving their first allegiance to their tribal and national identities. They will begin to see all of humanity as one. Because of combination of globalisation and technological interconnectivity, we are continually reminded that humanity has a shared planetary home and a common future. And as their education levels rise further, people are also increasingly likely to assume planetist values and practice planetist ethics.

10.2. Knowledge and Wealth

Learning provides the best pathway to long-term prosperity. As mentioned earlier, Buckminster Fuller told us that wealth is derived from a combination of two components: physical resources (ecosystems and natural resources) that must be conserved, and metaphysical resources (ideas, knowledge, and wisdom) that can only grow. This is *Bucky's Fullers Wealth Duet (FUTK10)*.

Wealth is generated through turning both physical and metaphysical resources into 21st century-relevant products, services, and technologies. What we know (our metaphysical resources) and what we can do (our skills sets) will increasingly become the basis of 21st century wealth. And we need to be, and can be, educated both more and differently to ensure we become the most successful builders of metaphysical future prosperity we can be.

10.3. The Two-Year-Old Learner

If we want to maximise our chances of success in a rapidly changing 21st century, we need to be continual and committed learners. The most motivated and purposeful learner is the two-year-old: two-year-olds are exemplars of those who *live to learn so that they can learn to live*. When they want to know something, they demand the relevant knowledge *immediately*, not tomorrow or next year, but *now*. And now all of us can learn as two-year-olds do throughout our lives, for the answers to all the questions we might ask can be accessed from an increasing number of sources such as the current World Wide Web and the emerging metaverse.

One of the goals for 21st century education, perhaps the biggest goal of all, should be to keep the two-year-old learner in all of us vital and alive throughout our whole lives. Our adult learner can simply be a more sophisticated version of our two-year-old learner. What follows is what I call the *21ˢᵗ century Learning Culture*. This describes how we can best learn using 21ˢᵗ century means.

10.4. The 21ˢᵗ Century Learning Culture

The 21ˢᵗ century Learning Culture is described in two parts. The first part, *The Seven Modes of 21ˢᵗ century Learning (FUTK27)*, refers to *how* we can learn in the 21ˢᵗ century. We can learn continuously from the world around us, including through the internet or the newly emerging metaverse, which functions as a combination global relationship building, communication, trading, and knowledge sharing and learning facility.

Once, we learned most of what we know from our parents or our elders, our peers in our local communities, and our schools and other education institutions. Our first teachers were our parents, but not all of us are lucky enough to have parents who are superb teachers. Many of us have been either advantaged or disadvantaged by the knowledge and understanding we received, or did not receive, from our parents. Most of us were blessed by the work of at least few high-quality teachers, in our schools and in our communities more generally. Most of us can recognise when we are being well taught, and we remember all our lives the superb and inspiring teachers and mentors we had.

Fifty years ago, apart from what we learned from our parents our knowledge mostly came from just two sources: from the knowledge of our various teachers and from the books we could buy or access from the library. Provided we knew how to read, of course, and many of us were disadvantaged because we were partly or significantly illiterate. Literacy still matters today but we can now learn as effectively from non-literary sources, just as two-year-olds still do. After all, two-year-olds learn rapidly even though they are illiterate!

As the availability of digital technology becomes ever more universal, everyone in our shared global village can potentially be our teacher and we can choose who these teachers will be and for what purpose. Then we can have access to universal teaching and learning.

The framework described below is a framework to guide future educational innovation, design, and planning. We can use this to build a superb 21ˢᵗ century-relevant global education system, one that will improve our ability to use the *Six Future Shaping Tools (FUTK40)* and embed in ourselves all the abilities we need to become 21ˢᵗ century successful people.

The second part of the 21st century Learning Culture refers to *what* we learn rather than *how* we learn. This second component seeks to answer the question *What core capabilities should and could be developed to ensure that we can process the information and knowledge we seek, and grow our capabilities and skills so we can secure our future success?* This is called the *Four Domains of Holistic Learning (FUTK28)*.

10.5. The Seven Modes of 21st Century Learning

In the discussion below, the first part of the 21st century learning culture is outlined. This is a framework for future innovation, design, planning and learning. Much of the detail has yet to be invented. If it is developed to its full potential, it can uplift the spread and depth of learning everywhere. Learning and education is already the second biggest industry on our planet. Most parents recognise that the biggest gift they can give to their children to uplift their chances of future success, is to maximise their educational and learning opportunities.

Education and learning can be expected to grow further. Education will most likely soon replace health as the world's biggest industry. And here we are talking not only about learning in formal education such as schools and universities, but learning from the exploding educational sector of informal learning providers. The opportunities to learn have never been greater and informal learning is growing faster that formal learning.

There are seven components to our global learning culture, which I call *The Seven Modes of 21st century learning.* They are life-long learning, learner-driven learning, Just-in-Time learning, customised learning, transformative learning, collaborative learning and contextual learning (FUTK27).

10.5.1. Lifelong learning

Fifty years ago, formal education was what we did when we were young and, for most of us, seldom did after our adolescence or at best our early twenties. Of course, we all learn throughout our lives, but for most of us this learning was haphazard and neither systematic nor formalised. Some sought to continue to learn throughout their lives, but this was a small minority. For example, professional people such as doctors had the opportunity to learn as part of their professional development.

But everybody should be able to learn whatever, whenever, and however they want to learn throughout their whole lives. From now on a good principle would be for all of us to be able to dedicate, and accept the responsibility for dedicating, up to 20% of our time and resources to continually learning. In our future work, we will preferably seek work arrangements that allow us to learn continually throughout our working careers. As we tread each step in our career path, we should have the opportunity to acquire new knowledge and skills. Lifelong learning could be universally documented by providing all people with a formal learning record that travels with them to different education providers and workplaces, just as a personal medical record does in the health industry. This record could also provide an educational passport by documenting the higher levels of formal learning acquired by the learner throughout their working lives.

10.5.2. Learner-driven learning

The two-year-old is an exemplar learner-driven learner, but in fact learning everywhere is increasingly being learner driven. The teacher's role is also changing. The old model of learning was to transfer knowledge from the teacher to the student. In the 21st century the teacher's role in a learner-driven-learning culture will increasingly embrace three responsibilities, that of being a:

- *Knowledge navigator*: introducing and guiding the learner into pathways for acquiring and understanding data, information, and knowledge
- *Mentor*: interacting with the learner-driven learner to turn data and information into knowledge and wisdom
- *Personal development counsellor*: ensuring that learning is relevant and customised to meet the learner's aspirations and promotes their personal and professional development

10.5.3. Just-in-time learning

The two-year-old is also an exemplar of just-in-time learning. They learn when their curiosity and their need to know and understand is greatest: that usually is right now! And they love to learn as well. In the past, this two-year-old learner-driven, just-in-time learning culture was crushed by the school learning culture based on uniform one-size-fits-all and school and teacher driven learning. Education was informed by Henry Ford's and Fredrick Winslow

Taylor's concepts of mass production and economies of scale. As Winston Churchill said, 'my education was only interrupted by my schooling.'

Throughout much of the 20th century, too many people reached adulthood remembering their school years as sometimes uninspiring and even unhappy experiences. Keeping the two-year-old learner alive well into adulthood would massively reduce such alienation from formal learning. Now lifelong, learner-driven, and just-in-time learning can be complemented by the provision of just-in-time knowledge navigation, mentoring and personal development counselling by teachers.

10.5.4. Customised learning

All learning opportunities and processes can be customised to suit the learner's preferred learning and thinking styles so that our learning is the most effective it can be. We are all different, and our minds differ in the ways we learn, process information, and create knowledge. Now because of progress in neuroscience we know the brain is adaptable, is neuroplastic, and that we can, over time, change and improve how we learn.

We can understand how we currently learn through several different methodologies and instruments. One of the best is based on the work of 'Ned' Herrmann, the Herrmann Brain Dominance Instrument (HBDI). There are others who have followed similar pathways. In the 21st century it is possible to create new learning modules customised to match every person's preferred learning and thinking style. Imagine a learning supermarket, where all learning modules, each customised for different learning and thinking styles, are on the shelves and can be accessed and acquired by any learner! Providing products and services, *ways and wares*, to achieve this will certainly be part of our education and learning futures.

10.5.5. Transformative learning

Our primary motivation for learning is because we want to transform ourselves, including for realising our visualised future self. We currently assess what has been learned by asking people to remember and regurgitate what they have learned in structured processes we call exams. Some of us do well in these conditions. Others do not. We know that our ability to become successful in the future often bears little relevance to how we perform in examination conditions. These exams measure what we can recall and our ability to perform under these conditions, not our capacity to be transformed or how much we have been transformed.

Often, people have a disability in one way and an ability in another, or they are disadvantaged in one way and advantaged in another. For example, psychologist Tony Attwood, well known for his work with people with Asperger's Syndrome, encouraged his clients to transform themselves by concentrating on further developing what he called their 'assets'. As we transform ourselves through our learning, we can focus on implementing mission-directed aspirations of considering how we might build and maximise ability and advantage, thereby building on our perceived strengths, rather than only on minimising or ameliorating our perceived weaknesses, our disabilities, and disadvantages.

Imagine some *ways and wares* we might develop so that we could assess our capacity to be transformed and how much we have been transformed by learning! We can assess our healing and wellness in health and medical services. We should also be able to do this in education services.

10.5.6. Collaborative Learning

In this book we have discussed collaboration many times. Being able to collaborate for mutual benefit is essential if we want to be successful in the emerging interdependent 21st century society. On the sporting field our competitive conditioning is so deep it is difficult to imagine a team sport based on collaboration rather than competition. But even in sport, we need collaboration. Good sporting teams are successful because their members can collaborate brilliantly. It is said that a *champion team* will defeat a *team of champions*.

The Japanese have a word, 'coopetition', meaning we should seek to individually collaborate more vigorously so that we can then compete as a team more effectively. The Japanese also have a business philosophy called *Kaizen*, meaning continuous improvement. It is the basis of Japanese workplace productivity. It is focused on teamwork, personal discipline, quality circles and workplace morale. Collaborative learning is central to *Kaizen*. In the increasingly interdependent 21st century world of work, the world could learn much from the Japanese.

In all our work, we will increasingly work in teams, including teams with different abilities and capacities. In many of these, we will be collaborating to visualise and realise one or more of our six futures. In the 21ˢᵗ century, success will increasingly go to those who collaborate best with others, including with their own suppliers and customers, rather than those who compete individually and ruthlessly. And new technology, digital technology such as *Zoom* and *Teams,* is facilitating collaboration between different professions and other differently skilled workers, and various organisations and groups. This enables differently skilled people and different cultures to collaborate and combine their talents in new *ways and wares,* such as digital conferencing to produce synergistic collaborative outcomes.

Of course, despite technology, outcomes might still be antagonistic. Imagine *ways and wares* that might enhance synergism and ameliorate antagonism in our collective endeavours.

In this regard, the work on *team building* and on *team roles* by both Will Schutz and Meredith Belbin provide excellent pathways to enable people to become the most effective team member they can be. Curricula in collaborative learning can include material drawn from these sources. Our capabilities in collaborating when we shape the future together will also uplifted by the conscious promotion of interpersonal emotional intelligence. Imagine *Interpersonal Intelligence Uplifting Ways and Wares!* Collaborative learning modules can be consciously built into any collaborative strategic action we undertake, including when we use any of *the six future shaping tools.*

In our increasingly interdependent 21ˢᵗ century, we should be able to learn collaboratively and for our mutual benefit. More and more we will be placed in situations where we need to be able to learn collectively rather than individually. The *interdependence trio (FUTK08)* and the *trust trio (FUTK09)* can be core building blocks for any successful future collaborative learning program and curriculum.

10.5.7. Contextual Learning

Two-year-olds learn in context. Stimulated by what they are observing or are being told, they usually ask questions that reflect what they need to know. Our genes have programmed us to learn best this way. We all ask questions to understand more about matters relating to what we are experiencing or witnessing at that moment, or to assist us to realise our aspirations. Young people learn best about nature when they are witnessing and experiencing nature. Experiencing is an essential component of effective learning.

Where possible, all learning should be put in context, surrounded by relevant reality, or if not reality then in simulated reality such as virtual or augmented reality. Modern technology can create simulated reality to make our learning more effective. We can expect that with further developments in digital technology there will be a creative explosion in contextual learning and virtual experience This will create limitless numbers of virtual reality experiences in simulated learning environments. Digital technology, including AI, VR, AR, the Internet of Things (IoT) and robotics will be increasingly used to provide simulated environments to enhance learning in context.

In coming decades, we will increasingly be able to learn in collaborative mode in groups in virtual reality as well. Imagine young people seeking employment, when asked about their experience, being able to inform the interviewer that 'I have only a few days of real experience, but I have completed a year of simulated (virtual) experience.'

10.6. Uplifting the Capability and Fulfilling the Potential of Our Mind

In the 21st century, we can not only become better learners by changing *how we learn* through *The Seven Modes of 21st century learning (FUTK27)* but also by uplifting *our capacity to learn and our ability to create new knowledge.* Here, we are referring to what we can do to improve the *processing power* of our minds, how we might uplift the processing power of the carbon-based computer that lies between our ears! This is what intelligence really is. In recent years, we have realised that we can change our brains and even increase our intelligence through what is called neuroplasticity.

So, the relevant question we could pose here is, *what mind processing capabilities do we need to grow to become the most successful people we can be?* If we can do this, then our 21st century life path and career path will become a more enriching experience, enriching in every meaning of the word. The answer lies in *The Four Domains of Holistic Learning (FUTK28).*

10.7. The Four Domains of Holistic Learning

The Four Domains of Holistic Learning are learning to learn, learning to think, learning to feel and learning to reflect (FUTK28).

10.7.1 Learning to learn

If we are to learn more effectively, it is important that each of us knows how we currently learn and what we can do to become more effective learners. We are all different. Learning authority Julia Atkin tells us that our preferred modes of learning depend upon which parts of our brain are dominant in our thinking and learning processes, and which parts of our brain are most easily accessed by us. In this context we can consider the brain as consisting of four parts: the cerebral left and cerebral right, and the limbic left and limbic right.

We all differ in how capable and powerful we are in each of these quadrants. Many of us are strong in one of these, moderately strong in one or two of them, and weak in a fourth. However, there are also some people who are equally powerful in all four of these. If we want to be as successful as we can be it is highly desirable to know how we currently learn and how we might improve our ability to learn. Atkin tells us that the four core parts of the brain and their related learning styles are:

- Upper left learning (cerebral left): learning by gaining information and facts
- Lower left learning (limbic left): learning by being able to do, acting out, applying
- Lower right learning (limbic right): learning by feeling emotions, experiencing, and doing
- Upper right learning (cerebral right): learning by making connections, understanding and insight

We will certainly know a lot more about how we learn in the coming decades. In the future each of us will be able to have our current means of learning assessed so we can then become more holistic in the way we learn, growing our capabilities in all four quadrants by accessing learning programs specifically customised to make our brains ever more capable of learning. Imagine new tools, new *learning style assessment ways and wares* that could help us identify how we currently learn and *learning improvement ways and wares* that could uplift our ability to learn more effectively in quadrants where we are currently weak.

The Herrmann Brain Dominance Instrument (HBDI) is a useful instrument for helping us begin to understand how each of us learns. In the next 20 years there will be great progress made in matching people's learning styles and preferences and in customising education products and services for different people. And we will also learn how we can better trigger and catalyse neuroplastic changes in our brains so that we can become more complete whole brain learners. And as our learning becomes less empirically and more scientifically based and as our knowledge of neuroscience grows, we will learn much more about how our brain works and how we can improve it.

Many people are concerned that artificial Intelligence (AI) will eventually surpass our natural intelligence in a runaway process of ever self-improving artificial super intelligence. This is the so-called *singularity*. Some have predicted that this will occur around 2040-2050. However, we can improve our natural ability to learn and ensure this threat never becomes a reality. We have already discussed a *mind augmentation industrial future.*

10.7.2. Learning to think

In the 21st century, our future wealth and prosperity will be dependent on what we know, and what we can do, our skills or our capabilities. These are our individual and collective metaphysical resources. The better thinkers we become, the better will be our ability to generate wealth from metaphysical resources. Those who are able to use their minds rationally, critically, and creatively, and who are effective learners, will become the best creators of 21st century metaphysical wealth.

The importance of learning of philosophy from an early age has already been mentioned, and this is strongly promoted here. See *kinderphilosophy.com* for ways in which this is already being done.

The main four core domains of philosophy relevant to shaping futures are:
- *Metaphysics:* which asks and answers the questions: *What do we know? What are the facts?*
- *Epistemology:* which asks and answers the questions: *How do we know? Are our sources of knowledge reliable?*
- *Reason:* which asks and answers the questions: *What can we conclude? What sense can we make from what and how we know?*
- *Ethics:* which asks and answers the questions: *What should we do? What is the right thing to do?*

So The Four Philosophical Domains for Future Shapers are Metaphysics plus Epistemology plus reason plus Ethics (FUTK25).

Imagine the *Ways and the Wares* that might be developed to ensure that all of us are more able to use these four philosophical processes in our future-shaping and decision-making tools throughout our lives. These *ways and wares* could include digital philosophical templates that can assist us to understand our status in the world better and guide our use of *the six future shaping tools.*

When we introduce a new technology, make a development proposal, or consider undertaking any important future shaping activity, we should be able to engage in a critical thinking process to decide whether we should proceed with our proposal, and then how we might proceed. The ethical question 'what we should do' is the key question here, but we should ask it only after considering the issue in terms of the other three philosophical questions.

We can seek to know the facts and assess any related evidence by asking and answering the metaphysical and epistemological questions. We can use reason to conclude what our situation is and how effective current practices are, the consequences of remaining where we are, or consciously changing our situation, and whether we should proceed or not with any proposed new initiative. We can consider the ethical question when we assess the proposal in terms of whether proceeding will uplift *the six pillars of liveability* or not, or whether proceeding with the proposal is sound in terms of emerging values environments such as the *nine values of planetism.*

These four domains of philosophy, used together and in this order, are a generic form of some existing decision-making processes such as doing due diligence, which is used to evaluate the worthiness of an investment proposal. They also inform other decision-making processes such as an environment impact assessment and a technology assessment.

10.7.3. Learning to feel

Howard Gardner in his book *Frames of Mind* suggested that two of his then seven multiple intelligences are emotional intelligences, that he called respectively *intrapersonal and interpersonal intelligence*. He now describes a total of nine multiple intelligences. However, these two intelligences respectively refer to being able to:

- Understand our own current emotional self and emotional status (intrapersonal intelligence)
- Access and comprehend the emotional status and world of others (interpersonal intelligence)

Our success in emerging 21st century society will depend on our being as emotionally intelligent as possible so we can construct and maintain harmonious and interdependent relationships. And, as already discussed, this also requires us to be as mature as we can be.

The *Six Emotional Pillars of Future Shaping (FUTK45)* have already been discussed, and how important it is to be able to access and use these six key emotions as we seek to shape 21st century society and visualise and realise our own future life and career pathways. The *Motivational Pairs Quintet* has also already been discussed.

There will be many *emotional intelligence ways and wares* invented in the next decades that can assist us to improve our ability to use our feelings to inform us as we seek to know our emotional selves better, relate to others, and shape the future by being better able to understand and access the emotional state of others. In previous times we thought that we could not alter brains to improve intelligence, but now we know better. However, the means we might use to raise all of Gardner's nine intelligences have for the most part yet to be invented. Imagine new *intrapersonal intelligence uplifting ways* and *wares and interpersonal intelligence uplifting ways and wares!*

10.7.4. Learning to reflect pathways to critical and creative thinking

The best ideas about our work, when our 'light bulb' moments occur, usually happen when we are not working. They occur when we are in reflective mode. It is then that some understanding or insight buried in our subconscious is facilitated to enter our conscious mind. If we think of *Rumsfeld's knowledge quartet (FUTK35)* we are talking here about *Unknown Knowns*, things we didn't know we knew, transforming themselves into *Known Knowns*, what we now know we know. By placing ourselves in reflective time and space we can gain access to this treasure trove of hidden knowledge in our minds. Yogis, Zen Buddhists, Taoists, Jesuits, and others who regularly meditate, have known this for centuries.

When we reflect in this way, we cease working hard and start working smart. Our mind can both enslave us and liberate us, and it can both make us ill and make us well. We sometimes reach a moment when our passage forward appears to be blocked, or when we are conscious that our present self and emerging future self might be endangered or disrupted. At such moments, we sometimes become conscious of a new concept or idea, when a new pathway forward, a new insight or a new future option magically presents itself to us. But for this to happen, for this perception liberation moment to occur, we must stop working and trying to meet targets in left-brain dominant mode. Instead, we have to relax, enjoy ourselves and give our minds the opportunity to transform unknown knowns into known knowns. We enter this reflective space best when we are doing something that fulfils us and which we enjoy, thereby giving our right brain the freedom, space, and time to release new insights and ideas from our unconscious into our conscious mind. This phenomenon shows that we can work both smart and hard *but not at the same time.* If we wish to work smart, we need to take sufficient time to reflect, by stopping working and relaxing. Indeed, when we are in reflective mode, reflecting on what we have before us or why we are in the situation we are, we can become the wisest person we can be. In the emerging knowledge-based economy of the 21st century, being able to reflect will be economically important as well as physiologically and psychologically important.

Human ecologist Stephen Boyden has introduced the concept of what he calls *meliors (FUTK37).* He tells us we all live in a continuum between the polar-opposite emotional worlds of *Distress* and *Bliss.* He describes as *stressors* those elements in our life that raise our levels of *distress*, by driving us towards the distress end of the continuum. *Meliors,* on the other hand, are elements in our life that raise our level of *bliss* by taking us towards the opposite end of the continuum, the *bliss* end.

What is a stressor or a melior is going to vary from person to person. One activity might be a *stressor* for one person and a *melior* for another. If we promote the idea that each of us should assemble our own imaginary *personal backpack of meliors* and regularly practice meliors by regularly taking *melior time,* we can place ourselves in *reflective time and space* more often. If we regularly practice melior time by reaching into our melior backpack and using one of our meliors when we need to, we can lessen our distress and uplift our bliss at any time we need to. Our capacity to uplift our wellness will not only be greater, so will our capacity to live and work.

10.8. Learning Innovations for the 21st Century: Effective Learning

Education and learning is the world's largest industry after health. The formal education sector is growing by about 11% annually and is projected to reach at least $US10 trillion in 2030. If we add to this the informal learning sector, a sector that is growing even faster, the total education and learning industry is likely to be US$15 trillion and be the world's biggest industry by 2030.

All the different elements of both components of the 21st century learning culture, the *Seven Modes of 21st Century Learning (FUTK27)* and the *Four Domains of Holistic Learning (FUTK28)*, can be sources of new designs, plans and innovations over the next decades. Imagine all the *ways and wares* that could be invented to provide such cutting-edge goods and services.

All aspects of the 21st century learning culture are really components of the current infant version of the *Mind Augmentation Industrial Future* of the 21st century. This will involve many new *Mind Augmentation Ways and Wares* entering global markets in the next generation.

The Buddhist Sociologist Barbara Lepani has suggested that the *Mind Augmentation Ware* presented in this chapter, which includes *The Seven Modes of 21st century Learning* and *The Four Domains of Holistic Learning*, could be called *Mindware*.

Chapter 11: Renewing the Agents of Change: Work and Career Futures

11.1. Worry About Work Futures

I keep on suggesting that our economic future is bright, and have nominated hundreds of *ways and wares* that could be innovated and marketed to generate virtually unlimited wealth and endless vocational possibilities. Some people think this is much too optimistic. They foresee a bleak vocational future due to jobs disappearing because they are in declining 20th century industries, they are being lost through automation, or they are victims of global recessions visited on us by economic crises in other parts of our interconnected global village. Others are concerned that many of the emerging new jobs, such as those in the gig economy, do not provide long-term work security, casualise work, and pay poorly. Some are worried that immigrants might steal their already 21st century-endangered jobs. Others are concerned that government cost cutting is not sufficiently assisting people who are losing their jobs to prepare adequately for future jobs. And many see the unfairness of government taxation policies that favour the already well off, and that are not doing sufficient to challenge greedy corporate leadership that is making itself richer while simultaneously minimising employee salaries and downsizing the numbers of their employees. I too am worried that many governments are more concerned with achieving economic efficiency driven by more automation and fewer workers and extending the life of declining 20th century industries than with becoming midwifes to the birth of 21st century-relevant industrial futures.

However, I believe that the long-term trends outlined in this book will further undermine the declining 20th century Modernist nation-first political culture that continues to cause many of these undesirable work outcomes. I also believe that too much of our so-called political and corporate leadership is practicing management rather than leadership: it practices too much cautious future-taking and not enough purposeful future-making. Too much of it lacks purpose other than trying reactively to minimize harm rather than seeking to maximise good outcomes. And I further believe that the same applies to much of the union movement as well. A cultural and political environment of future-making leadership is needed everywhere.

Some people have told me I'm being too idealistic. They say *not everyone can be an entrepreneur or a leader!* But I firmly believe that everyone can be an entrepreneur and a leader of self, just as they can also become their own futurist. History shows that people from unpromising environments can achieve amazing things. Think Henry Ford, Marie Curie, Captain James Cook, Mary Anning (the fossil hunter), Gerty Cori (Nobel Prize in science), Helen Taussig (founder of paediatric cardiology), Barbara McClintock (Nobel Prize in Physiology or Medicine), Rachel Carson (author of *Silent Spring*), Charlie Chaplin, Leonardo Dicaprio, Oprah Winfrey, Anthony Albanese.

11.2. Looking More Closely at Work

Life is unimaginable without work. Work, second only to globalisation itself, is the biggest prosperity uplifting machine humanity has ever invented. But it is work as described here, not work as it has been: as something one does, and often would rather not do, to earn income and to live. I am talking about metaphysical work that in the coming decades will deal successfully with the key issues facing our world.

The word 'work' currently has several different meanings. So that we can fully explore work in the 21st century, I have sought to use some specific words to describe different aspects of work. Our *work* is what we do *that gives meaning to our lives.* For many this involves fulfilling one's *destiny*, using one's *aptitude* and one's *passion* to build one's future career path and realise fulfilment in our work. *Vocation,* on the other hand, is *that which we do to give us the financial means to support ourselves.* In the past, people often held jobs that gave them economic security but that rarely had much in common with either their personal interests or their aspirations. And of course that is still true today, albeit less so. And finally, work can be an *avocation*, which is *doing what we love to do.* People often use the word 'hobby' to cover this aspect of our working lives. Many people do *work* that is their *vocation*, and others do *work* that is also their *avocation*. These people are already more fortunate that most. I believe that in future there will be an increasing number of these work-related combinations of *work/vocation* and *vocation/avocation* and indeed all three of these simultaneously. My vision is to facilitate the development of career paths of all who wish to enter a world of perfect work that involves us combining our *work* and our *vocation*, and even our *avocation* as well, into a single entity and career. Imagine a future world, a *working heaven*, where everybody could accomplish that outcome!

This work-related concept is called *The Occupation Trio*. It consists of work plus vocation plus avocation *(FUTK24)*

11.3. How We Think Matters

In Chapter 4, it was suggested that *any wind shift will be perceived to be an ill wind shift by a sailor who has no course.* If we have already set a course to take us to the future that is based on our own aspirations, we can tell whether any change is either a threat or an opportunity.

Our vulnerability or resilience to change will depend on how we perceive it. If we are making a change happen and actively shaping the future as a proactive future-making leader of self, we will be much more resilient and less likely to be disrupted by change. If change is happening to us and we are responding as reactive future-talking managers of self, we can become very vulnerable to change. I believes this mindset is at the centre of all our concerns about the future of work.

As already mentioned, there is a great deal of public concern that emerging technology such as robotics and artificial intelligence might cause massive job loss and economic havoc. Writers and commentators often use the word 'disruption' to describe social and technological change that will significantly damage employment. And it is likely that, if we remain in *future-taking mode and* seek to *future proof* ourselves against the further penetration of our vocational world by intelligent machines or by social or technological threats of any kind, we will become collaborators in realizing these dire predictions.

But if we become *purposeful future makers*, our work and vocational options can be without limit. We need to have 21st century-relevant visualizations of the future we seek to create for ourselves, including understanding our *destinies* and visualising the future occupations we might create in the future. And we can set out to realize our visualisations. This is equally true whether this visualization and realization of the future relates to an individual, an organisational or a community future.

However, when we are thinking about creating industrial and occupational futures our thinking should never be directed only at new physical resource based industrial futures. There will be a time when a key physical resource might be exhausted or made obsolete by social and technological change, or become unavailable for another reason, and cause a new economic crisis. If we want to ensure we can thrive in the 21st century our thinking should be about consciously building a 21st century-relevant metaphysical resource based industrial future for ourselves. We can accomplish this by committing ourselves to continuously creating both new knowledge through research and development, and establishing new institutes of learning to consciously create exemplary vocational skilled people and career paths in the 21st century relevant industrial futures we are seeking to build.

A favourite scenario I put to clients foreseeing a bleak future and needing to develop a new long-term social and industrial future vision for themselves is, *This community is a world centre of excellence in X. X is a 21st century industry that did not exist a generation ago.* This is followed by the question, *what is X?* Rather than trying to protect a current industrial base that is already, or soon to be, in decline, an organisation that wants to be resilient needs to put its energy into answering this question.

Coalmining communities, for example, should not be telling us to buy and use their coal because it keeps them employed. It is now absurd to try to future proof a coal region. What they can do instead is use the value of the still somewhat valuable coal asset to raise the capital to visualising and building a new 21st century relevant future for themselves such as a green hydrogen or green ammonia industrial future.

We have already discussed the reason why robotics was first developed in Japan was because Japan got to the future first in terms of demographic ageing. Japan was farsighted enough to be concerned that it was likely to face worker shortages rather than worker surpluses in the coming decades. It prepared itself well for an ageing Japan. Most of our nations are demographically ageing. From now on, our vocational and industrial futures will more likely be characterized by labour shortages rather than labour surpluses. Yet many people in Eurocentric cultures have, until very recently, continued to regarded automation as a disruptive threat!

Technology will certainly destroy many current jobs, but it will also enable us to create many other jobs and whole new careers, most of which have never existed before. All of these will be creating new 21st century relevant *ways and wares*! But we need to operate primarily in *future making (leadership)* mode if we wish to realise this outcome.

Throughout history jobs have disappeared because of social and technological change. In the early 19th century, there was resistance to the automation of the cotton industry by the followers of Ned Ludd, who inspired the *Luddite* movement named after him. *Luddites* feared the end of artisanship. This did not occur. Fabric and garment making in the digital age is full of magnificent creativity and artisanship! Jobs for executioners largely disappeared when most of humanity did the right thing and ended capital punishment. Nobody complained about that. We correctly regarded this as human progress. Jobs in the coal industry are disappearing now and soon they will disappear in the oil industry as well. However, jobs in renewable energy are appearing much faster than predicted, and here future-making public policy can make a big difference.

Japan has, for example, decided that within a decade all its motor vehicles must be either solar/electric or solar/ hydrogen/electric. Japan will get to the future first and benefit economically from becoming a leader in both solar hydrogen/ammonia technology and in creating the first generation of zero carbon emission motor vehicles that it can then export to the world. The end of the fossil fuel era will not damage Japan, but it will damage others who let themselves be dominated by future-taking mindsets. If any country continues to let its oil industry continue to reign, the consequences of the inevitable and desirable demise of the oil industry will be a significant disruption of its industrial base. The USA under Donald Trump would have headed for a massively disrupted industrial future had he been re-elected. Fortunately, Joe Biden has now committed the USA to a solar /electric motor vehicle future.

The rewards of changing strategic directions early and consciously seeking to get to the future first can offer immense rewards. For example, Elon Musk wants to make the USA a leader/future maker in electric motor vehicles. In 2020 Tesla was by monetary value the biggest automotive company in the world. Musk was therefore very well situated for the arrival of the Biden administration. And he is not only getting to the future first, he is also finding partners and collaborating across our global village to co-realize his vision with him when he does. He is getting his vehicles made in China as well as in the USA, just as Apple is making its smart phones there. Global collaboration not national competitiveness is driving these changes. And this means that despite the archaic and neurotic modernist mindsets of defence planners and conservative Republicans, China and the USA will inevitably become more interdependent in the future than they are now.

The promotion of metaphysical innovation to get the future first, and then be a planetist collaborator with others when you build new products and services, will provide the most promising highway to future success for all of us. Increasing interdependence between commercial corporations across the planet is both inevitable and desirable in our emerging global village. Planetist (cosmonaut) capitalist investors are more prescient than are defence planners. They know which companies have 21st century-appropriate agendas and will increase in value, and which have 21st century inappropriate agendas and will decline in value. This is a classic example of how values are increasingly shaping investment decisions in the 21st century. All the *future proofing* in the world will not save a motor vehicle manufacturer perceived by customers and investors to be a yesteryear motor vehicle company.

11.4. Imagining Emerging 21st Century Work and Career Paths

It is relatively easy to predict where jobs will never disappear. We will need doctors or teachers forever but what doctors or teachers might do will significantly change. In Chapter 10 we discussed how what teachers do will change, how they are likely to become a combination of knowledge navigator, mentor, and personal development coach. We also know that some jobs will disappear forever. We have already mentioned executioners and jobs in the coal and oil industries. And we have described occupations that will appear and grow, such as those in ecological restoration and regenerative medicine and agriculture.

How can we understand what totally new and not yet visualized vocations will appear in the future? First, it is self-evident that new occupations and vocations will only appear if there is a demand for a product or service provided by that occupation. Chapter 1 outlined how we can predict how the demand for new products and services, or new *ways and wares*, will change by linking the dots between five words: evaluate, values, value, valued and valuable. This will lead to understanding the purposes of emerging occupations that will supply the products and services to the global market in coming decades. These will appear because of the same social and technological changes that are causing the abolition of other vocations.

This book has listed many *ways and wares* that are likely be in demand in emerging 21st century markets. This will include supplying the ways and wares enabling us to be as comfortable and fulfilled in a global village at least as much as we were in a small village a century ago, needs which were set by the requirements of genes that have been naturally selected for over millions of years.

There also will be an ever-present and growing market demand for ways and wares that makes our emerging global village more liveable, by uplifting *the six pillars of liveability.*

So far, we have been discussing the evolution of the market demand that will shape our vocational futures. But we also need to think about the vocational supply side; that is, how we best provide the capable and knowledgeable people who will be able to create these new products and services for these emerging industrial futures. Chapter 3 outlined several insight, hindsight, and foresight-based tools that can enable a person, group or organization to understand their *destinies* and then make wise choices about their future career paths. As well, in the previous chapter, we discussed how education and learning could change to ensure that all of us are as prepared as best we can be to build and tread 21st century successful career paths and a 21st century global metaphysical resourced prosperity. As discussed earlier, we can envision and then realize future work, vocations, and avocations by examining the following components of Future Knowledge's Futures curriculum:

- *the nine values of planetism, (FUTK05)*
- *the six pillars of liveability, (FUTK46)*
- *the six futures (FUTK41)*
- *the six future shaping tools, (FUTK40)*
- *the future shaper's quintet, the 5Vs (FUTK43)*
- *the six emotional pillars of future shaping, the Six Cs, (FUTK45), and*
- *the five drivers of social innovation, (FUTK56)*

11.5. Building Exemplar 21st Century Work and Workplaces

Fairness is more than an absence of unfairness, just as peace is more than an absence of war, or wellness is more than an absence of illness. In the modernist era of the early-mid 20th century, work and workplaces were not required to be fair, and were mostly unfair. And as discussed in Chapters 1 and 2, modernist globalisation was unfair as well. The modernist values of competition, self-interest, and win/lose dominated all our relationships, including work and workplace cultures. Fairness in work had to be fought for everywhere and was, for the most part, begrudgingly given. The Modernist Fordist/Taylorist workplace culture based on mass production and time and motion studies sought to create economies of scale to maximize efficiency and productivity, frequently to the detriment of employee wellbeing. The battle for fairness in work grew with the emerging labour movement challenging autocratic Modernist capitalist workplace administrations, using as its weapons employee solidarity and confrontational collective bargaining. Without the massive contribution of the labour movement, little improvement would have been achieved. Unfairness was lessened incrementally, but the question of what might constitute future fair work and fair workplaces was neither asked nor sought. It was world of ideological confrontation.

The mental baggage carried by many of those involved in these struggles persists to this day, and this is preventing many people from seeing the 21st century as it is, as a much less ideological and a more values based political era than were the 19th and 20th centuries. Postmodern and emerging Planetist values such as collaboration, mutual interest, and mutual benefit (win/win) will increasingly inform dialogue between the various stakeholders shaping work and workplace futures. In the 21st century work and workplaces where wealth will increasingly come from metaphysical resources, we will have no choice but to design and build democratic work and workplaces that enable all involved to thrive together, and where nobody is abused or exploited. If we do not do this the people who create metaphysical wealth in work will simply walk out the door to other workplaces where they and their work will be more appreciated.

Buckminster Fuller suggested that if we want to successfully shape the future and drive change it is better to stop fighting and chipping away at the old model, and instead to imagine and build a new model that makes the old one obsolete. I suggest that the global labour movement should now give itself a new brief of visualising and realising 21st century work and workplace perfection for the metaphysical economy of the 21st century. We know what we don't want, the still existing 20th century *impediments* that create dysfunctional workplaces. However, do we know what new 21st century-relevant *initiatives* we want to add to work and workplaces, and what *improvements to current work and workplaces* we want to make? Not enough people seem to be doing this work. It is about time more people did. If the global labour movement took the role of being a leader of this movement, one that sets out to determine and advocate what constitutes 21st century work and workplace perfection, it could play a major role in shaping the future of 21st century work and workplaces. To paraphrase George Bernard Shaw, we must *dream what could be, and say why not!*

Can we imagine what 21st century *working perfection* might look like? It is likely to be work and workplaces that optimally combine high knowledge, high learning, high productivity, high conviviality, and high liveability. And it will require less problem-centred managerialism and more mission-directed leadership from all involved in shaping work futures. I also contend that 21st century work cultures will promote the professionalisation of all work. Professional people have careers and follow career paths. They do not seek and get jobs. The concept of jobs, and the politics of 'providing' jobs that so dominated 20th century political conversations about work will disappear in the 21st century. In coming decades all workers will become knowledge workers, and many of these will become wisdom workers as well. Robots and other forms of automation will do the lower skilled work.

Truly liveable 21st century workplaces, wherever they are, will be built by uplifting all the six pillars of liveability. They will be informed by a Planetist moral compass that will include the values of interdependence, democracy, communitarianism, gender equality, and respect for difference. More liveable workplaces will be more productive workplaces. Just as relationships and trade in the 21st century are becoming ever more based on communitarian collaboration and less of individualistic competition, the same will be true for work and workplace cultures. Work collaboration ways and wares such as Zoom and Teams are already being developed to enable us to continue to collaborate even if we are working during a pandemic or collaborating across our global village.

Two of the most important elements of 21st century planetist work and workplace cultures will be interdependence and trust. The *Interdependence Trio* involves utilizing the Golden Rule, making mutual obligations, and seeking win/win outcomes. The *Trust Trio* says that for trust to exist we must have honesty, reliability, and competence. Imagine *workplace interdependence ways and wares* and *workplace trust assessment and building ways and wares!*

In the 21st century workplaces can and should be as least as mutually beneficial and fair as trade and commerce are becoming. Humanity can establish a set of universal rules and standards for the building and management of workplaces all over the planet, just as it is doing for global trade and commerce. Those who develop a vision of what 21st century work could become and who can envision exemplar 21st century liveable, convivial, and productive workplaces, can get to the future first and shape workplace futures everywhere.

Work has always been a major means for turning both physical and metaphysical resources into prosperity. It will continue to be a massive prosperity-uplifting machine, one that will be second in importance only to globalization itself.

At present commercial corporations and NGOs of all kinds are globalizing successfully. Even organized crime is globalizing. However, the same levels of globalization are not occurring in the labour movement. The labour union movement should seek to fully globalize itself so it can ensure that 21st century work and workplaces everywhere in our emerging global village are as fair and productive as they can be. A new vision of 21st century work and workplace perfection should be developed by all parties shaping the future of work in the 21st century. This brief could be added to the labour movement's current focus on protecting the rights and conditions of workers in the work they do today. As well it can work for the professionalization of all work and support a work future based on creating liveable workplaces with Planetist work cultures. The question that the employee/labour movement can ask of itself is, *if the current employee movement is not as 21st century appropriate and successful as it could be, what must it become to be as 21st century relevant and successful as possible?*

Chapter 12: Renewing Our Economic Mindsets for Building and Managing a Planetist Global Village

12.1. The Growing Planetist Moral Compass

Planetist values are informing the moral compasses of an increasing number of people. The Planetist moral compass tells us that:

- We should give our first allegiance and loyalty to planet over nation or to cultural/religious identity, for we live on a shared world and have a common future.
- Human beings are social creatures and happiest and most productive when living in convivial cooperative environments that facilitate greater interdependence, harmony, security, and respect of difference.
- Opportunity should be universal irrespective of race, culture, gender, sexual orientation, religion, or disability. Our *Circles of Identity* should include all humanity and not just some of it.
- People should decide who governs them: democracy is the most appropriate form of governance. They will increasingly take a dim view of and will resist autocracy and autocrats.
- The wellbeing and needs of both current and future generations should always be considered in our future-shaping decisions.
- Humanity is part of nature and we should conserve and not collaterally harm nature, just as we seek to conserve and not cause net collateral harm to ourselves.

These values will underpin our conceptual thinking as we construct our 21st century world.

Many Modernists, including political leaders who are Modernist populists like Trump or Modernist autocrats like Putin, will continue to give first allegiance to nation or tribe. They will dislike and conflict with those who are different and believe that confrontation and even war can solve global differences. They will favour competition and win/lose over collaboration and win/win, and they will favour autocracy over democracy. They will also treat women as inferiors and that they can trash nature in the name of progress. But this cohort is in decline. An ever-growing number of Planetist customers and voters will judge these Modernist people and governments increasingly harshly. If these Modernist leaders persist, they will become misfits and even pariahs in an ever more Planetist 21st century simply because they will offend more people because they not practicing 21st century ethics. Putin has already sunk to the same global status as Kim Jong-un. Those political and community leaders and commercial corporations with Planetist virtues will be rewarded by greater loyalty from their voters and followers, or their shareholders, suppliers, and customers.

Individual rights are not becoming less important. We have fought very hard to achieve current individual human rights and freedoms, and there is a significant portion of humanity who have not yet achieved this level of freedom. However, it is also true that from now on in our increasingly interdependent and communitarian 21st century, humanity will need to recognize that individual rights must now be balanced fairly with reciprocal responsibility to community and planet as well. The concept of *sustainable individualism* (FUTK64) is my suggestion to assist us to keep this balance at where it needs to be in our rapidly changing world.

We also know that some of our less admirable human traits are not going to vanish overnight. Greed and corruption by individuals, companies, and governments will not disappear anytime soon. They will, however, also be judged ever more harshly in an increasingly interdependent planetary society. The greedy and the corrupt will face the *Planetary Pariah Punishments (FUTK11)*, increased global shaming, and an ever more effective regime of national and international laws, such as through the International Criminal Court and the proposed Anti-Corruption Court.

Cultural values shifts of this kind and magnitude can take up to a generation to complete. I believe that the global society of 2045-2050 will be much more deeply interdependent and more willing to adhere to the three key elements of the *Interdependence Trio* of the Golden Rule, mutual obligations to shared destinations, and win/win outcomes. And where this is still necessary, we will seek to ensure that our negotiations are based on Garrett Hardin's *mutual coercion mutually agreed upon.*

Most parents want to leave a bigger legacy to their children that they received from their own parents. They also recognise that equity should be intergenerational as well as intra-generational: we should not steal from future generations just as we should not steal from others in our own generation. An Australian Environment Minister, Moss Cass, said to an OECD meeting of Environment Ministers in 1974, 'We have not inherited the natural world from our parents to do with what we like, we have borrowed it from our children, and we must act as if we hold it in trust for them.' In 2021 the Federal Court of Australia made an historic decision that reflects this view: it ruled that the Australian Environment Minster should, when she considered approving an extension of a coal mine, evaluate its impact on global heating and on the future wellbeing and safety of today's children. This decision and similar ones that will follow will have a massive impact on how we make all our future-shaping decisions. Intergenerational equity will become an ever more important consideration in our management of all environmental issues, and indeed in our considerations in all six pillars of liveability.

Planetist values in coming decades will inform an even stronger moral compass to guide the actions 21st century political, corporate and civil society leaders. This emerging global moral compass recognizes that the rising tide of globalization can and should be used to lift all boats not just some boats. As Nelson Mandela told us, we must globalize responsibility. Any global change program or political movement informed by Modernist mindsets, or seen to be undermining *the six pillars of liveability*, will be increasingly opposed. Win/loss is no longer an option in the 21st century. We will either succeed together or we will fail together.

12.2. Following in the Footsteps of Three 20th Century Visionaries

I have sought to build upon the combined legacies of three great 20th century visionaries: Marshall McLuhan, Kenneth Boulding, and Richard Buckminster Fuller. The British Prime Minister Tony Blair said in the year 2000 that the 20th century was the century of ideology, but he believed that the 21st century would be the century of ideals. I believe Blair is right, and that these ideals will be Planetist ideals. Those who continue to look at the world through Modernist ideological lenses, or even ideological lenses of any kind, will misunderstand and misconstrue what they see happening before them.

12.3. Realising the Vision of Kenneth Boulding

In 1989 the Soviet Union disintegrated. With this collapse one side of the great ideological divide that traumatized humanity for much of the 20th century also dissolved: communism. With this collapse, one form of capitalism, state or command capitalism, which is based on shaping economic and industrial futures through conscious government capital investment, fell from favour. What was left standing was free market capitalism and with it what was regarded as a mean and often brutal form of free market capitalism, namely neoliberalism. Command economies in Modernist times could deliver generosity and fairness, but fully free market economies rarely did. Both command capitalism and then the dominant form of neoliberal market capitalism were flawed. The command economy of state capitalism was bureaucratically encumbered and inflexible. Although it could deliver fairness and generosity it was structurally inflexible and not sufficiently resilient to social and technological change. And while the market economies were flexible and adaptable and could operate freely without government interference, they often delivered unfair outcomes.

Economics is called *the dismal science*. Traditionally it has focused on the management of scarcity. And budgets are devices that decide to whom we will be generous and to whom we will be mean. We assumed that scarcity would always be with us because we had not yet recognized the potential of metaphysical resources to create wealth without limit.

Neoliberalism, more generally, has been dedicated to limiting governments and expanding the private sector. Adherents to neoliberal economics did nothing to encourage intervention by individual governments to make economies more generous, humane, and fair.

In 2020 neoliberalism hit a wall. The economic disruption caused by the COVID-19 pandemic laid bare the inadequacy of Modernist neoliberalism for delivering the fair economic stimulation that was then urgently required. Keynesianism, which since the 1960s had fallen from favour, returned strongly to economic public policy in 2020-2021, to stimulate individual national economies to recover from the pandemic. Many people continue to believe that more government-led Keynesian interventionist public policies by national governments will always be needed. For them, no other route to fairness is perceivable. Most people noticed that Keynesian stimulus did indeed work very well in resurrecting economies damaged by the COVID-19 pandemic.

Many people now believe that any free-market economy operating without government intervention and across regional and global economies can never be fair. However, I believe they are being overly pessimistic.

Neoliberalism is not intrinsically unfair. The fact that neoliberalism was championed by many conservative governments has shaped many people's negative perceptions of neoliberalism. But these conservative governments carried moral compasses based on the Modernist values of individualism, self-interest/national-interest, competition, and win/lose. It was these Modernist values that made neoliberal economic outcomes unfair.

Is it possible that neoliberal economics could also be guided and managed by people with a Postmodern/Planetist moral compass? Can we construct a neoliberal global economic system and market that both operates free of government intervention and simultaneously delivers much fairer outcomes to all global villagers?

In fact, there were governments after 1980 that were both functionally neoliberal and informed by Postmodern moral compasses. The first of these were the Hawke and Keating governments in Australia, followed by the Blair and Brown *Third Way* governments in the UK, the Clinton administration in the USA, and most recently the Macron Government in France. If economic scarcity is ultimately replaced by metaphysical-generated economic plenty, as I believe will be the case, we will not need meanness dispensed by neoliberal economics at all. We will need instead new economic management tools that are appropriate for these emerging 21st century realities.

As the year 2000 approached, unfair outcomes as part of globalization were still accepted by many with their hands on the levers of economic public policy and corporations. However, by then enough people were also fed up with the injustice associated with modernist economics to begin to clamour for change. What these people believed the world needed was not only *free trade* but *fair trade* as well. And people began to realize that fair trade meant more collaboration and less competition, mutual interest, and shared benefit or win/win outcomes. They also realised that managing the global economy could no longer be left to individual nation states to manipulate at their will and in their own interests. Global collaboration was now needed to negate the excesses of self-interested win/lose operators such as the Wall Street banks whose actions had caused three global financial crises in 1986-87, 1997-1998 and in 2007. The increasing demand for fairness became a driver for economic reform. Most people wanted greater fairness, but most people believed, and many still do, this might be an impossible dream if we continue to let neoliberalism dominate our global economic management and trading culture.

In first decade of the 21st century those supporting neoliberal economic management were also beginning to realise the harm caused by the current Modernist economic orthodoxy. They now recognized what had been obvious to others for many decades: that there were alternative concepts and approaches to Modernist neoliberalism, alternatives that had been in mainstream global conversations since the 1960s.

So to take this exploration further, let us go back to the 1960s and the *Apollo Program* and the *Earthrise* narrative. Many people then were concerned about where globalization might ultimately take humanity. In 1962, Marshall McLuhan prophesied that globalization would ultimately create a *global village*. He specified a *village* not a *town* or a *city*. His choice of the word *village* was prescient and important. He did not suggest a city where most of us would be strangers to each other and did not trust each other, and where people accepted that they did not even need to trust each other. Villages are mostly friendly places where everyone knows everyone else and where most people like to befriend and collaborate with everyone else. This was a far cry from the prevailing Modernist brutal and friendless survival-of-the-fittest economic reality of the last quarter of the 20th century.

Besides McLuhan there were two other visionary giants in the 1960s, the economist Kenneth Boulding and the futurist architect, systems theorist and inventor, Richard Buckminster Fuller. These two began to use the term *Spaceship Earth* in their work. In his 1966 essay *The Economics of the Coming Spaceship Earth,* Boulding prophesied that both national and global economies should/would transform from what he called *Cowboy economies* to what he called *Spaceman/Spaceship economies*, though he did not outline how such a transformation might occur. To me, this essay was both a *Probable future prediction* and a *Preferred Future vision*. In 1969 Buckminster Fuller built upon Boulding's work when he published his extraordinary book, *Operating Manual for Spaceship Earth.* Perhaps needless to say, the work of these three visionaries kickstarted and inspired my own work.

Besides Kenneth Boulding's important essay *The Economics of the Coming Spaceship Earth,* my thinking has also been guided by Garrett Hardin's essay *The Tragedy of the Commons*. Hardin told us that humanity's dialogues in the 21st century will increasingly recognize our interdependence and that we will increasingly be obligated to negotiate what forms of mutual coercion we can mutually agree upon. This will be a question that will increasingly shape virtually all global dialogues and negotiations if we are to successful build a shared fairer future with effective and mutually beneficial global political, social, and business relationships and create a world that is liveable for all. A good example of mutual coercion mutually agreed upon is the tortuous global negotiation processes currently under way as humanity battles to meet the challenge posed by global heating.

As a disciple of both Boulding and Buckminster Fuller, I asked this question based on Boulding's concept of a *Spaceship Economy*: If I were the leader of a spaceship with a multicultural crew travelling on a 20-year journey to a distant planet, what values and practices would I promote to ensure the mission were successful? Clearly, we would need to look after our shared spaceship home to ensure it completes the journey by returning us safely to Earth. This means we must have first allegiance to our vehicle, our *Spaceship Earth*. We would also need to build a state-of-the-art liveable environment for the spaceship's crew and promote planetist virtuous behaviours by that crew. This led to identifying much of my curriculum, including the *nine values of planetism,* the *six pillars of liveability,* the *four domains of sustainable prosperity, the interdependence and trust trios,* and the *cosmonaut economy quintet,* the last of which will be described shortly. I recognised that all these concepts were already becoming more ascendant in global values shifts, particularly in the rapidly growing global educated middle class.

As mentioned earlier, Boulding was also clearly aware that there are two sciences with names derived from the same Greek word *Ecos,* meaning *home*: the social science of Economics, which means managing the home, and the natural science of Ecology, which means understanding the home. In the 1980s an *ecological economics* movement was born. This form of economics seeks to honour and build on the work of Boulding, to bring the two home-focused sciences of economics and ecology into a single future shaping framework and tool. *Ecological economics* focuses on sustainable and fair outcomes in both intragenerational and intergenerational terms. *Feminist economics* was also born in the 1980s. It focuses on gender equality, inclusion, and social justice. These two movements are major contributions towards creating a new economics that is more appropriate for managing humanity's shared 21st century home. They are contributions to humanity's attempts to include into mainstream 21st century economic management frameworks all the considerations that we recognize were previously excluded from modernist orthodox free market economics including neoliberalism. These are the elements that were called *externalities* by Modernist economists. However, I suggest that my own *planetist (cosmonaut) economics* is more holistic than either or both of *ecological economics and feminist economics* and more completely fulfils the brief humanity needs to realize Kenneth Boulding's *spaceship economy* vision.

If we can imagine a form of economics informed by Planetist instead of Modernist values, we can begin to imagine the economic management machinery that will be needed to manage our ever more integrated and interdependent global economy and village. Any unilateral economic intervention by an individual national government acting in its own self-interest from now on can increasingly cause collateral harm to others in other nations and even disrupt the global economy. We will need many new collaborative arrangements to ensure our global economy becomes as fair as it must become, and as resilient to such interventions as is possible. And such collaboration is now the biggest game on our planet. The EU, the G7 and the G20, the OECD and ASEAN, the hundreds of global NGOs, the ever-growing number of multilateral and bilateral trade agreements, and the International Criminal Court, are just a few examples of this planetary collaboration boom. The UN system is now only one part of this growing global collaboration infrastructure

Humanity will need to collaborate to create of a common global currency. It will most likely operate besides national currencies as second global currency and it will replace the current de facto role the US dollar now plays. This will be needed for the same reasons we need a shared global second language such as Esperanto. And for the same reasons this currency should not be an upgraded national currency that is given a new global role. It will need to be a totally new fit-for-purpose second currency. Strongly backed by global financial institutions, this global currency could significantly reduce disruptive currency speculation and over time eliminate it all together. Over time it might replace an increasing number of national currencies. But this decision would be up to individual nation states and regions like the EU. But, irrespective of what each nation state or regional administration does, our global trading and investment system would be able to function well and safely. The basic essential is that our emerging global economy needs economic management rules and processes that ensure it is never vulnerable to interference by individual national governments, organised crime, and financial speculators and manipulators, and that it is as resilient as it can be to those who seek to harm or exploit it.

To sum up, there are currently two coexisting modes of globalisation and capitalism. A global economy informed by a Modernist moral compass describes Boulding's *cowboy economy* while a global economy informed by a Planetist moral compass would include the core ingredients of Boulding's *spaceship economy*. The *cowboy forms* are in decline and the *cosmonaut forms* are in ascendance

12.4. Consolidating the 21st Century Cosmonaut Economy

While the long-term trends are slowly delivering a *Planetist (Cosmonaut) Future*, what future-shaping public policies could be initiated to more thoroughly consolidate this emerging *21st century Planetist (cosmonaut) economy?* I believe there are five of them, which I have called *The Cosmonaut Economy Quintet*. This consists of aiming to grow metaphysical wealth, stimulate and reward innovation, promote Planetist values, foster liveability, and manage plenty as well as scarcity *(FUTK68)*. These are discussed below:

12.4.1 Grow Metaphysical Wealth

Richard Buckminster Fuller told us in his 1976 book *Approaching the Benign Environment* that 'Wealth consists of the physical that must be conserved and the metaphysical that can only grow.' He is telling us that our ability to prosper will now increasingly be generated by human ideas, by our creativity and imagination, and by our conceptual thinking and our entrepreneurship. There is now no limit to how much humanity can prosper. The only limit will be our imagination, our innovation, and our enterprise. If a society can expand its critical and creative thinking capability, it can also uplift its metaphysical wealth. China, for example, which has a future-shaping mindset, is already focussed on growing its metaphysical wealth and is opening a new university every week.

Many ways of producing a world full of knowledge based (metaphysical) future makers have been discussed. These include promoting the *four philosophical future-shaping tools* (FUTK25) which stimulate the learning of philosophy from the primary years of school onwards, the *seven modes of 21st century learning* (FUTK27) and the *four domains of holistic learning* (FUTK28).

12.4.2 Stimulate and Reward Innovation

Invention, the creation of new ideas and new thinking, will be the major source of 21st century metaphysical prosperity. But *invention is not innovation. Innovation* involves turning *inventions* into new tradeable products or services. *Innovation* involves finding the means to *do old tasks better and new tasks first.* I have suggested that an innovation culture can be consciously promoted across the whole of society to stimulate new modes of thinking. The *innovation duet,* which consists of ways plus wares *(FUTK53),* can be critical, for it can be a tool for focussing on turning *inventions* into *innovations.* I have also suggested that there are *five social drivers of innovation (FUTK56).*

In their 1996 book *Competing for the Future,* Gary Hamel and C. K. Prahalad told us that 'success goes to those who get to the future first.' They did not say that those who compete most ruthlessly in the management of the current generation of businesses would win. Being a ruthless competitor in a then Modernist world was yesteryear's brutal formula for becoming wealthy. Now success will go those who first and best innovate the *ways and wares* to supply the emerging demands of the markets of our growing global village. Now we need to be innovative to get to the future first and then act with enlightened self-interest by collaborating and sharing benefits with others (win/win) if we wish to be become 21st century successful. We can and should imagine and then build new 21st century appropriate industrial futures, including industries that uplift liveability, create *sustainable prosperity,* and affirm and grow the *nine values of planetism.*

Elon Musk is one of the world's richest people because he has been able to get to the future first in in two categories: electric motor vehicles and aerospace technologies/services. There will be many more 21st century metaphysical innovators who will identify many *new innovation arenas,* and new *ways* and *wares* in these arenas, who will build the Planetist global village in the coming decades and grow global metaphysical wealth.

12.4.3 Promote Planetist Values

The values we have used to grow and manage a series of national, often monocultural Modernist communities will be inappropriate for growing and managing a multicultural and integrated 21st century global village. The values of Modernism, such as independence, self/national interest, individualism, competition, and win/lose outcomes are 21st century inappropriate and will undermine our ability to thrive in the 21st century. In the third decade of the 21st century we are offended when we see yesteryear-thinking Modernist decision makers making catastrophic 21st century-inappropriate decisions. In the corporate sector Rio Tinto and BHP destroy and mutilate sacred indigenous heritage and oil companies continue to search for more oil as if it will be in demand forever. There will now be a huge global clean-up required to restore the collateral damage caused by 250 years of fossil fuels production and to turn Blake's dark Satanic Mills back into a green and pleasant planet. But this will provide an economic opportunity. Fossil fuel production and use was a generator of wealth in the Modernist past. Cleaning up the collateral damage caused by it and innovating clean alternatives to it will now be a generator of wealth in the Planetist future. In the national government sector Bolsonaro's Brazil trashed priceless rainforests and sought to undo all the progressive environmental legislation brought into being since *Earthrise*. In the USA a Modernist populist Republican Party aspires to do the same. The Planetist part of humanity looks on amazed, and asks *what kind of yesteryear mental universe do these people inhabit?*

If we want to become 21st century successful people we must take on 21st century Planetist values and practice 21st century Planetist virtues. In turn, these values will determine what people will value and seek in the markets of our emerging global village. Market economies will be increasingly informed by the values of Planetists, who will number 5 billion in 2030. This is because those with Planetist parents or mentors are more likely to become Planetists themselves, as will those who complete any form of tertiary education.

Investors will invest in what they believe will be successful ventures in 21st century society. These ventures will therefore need to be compatible with *the nine values of planetism, the six pillars of liveability,* and the *four domains of sustainable prosperity,* not only because there will be so many Planetists but because those who cause net economic, ecological, social, and cultural collateral harm will increasingly become planetary pariahs.

12.4.4 Foster liveability

Educated middle class people want to live in environments that are as liveable as they can afford. Uplifting *the six pillars of liveability,* namely prosperity, harmony, inclusion, sustainability, health and security, is a core purpose of most government public policy everywhere. Improved liveability is both a reward for past accumulated wealth and a generator of future wealth. Industries and ventures that increase liveability will be major contributors to the 21st century *cosmonaut economy.*

Incidentally, we could use *the six pillars of liveability* to create new 21st century-relevant assessment indices for the measurement of *human progress* in our emerging Planetist global village to replace the archaic and useless GDP.

12.4.5 Manage plenty as well as scarcity

Economics has significantly involved itself in the management of scarcity and how this scarcity might be fairly apportioned in the interests of all. No wonder it is called the dismal science. Economic management has largely been directed at considering the management of meanness and generosity, and politics and budgets are largely based on the management of scarcity, for they decide who receives the generosity and who the meanness. Modernist budgets were dominated by win/lose.

In the 21st century we will become more concerned about the management of plenty and win/win in the interests of all. Until the Postmodern era, most of us believed that the source of wealth came from our use of physical resources, with or without value adding. We also believed that scarcity would always be present because physical resources are limited and that there would always be limits to growth itself and to how prosperous we might become. Because economic management and public policy is largely about managing scarcity we have developed many economic tools (both ways and wares) to manage scarcity effectively. Because we know now that a world of plenty is possible because humanity's capability to create new metaphysical resources is potentially unlimited, we will now need to learn how to effectively manage both generosity and plenty.

We now need a set of economic management tools that enable us to manage our global village to maximize the benefit we receive from natural resources while conserving and not collaterally harming them. We also need them to facilitate the development and spread of metaphysical wealth, and with it the management of plenty. The management of plenty includes policies to reduce corruption and punish cowboys (Modernists) who are still seeking to steal and promote win/lose. In the future plenty must be as fair as the management of scarcity and must be seen to be so.

In the coming decades humanity will promote planetist integrity in all global villagers. Philanthropy is one form of generosity that abides within the market economy. In fact, philanthropy is becoming a mainstream activity in the 21st century. Many people who have built high levels of metaphysical wealth and who have planetist values have become the biggest philanthropists who have ever lived. Can we imagine other *generosity delivery ways and wares* that can also operate within a market economy? These will certainly appear in the next decade, for there will be people who will have the appropriate values and mindsets and who be able to imagine and build such innovations.

We can also use new emerging global anti-corruption legal instruments and *planetary pariah punishments (FUTK11)* to punish recalcitrant modernists who will increasingly become the planetary wicked in the 21st century. This might include *integrity assessment and integrity building ways and wares.*

I would like to ask the planet's economists and public policy experts to develop the management instruments, the *cosmonaut economy ways and wares,* that can enable this *cosmonaut economy quintet* to be internalised into 21st century economic management tools. These would enable all 21st century future-shapers, including government public policy initiators and all investors, to act with enlightened self-interest to shape the future of humanity's 21st century global village in the interests of all.

12.5. Investing in the Planetist Future

Cowboy globalisation is receding and *cosmonaut globalisation* is replacing it. A new 21st century equivalent of the ancient, mutually beneficial form of interdependent globalisation conducted along the Silk Road and over sea routes is emerging. But this time it will be truly global. At its centre are programs such as the immense Chinese-driven *Belt and Road Initiative* (BRI). This is where foreign aid will increasingly be directed, to enable all to help themselves and prosper sustainably through being able to trade in a global village. The net result of all the global change described in this book will be a 21st century world trading and investment system more free and fair and beneficial for all. Ultimately most of us, except some political autocrats, international crime bosses and religious extremists, want a future world that is beneficial and fair to all.

More investors, traders, and political leaders are committed to Planetist-informed economic and social development and to building an increasingly powerful global trading and investments regime governed by a set of universal rules. These rules will be guided by a planetist moral compass. These rules will be negotiated and used to conduct political and economic relationships, and for dealing with emerging crises such as global heating, pandemics, and peacebuilding in zones of conflict. A worldwide legal regime will be put in place. This will include the current International Criminal Court and the proposed Anti-Corruption Court. Civil society NGOs such as Amnesty International, Transparency International and the WWF will have planet-wide watching briefs. These organisations already have Planetist values and practice Planetist virtues. They will work to both promote good planetary behaviour and blow the whistle on bad planetary behaviour. The collective outcome of all these components working together will be a Planetist form of globalization, a *cosmonaut globalisation* that will build Kenneth Boulding's *spaceship economy*.

Cowboy *capitalism* probably reached its zenith in the late 1980s and has been in slow decline ever since. However, for a while we will probably continue to be vulnerable to both selfish cowboy behaviour and our own ultimately destructive collective decision making if this continues to be informed by nation-first cowboy mindsets.

History will judge *modernist populists* and *modernist autocrats* who initiate conflict harshly, as it will those unwilling to collaborate with others even in our planet's hours of need. It will note, for example, that when the COVID-19 crisis was upon us China collaborated and sought to be part of the solution, while Trump's USA did not. The USA remained part of the problem until the timely arrival of the Biden administration. It is noteworthy that Modernist populists such as Trump and Bolsonaro, who practised change denial, division and confrontation rather than follow the scientific evidence and collaborate with others to meet shared global challenges, were also the political leaders who failed most spectacularly in containing the damage caused by COVID-19 within their own jurisdictions.

Some people still believe that most of those who trade and invest are mostly, or even only, self-interested. And some still believe that capitalism is inherently flawed and cannot be reformed. I do not share these views and have already outlined the changes happening to capitalism itself: the transformation of capitalism from 20th century *cowboy capitalism* to 21st century *cosmonaut capitalism*. The investment community is also increasingly informed by the values of Planetism and will progressively invest in activities that uplift *the six pillars of liveability*. They will want to make their investments informed by Planetist ethics. Any Planetist-informed investor will know that if they invest in fossil fuel, for example, they will become planetary pariahs and leave themselves saddled with stranded assets. They also believe they can do economically well by doing ecological, social, and cultural good, not bad. After all, most of these investors and bankers need to justify what they do at work to their own children over the breakfast table: the same children they are seeking to educate well and who will therefore most likely have Planetist values.

This transformation is already well under way in philanthropic communities. It can be seen in, for example, The Giving Pledge, a campaign initiated by Warren Buffett and Bill and Melinda Gates. Most of these ultra-wealthy people have generated their wealth from metaphysical resources and they already hold Planetist values. They donate to address planet wide issues such as global heating rather than national issues.

Modernist investors, or cowboy capitalist investors, were mostly motivated by narrow self-interest and win/lose. They believed prospering economically while causing ecological, social, and cultural harm, was acceptable behaviour. They were guided by what was legally permitted rather than what they believed was ethically right. Whether they recognize it or not, their behaviour is informed by a modernist moral compass. Planetist investors, cosmonaut capitalists all, are more likely to be guided by enlightened self-interest rather than narrow self-interest. They are unlikely to invest in proposals that might cause net collateral harm in any form: to people, to communities, to other species, or to our planetary environment. These Planetist investors will more often want to seek win/win/win: a triple win, first for the investee, second for the investor, and third for our planetary home. Many of these are *socially responsible investment (SRI) organizations or Ethical investors* who are already making investments guided by planetist informed moral compasses.

In late 2020 the demise of the Trump administration and the election of the more collaborative and internationalist Biden administration heartened Planetists everywhere. This change will enable nations to initiate and negotiate a more global collaborative and win/win approach to corporate taxation. Some people fear a return of Modernity. However, Modernists will only succeed if they actively rig the whole democratic system to suit themselves and the rest of us allow them to do this. I think the sun is already setting on them.

Meanwhile, Planetist-informed global collaboration is already working for the rest of us. The G7, the G20 and the OECD are now beginning to build the long-sought fair-to-all global taxation regime that will be required for the effective management of our interdependent global village. This includes a universal approach to assessing and setting the rights of national governments to tax the profits of multinational corporations depending on where the corporation's customers live instead of where the corporation chooses to reside. This initiative has also set a universal minimum corporate tax rate of 15% with so-called 'top-up' provisions to discourage nations from competing in a race to the taxation bottom to attract tax-avoiding multinational corporation residents to their jurisdictions. These two things will create disincentives for corporations to minimise their taxation by shifting their profits to nations with low corporate taxation regimes or to tax havens. Such planet first collaboration and win/win approaches will increasingly be used to mould emerging global financial arrangements.

One feature of the early years of *cosmonaut capitalism* will be an ever-increasing internationalisation of revenue raising that will be used to both to improve liveability and the governance of our emerging global village. Given the realities of national politics it is unlikely that an already existing national tax will be handed over by nation states to facilitate more effective global governance. It is likely, therefore, that a new tax arrangement will be required to finance this governance. These taxes will probably be based on the ever-growing interdependence between nation states and commercial and non-commercial NGOs organizations. In 1972 the economist James Tobin proposed that a new planet wide tax on the movement of capital across national boundaries be introduced. I believe this so-called *Tobin Tax* will most likely be the first of several new international taxes. The revenue raised could then be used to fund the work of the United Nations and its successors, and also fund the development of the new planetary governance arrangements that will need to be introduced during the remainder of the 21st century. The current arrangements of funding global governance through the levying of nation states will need to change. It is not acceptable to permit powerful individual nations to control all the purse strings that finance the governance of our shared 21st century global village. Such control by nation states over global finances has stymied the work of the UN since its inception. Over time we can expect that the emerging Planetist moral compass will encourage all organisations and individuals who expect to economically benefit from our increasing global interdependence to become more willing to pay planet wide taxes.

An ever more liveable and sustainably prosperous planet can be the outcome of our collective investment should we choose to build a framework that can guide all our decision making towards realising a more liveable future. In the 21st century national governments are becoming relatively less powerful because their capacity to generate change is limited by the fact they can mostly only act alone within their own political jurisdictions. The exception is when they invest in projects and developments that consciously promote increased interdependence between governments, businesses, and communities, as the Chinese government is doing with their Belt and Road Initiative.

However, there are no such limitations on private wealth. It can be spent anywhere, and private wealth is increasingly being invested as if there were no national boundaries any more. An increasing number of these private investors are seeking to do economically well by doing social, ecological, and cultural good, and on a planet wide scale. They are creating what we can call *sustainable investment*, investment that avoids net collateral harm and uplifts *sustainable prosperity*. These private investors, and some national sovereign funds as well, are investing according to their values and increasingly these values are Planetist values.

I am interested in providing this large group of actual or potential investors, most of who will have Planetist values, to put planet first and invest in projects compatible with their values. I seek to provide them with a curriculum that can enable them to realise such an aspiration.

The proportion of people whose choices and behaviours are influenced by Modernist values will continue to shrink as the 21st century progresses. We are now entering an era where Planetist values, and the aspirations of billions to live in a liveable global village, will increasingly influence the choices people make about what they should or should not ethically do and support, what they should purchase, how they should invest their time, energy and money, and what career choices they want to make for themselves. And social media, and the global media more generally, will be ever more powerful drivers of this change, despite the recalcitrant efforts of some of the remaining cowboy media such as a Fox News.

Our struggles to create a climate safe and pandemic safe world, and a peaceful future, will remind all of us that collaboration rather than competition will be obligatory from now on if we want to ensure that humanity can thrive in its shared planetary home. Our news is now as least as much dominated by what is happening beyond our national borders as what is happening within them. We are concerned about what the leaders of governments other than our own are doing, and our heroes, villains and celebrities now live on a global stage and communicate with global audiences.

John Donne's words 'No man is an island … I am involved in mankind. And therefore never send to know for whom the bell tolls; it tolls for thee,' were written nearly 400 years ago. In the 21st century his view of our world has finally moved from the idea margin to the idea mainstream.

Chapter 13: Conclusion

During the COVID-19 lockdowns many of us have had the opportunity to become more reflective, to spend a greater proportion of our time in reflective mode. Yes, the COVID-19 pandemic has caused widespread human illness, misery, and grief, and much economic disruption. However, good might come out of it as well. Humanity certainly will want to ensure that next time we are threatened by a pandemic it will be much better prepared. Indeed, this reflective time out might prove to be a big gain. In Chapter 8, I suggested that humanity can work smart or work hard but not at the same time. During COVID-19 many of us could not work hard, but many of us will have used the reflective time to find new means to work smart and to review whether a personal or collective *probable future* we have been heading towards continues to be where we still want to go. Perhaps we created for ourselves new *preferred and possible future* destinations that might be more enticing destinations for us rather than those on our current *probable pathway*.

Optimism was discussed very early in this book. Clearly I'm an optimist, but is there evidence we can be as optimistic I claim we should be? Let us explore some of the evidence that the realization of a universally prosperous and state-of-the-art liveable global village in the 21st century is not unreasonably optimistic. Here are some of the key pieces of evidence:

- Globalization is the biggest economic prosperity-uplifting machine that has ever been created. International trade and investment both continue to grow. And wealth is expanding to an increasing number of people.
- Education is rising everywhere. It is also broadening, with more people being educated; and it is deepening, with more people are being educated for longer. Informal education is growing massively as well. Most of us are having more opportunities to learn whatever, whenever and from whoever we wish to learn. Educated people can prosper economically by transforming what they know, the metaphysical resources they possess, into prosperous and fulfilled work, thereby generating more wealth both for themselves and for society.

- Economic prosperity is rising rapidly around the world. The educated middle class is growing by the population of New York City every three months. It will reach 5 billion by the year 2030. Wealth generated from metaphysical resources, unlike prosperity generated from our planet's limited physical resources, can grow without limit as it will only be limited by the capability of our creative minds and our collective entrepreneurship and enterprise.
- As more people are educated and educated for longer, Planetist values and ethics are being absorbed by, and informing the behaviours of, more people. These behaviours include what we buy, sell and invest in, and what career paths we choose to build for ourselves.
- During the Modernist period when wealth was largely created from the utilisation of natural resources it was to be expected that the rich could become richer while the poor might remain poor or even become poorer through a dominant *Modernist* win/lose culture. There was general acceptance that poverty would always be present because wealth would be limited by the availability of natural resources, and by the control over the use of these by a limited number of self-interested people. However, if economic prosperity is based on the use of metaphysical resources, on what we know and can do, there need not be any limits to humanity's wealth and prosperity. Therefore, the conclusion is that the rich can become richer and the poor can also become richer. Universal prosperity is possible, and poverty can be eliminated, and even more rapidly so if a *Planetist* win/win global culture continues to develop.
- As more people become economically prosperous, they will want to invest more of their wealth in making their world more liveable for both themselves and others. They can accomplish this by uplifting not only their own economic prosperity, but by uplifting the five other pillars of liveability, namely harmony, inclusion, sustainability, health, and security.
- Nelson Mandela pointed out in the year 2000 that humanity must *globalize responsibility* to ensure it avoided creating *islands of plenty in seas of poverty*. Planetists are committed to *globalizing responsibility* while the declining numbers of Modernists are not so committed. As people become more educated their *circles of identity* and *circles of concern* expand until these eventually cover the whole planet, all of

humanity and all of nature. These expanding circles are the driving forces of *the globalization of responsibility*. People with expanding *circles of identity and circles of concern* are increasingly investing their income in not only their own liveability but, by investing in initiatives that uplift all the six pillars of liveability everywhere, in creating a more liveable world for all. Planetists primarily invest according to their values. They want to invest to do economically well while they are also doing ecological, social and cultural good. More than $100 trillion will be transferred between generations in the next decade. The recipients of this wealth transfer will be the most highly educated generation that has ever lived: for the most part this generation will embody Planetist values.

- The ability of nation states to invest capital and resources to change the world is limited by the fact that they must always give priority to the interests of their own people and their own national interests more generally. On the other hand, private wealth can be spent anywhere and this will increasingly be spent by people who put planet first. There are no limits to the capacity of private creators of metaphysical wealth to invest in whatever and wherever they wish. They are free to make decisions guided by both enlightened self-interest and altruism.

So we can be optimistic that wealth and particularly private wealth and investment will grow in magnitude and will also become more globally responsible. Whatever kind of future world humanity might aspire to realise, there will be sufficient financial resources and an ever more integrated interdependent global economy that will be able to realize any aspiration humanity might seek to build.

So, if an ever more prosperous humanity does develop a shared vision for its future as I have suggested it should, what might that shared vision be? Any visualized aspirational future scenario should be clear, and also exciting enough to engage us so that all of us are motivated to commit ourselves to realizing it. It should also be flexible enough to enable different approaches and contributions from different cultures to be embraced by all. I believe that the United Nations *Millennial Development Goals* (for the years 2000-2015) and the *Sustainable Development Goals* (for the years 2015-2030) described in Chapter 7 could be precursors of something bigger to come. What should that be?

Throughout this book the suggestion has been that humanity *could first visualize and then realize a global village that is a liveable as we can make.* Perhaps we can imagine and create *Liveability Heaven!* Such a shared vision could provide such an uplifting *utopian realistic* vision for the next three decades through to the year 2050.

Who does not want to live in a more liveable world? We can conclude that this is pretty much nobody except maybe some religious and cultural extremists. The term *liveability* combines sufficient clarity and sufficient breadth to engage the commitment of most of the world's diverse cultures. It can be customized for different cultures and so create rich cultural diversity. In Chapter 6, I discussed liveability as *plausible, preferred, and possible future scenario*s for the human race in the 21st century. I believe that the innovation of *liveability uplifting ways and wares* and the growing market demand driven by the values of the educated middle class will make it a more *probable future scenario* than most people might imagine. The collective building of a liveable global village through uplifting the *six pillars of liveability* can become the major engine for creating universal economic prosperity in the 21st century. Chapter 6 outlined a global liveability industrial future that could realize this outcome. Any global program to follow the UN Sustainable Development Goals and recover from global setbacks such as financial crises or post pandemic economic crises could focus on uplifting global liveability! It can also create appropriate indices to enable it to assess the progress humanity is making to create an ever more liveable future.

This book has set out to provide a curriculum and a set of tools to enable anyone to create 21st century success for themselves. Here 'anyone' can refer to individuals, organisations, communities, or nations. Sixty-nine concepts and tools have been presented throughout this book and are listed in the Appendix.

Seeking to innovate a liveable future for all humanity is not only ethically right; it is also a pragmatic and smart thing to do. People who are excluded and left behind will direct their consequential disappointment and anger into seeking to undermine or even destroy the good works of others or they will seek to threaten our collective security: it is important that we commit ourselves to maximizing inclusion as we work together to shape humanity's collective future as well as our individual futures. The challenges posed by global heating and pandemics have reminded us that our future must be seen as a collective future. We cannot any longer choose to opt out. We are all part of every global problem and solution whether we like it or not.

This book is possibly the first time anybody has attempted to create anything like an integrated curriculum for understanding the 21st century and for thriving in it. It aspires to enable everybody to become their own futurist and not have to seek advice from others when they need future-related knowledge. We all should be able to acquire the future knowledge and the understanding we need for ourselves and not leave this to experts. We should be able to shape the future simply because we all have a future that is there for us to shape, even if for some of us that future will be longer than for others! The shaping of futures should be such a fundamental capability that we all should seek to develop it.

At the beginning, I stated that the primary purpose of this book was to create a holistic toolkit for doing two of the most important things that humans do: shape the future; and initiate, build and amicably end relationships. So far our education systems have collectively done precious little to develop either of these critical capabilities. *The Future Knowledge Compendium* offers a futures curriculum designed to fill this void. However, there are many places in this concepts bank and tool kit where others could add value to what has been created so far: for example, adding new *ways and wares* to the *liveability industrial future*. I will be providing opportunities for people to get in touch with me about this.

The Future Knowledge Academy wishes to become a global network of organizations and individuals who want to work with it to further develop *future knowledge*. Our aim is to build a global future shaping capability around its core purpose of building a 21st century on Planet Earth that is fully liveable (that is prosperous, harmonious, inclusive, sustainable, healthy, and secure) for all its residents, both human and non-human. We want to invite all actual or would-be *utopian realists* who share our aspirations to contribute. There are many new innovations already appearing in global markets that can enable us to do this well. And because we have announced our intentions, we believe others will come forward with suggested innovations that can better facilitate our aspirations.

Too much of our current so called 'leadership' still possesses deeply held 20th century values and management dominated conceptual thinking that is unsuitable for guiding humanity's journey towards our planet's emerging global village, the vision first suggested by Marshall McLuhan in 1962. This narrative of the birth and development of our global multicultural and interdependent, planetist informed, global village will be, I believe, the biggest story of the 21st century.

In the coming two decades current 21st century inappropriate leadership will be replaced by an educated Planetist leadership drawn from the 5 billion educated middle class people who will possess Planetist values. By 2035 the *Modernist populist* movement, and the remaining *Modernist autocrats* as well, will be history. The Future Knowledge Academy has as one of its core goals to ensure that this emerging political, academic, research, corporate, religious, and educational leadership will embody more of the concepts outlined here in *The Future Knowledge Compendium* and be taught in the *Future Knowledge Academy,* and hopefully many other places as well in the coming decades.

A liveable Planet Earth and shared sustainable prosperity in the 21st century is what most of us want for ourselves and our children and grandchildren. It requires humanity to become the best collaborative builder it can be. To create this future humanity will need to feel and share some pain to achieve shared gain. There even will be moments where the pain of Garrett Hardin's *mutual coercion mutually agreed upon* will be required. But the gain will be there for all of us to share, and it can be synergistic (2+2=5) gain. The alternative narrative offered to us by the remaining Modernist populists in their declining years will be more antagonistic loss (2+2=3) or even a zero-sum gain or worse. Modernist populists can only offer their 20th century yesteryear mindsets, and they will trade on fear, hostility to difference, and nation/tribe first. I am certain that most of humanity is too conscious and smart to accept their offerings and be taken to places where it is not in our long-term interests to go: to a divided, hostile, violent and trashed planetary future.

As the 21st century further unfolds before us we will increasingly recognize that we have no choice but to collaborate and share the responsibility of shaping humanity's future on Planet Earth. This future can be what collective humanity wants it to be, a preferred future global village that we will shape and design, a global village that is as liveable as we can make and in which humanity and other species can thrive and not just survive. Humanity should not settle for anything less.

The End

Appendix: The Future Knowledge Curriculum

- Twelve Mindsets for 21st century Futurists: Maximise your imagination + be both Prophet and Visionary + be a Manager and Leader of self and other + embody Planetist Values + build Positive Futures rather than eliminate Negative Futures + embed sustainable behaviours in yourself +.understand and grow interdependence + value Questions and Treasure Reflection + be a Utopian Realist.+ expand your Circle of Identity + recognize the role of, and embody all of the six future shaping tools + build a Liveable Future (FUTK01).
- Fourteen Global Trends: Growing Interdependence and interconnectedness + Rising Educational levels. + Increasing Global Wealth + A growing Educated Middle Class + A Single Integrated Global Marketplace. + Growing Communitarianism + Rising Democracy+ New Planet Wide Punishments + Increased Multilateralism + An emerging integrated global financial and investment market. + An ageing planet + Religion under Pressure. + Rising Sustainability + A global village customized for difference. (FUTK02).
- The nine values shifts from modernism, via post modernism, to planetism (FUTK03).
- The Three Global Paradigms: Modernism + Post Modernism, + Planetism (FUTK04).
- The nine values of planetism = first allegiance to planet + collaborate with those who are different+ communitarianism + governance through democracy + humanity part of nature + sustainable behaviours + gender equality + resolve conflict through collaboration/negotiation + safekeeping through security (FUTK05)
- The Three Relationships: Dependence + Independence + Interdependence (FUTK06).

- The Three Primary Allegiances: Tribalism (first allegiance to Culture/Tribe) +Nationalism (first allegiance to Nation) + Planetism (first allegiance to Planet) (FUTK07).
- The Interdependence Trio = The Golden Rule + Mutual Obligations to achieve shared aspirations+ Win/Win outcomes (FUTK08).
- The Trust Trio: Trust = Honesty + Reliability + Competence. (FUTK09).
- Bucky Fuller's Wealth Duet: Wealth = Physical resources + Metaphysical resources (FUTK10).
- The Planetary Pariah Punishments = Trade Sanctions + Customer Boycotts + Investment Strikes + Frozen Bank Accounts (FUTK11).
- Destiny Duet. Destiny = Aptitude + Passion (FUTK12).
- Destiny, Description = Domain Descriptor (an adjective) + Activity Descriptor (a noun) (FUTK13).
- The Four Domains of Prosperity and Poverty = economic + ecological + social + cultural (FUTK 14).
- The Four Domains of Sustainable Prosperity = economic prosperity + ecological prosperity + social prosperity + cultural prosperity (FUTK15).
- The Ecological Prosperity Quintet = Live solely on perpetual *solar income* + Learn from nature + Create circular economies + Use resources *JEPAT* + Protect and nurture Biodiversity (FUTK16).
- The Social Prosperity Quintet. The Social CHOIR. = **C**ohesion + **H**armony + **O**pportunity + **I**nclusion + **R**esilience. (FUTK17).
- The Cultural Prosperity Quintet. Cultural POWER. = ***P**articipation* + ***O**riginality* + ***W**ealth*: + ***E**steem*: +***R**esilience* (FUTK18)
- The Three Sights = Insight + Hindsight + Foresight (FUTK19).
- The Three Dialogues = Destiny dialogue + Derivation dialogue + Destination dialogue (FUTK20).
- The Three Selves = The Past Self + The Present Self + The Future Self. (FUTK21).
- The Derivation Duet: Derivation = Heritage + Baggage. (FUTK22).
- Destination Duet: Destination = Prophecy + Vision = The Visualization Duet. (FUTK23).
- The Occupation Trio = Work + Vocation + Avocation (FUTK24).
- Four Philosophical Future Shaping Tools = Metaphysics+ Epistemology+ Reason+ Ethics (FUTK25).

- The Exemplar Manager and Leader = Resilient Future Taker + Purposeful Future Maker (FUTK26).
- The Seven Modes of 21st century learning = Life-long learning + Learner driven learning + Just in Time learning+ Customized learning+ Transformative learning+ Collaborative learning + Contextual learning. (FUTK27).
- The Four Domains of Holistic Learning = learning to learn + learning to think + learning to feel + learning to reflect. (FUTK28).
- Sustainable Behaviour = Zero net collateral harm /damage to other (FUTK29).
- Healthy behaviour = Zero net collateral harm to self (FUTK30).
- The Hierarchy of Knowing: data, data + purpose = information, information + culture = knowledge, and knowledge + experience + refection = wisdom. (FUTK31).
- Collaboration Trio: synergism (2+2=5) + sum (2+2=4) + antagonism (2+2=3) (FUTK32).
- Ten Capabilities for Responsible Adulthood = Have a realistic understanding of one's capabilities and destiny+ Build career paths that provide economic security + Be leaders of self + Build, maintain and amicably end, interdependent relationships+ Respect others who are different + Recognize that individual rights should be reciprocal with community rights + Practice healthy and sustainable lives + Be capable parents and carers of others + Be lifelong, learner-driven learners + Value, and avoid collaterally harming, the environment and other species (FUTK33).
- Peter Singer's Circle of Concern (FUTK34).
- The Circle of Identity (FUTK35).
- Anthony Giddens' Utopian Realism = *Utopian* Visualization + *Realistic* Realization (FUTK36).
- Stephen Boyden's Stressors and Meliors: *Stressors* increase Distress + *Meliors* increase Bliss (FUTK37).
- Donald Rumsfeld's Knowledge Quartet = Known knowns + Known unknowns + Unknown Knowns + Unknown Unknowns. (FUTK38)
- The Two Strategic Modes = Problem Centred Strategist + Mission Directed Strategist. (FUTK39).

- The Six Future Shaping Tools = Management + Leadership + Planning + Design + Innovation + Learning. (FUTK 40).
- The Six Future Questions and The Six Futures = Plausible futures + Probable futures + Particular futures+ Prospective futures+ Preferred futures + Possible futures (FUTK41).
- The Ten Complementary Capabilities of Managers and Leaders (FUTK42)
- The Future Shaper's Quintet = Visualization + Values + Venturers + Voyages + Vehicles. (FUTK43).
- The Moral Compass Duet = Values (Values embodied) + Virtues (Values practiced) (FUTK44)
- The Six Emotional Pillars of Future Shaping = Confident + Courageous+ Committed +Considerate +Courteous +Compassionate (FUTK45).
- The Six Pillars of Liveability = Prosperity+ Harmony+ Inclusion +Sustainability+ Health +Security (FUTK46)
- The Harmony Duet. Harmony = Trust + Interdependence (FUTK47).
- The Security Trio. Security = Intelligence + Surveillance + Vigilance (FUTK48).
- The Two Stages of Foresight = Visualization + Realization (FUTK49).
- The Strategic Action Trio = Impediments + Improvements + Initiatives. (FUTK50).
- The Resources Duet = Capacities + Capabilities (FUTK51).
- The Wellness Duet = Wellbeing + Well becoming. (FUTK52).
- The Innovation Duet = Ways + Wares (FUTK53).
- The Venturer's Duet = Seafarers + Supporters (FUTK54).
- The Two Strategic Modes: Problem Centred Strategist (Management Initiated strategic action) + Mission Directed Strategist (Leadership Initiated strategic action) (FUTK55).
- The Five Social Drivers of Innovation = Make human effort more productive + Extend Mental Capability + Build more fruitful and fulfilling relationships + Shape the future + Uplift Liveability (FUTK56).
- Two Modes of Globalisation = Modernist (cowboy) globalization + Planetist (cosmonaut) globalisation (FUTK57).
- Two Modes of Capitalism = Modernist (cowboy) capitalism + Planetist (cosmonaut) capitalism (FUTK58).

- The Future Narrative Trio = future self + future present + future history (FUTK59).
- The Five Ws of Strategic Foresight: Who + What + When + Where +Why (FUTK60).
- The Identity Duet = Identity adaptable/*identity renovation* + Identity unadaptable/ Modernist *populism* (FUTK61).
- The Commitment Trio = unconditional + conditional + transactional (FUTK62).
- The Four Generic Technologies = digital technology + biotechnology + nanotechnology + new materials technology (FUTK63).
- Sustainable individualism = individual behaviour that causes zero net collateral harm to people and zero net damage to place (FUTK64).
- The Tourism Quartet = appreciate nature + appreciate society + appreciate culture + uplift wellness (FUTK65).
- The Four Communities = Locational + Cultural + Experiential + Aspirational (FUTK66).
- The Motivational Pairs Quintet = hope/fear + kind/cruel + respect/disrespect + love/hate + generous/selfish (FUTK67).
- The Cosmonaut Economy Quintet = Grow metaphysical wealth+ Stimulate and reward innovation + Promote planetist values + Foster liveability + Manage plenty as well as scarcity. (FUTK68).
- The Innovation arena: the conceptual framework that defines the purpose of particular social and physical innovations (ways and ware) (FUTK69)